# The United Nations as Leviathan

# The United Nations as Leviathan

## Global Governance in the Post-American World

Roland Rich

HAMILTON BOOKS
AN IMPRINT OF
ROWMAN & LITTLEFIELD
*Lanham • Boulder • New York • London*

Published by Hamilton Books
An imprint of The Rowman & Littlefield Publishing Group, Inc.
4501 Forbes Boulevard, Suite 200, Lanham, Maryland 20706
www.rowman.com

86-90 Paul Street, London EC2A 4NE, United Kingdom



British Library Cataloguing in Publication Information Available

**Library of Congress Cataloging-in-Publication Data**

Names: Rich, Roland, author.
Title: The United Nations as Leviathan : global governance in the post-American world / Roland Rich.
Description: Lanham : Hamilton Books, an imprint of Rowman & Littlefield, [2023] | Includes bibliographical references and index. | Summary: "The world needs a UN 3.0. The extent and severity of global crises are such that business as usual provides no solution. Roland Rich's Leviathan describes the necessary next version of the United Nations and the first step of how to put it into place"—Provided by publisher.
Identifiers: LCCN 2022033692 (print) | LCCN 2022033693 (ebook) | ISBN 9780761873723 (trade paperback) | ISBN 9780761873730 (epub)
Subjects: LCSH: United Nations. | International organization.
Classification: LCC JZ4984.5 .R53 2023 (print) | LCC JZ4984.5 (ebook) | DDC 341.23—dc23/eng/20220919
LC record available at https://lccn.loc.gov/2022033692
LC ebook record available at https://lccn.loc.gov/2022033693

The paper used in this publication meets the minimum requirements of American National Standard for Information Sciences—Permanence of Paper for Printed Library Materials, ANSI/NISO Z39.48-1992.

*For my grandchildren*
*Ace, Golda, Zadie, Raya . . .*
*May their children inherit*
*a livable planet*

# Contents

# Chapter 1

# Why the Leviathan?

We are living through a period of unprecedented change. It is without precedent because of its breadth, depth, and rapidity. Change is affecting climate, society, and the economy. Directly or indirectly, it is affecting everybody on the planet. And whereas phenomena like climate change used to take eons to play out, the periodicity is now down to generations or even decades. Generally, humans are averse to rapid change. Generally, humans are not placated by complexity. Generally, humans are discombobulated by capricious uncertainty. Such circumstances put a premium on the need for effective governance. Muddling along is no longer a luxury at our disposal.

The problem of managing rapid change is one borne by all levels of governance—local, provincial, national, and regional. This book focuses on the higher and overarching level of global governance. For the past seventy-five years, the world has relied on a system of occasional international cooperation facilitated haphazardly by international organizations and guaranteed grudgingly by the United States. The system of global governance in place could be described as muddling along, occasionally working but often breaking down. We no longer have the luxury of retaining this system because the world has entered the Anthropocene epoch whereby the greatest influence on the capacity of planet Earth to sustain its current ecosystem is the effect of human actions. Global cooperation through global governance is now a necessity.

This is an optimistic book in that it argues that effective global governance is within our reach. There is no reason why humanity cannot achieve it. But it requires change. Surely, it stands to reason that if the circumstances are changing deeply and rapidly, the response cannot be fixed. Nor can the global architecture to deliver that response remain fixed. The world needs a far more effective and impactful form of global governance, and this book describes the key elements of it.

The introductory chapter begins by describing the theoretical structure within which effective global governance can be achieved. After a brief discussion of some thoughts of Thomas Hobbes and Hedley Bull that demonstrate the "all against all" nature of our global society dominated by nation states, the chapter will explain the meaning of the concept of the twenty-first century Leviathan and will examine whether any nation or institution can perform this critical role. The United States has abdicated. The only viable candidate is the United Nations. The balance of the chapter will provide a keyhole peek at the ways in which this institution needs to be changed so that it can play its necessary role in global governance. Succeeding chapters will spell out the details.

## HOBBES'S LEVIATHAN

The title of this book sounds like the punchline to a joke. The United Nations is many things, good and bad, but a Leviathan is not a description that would readily come to mind. But the world needs a benign Leviathan, and the UN is the best institution to be shaped into that role. The term is borrowed from Thomas Hobbes's book, published in 1651.[1] The UN as Leviathan is therefore not a description, it is an aspiration.

Thomas Hobbes, along with Galileo, Descartes, Spinoza, and others was one of the great thinkers who paved the path to modernity.[2] He was well ahead of his time in his rigorous empiricism, his realism about the state of human nature and his prescription for the need for a mighty sovereign. He famously rejected previous theses that humans were born either good or bad but, rather, understood that they strove to maximize their power in a survival of the fittest context that anticipated Darwin by two centuries. Being an empiricist, he rejected any notion of spiritual intervention in human affairs and fell afoul of the church, the clutches of which he had to escape to be able to write *Leviathan*. He is famous for coining the phrases "state of nature," the universal and inevitable initial condition of humankind, in which life is "solitary, poor, nasty, brutish, and short" and where people are engaged in "the war of all against all."

Hobbes anticipated, though without direct reference, the impact of the Treaties of Westphalia signed in 1648, three years before the publication of his opus. It was, eventually, these treaties that initiated the modern world of nation states in which each was considered to be sovereign. It is in this sense that the term "Westphalian" is employed. Today, we think of such nation states along the lines of the Max Weber formulation that "a state is a human community that (successfully) claims the monopoly of the legitimate use of physical force within a given territory."[3] Or perhaps, drawing from the Charter of the United Nations, as simply being a peace-loving polity that is accepted for membership by the General Assembly.[4] But in the time in which

Hobbes lived, wracked by civil war and religious persecution, the notion of preferring an all-powerful sovereign, a Leviathan, who would reign unopposed and thus put an end to the war of all against all, was a novel concept.

The novelty, though, was not in the notion of the all-powerful prince. After all, Hobbes lived in the age of absolutism which had, during his lifetime, been further emboldened by the doctrine of the divine right of kings. He was familiar with sovereigns asserting power, nothing new there. It is the notion of the acceptance of the sovereign's power by the people through a social contract that gives Hobbes his originality. We need to be careful not to attribute virtues heedlessly. Hobbes was not a democrat though he may have had a role in preparing the way for modern democracy. His notion of the social contract was vague and not practical; philosophical and not applied. In fact, it can be compared to a concept Hobbes probably knew nothing about—the Chinese idea of the mandate of heaven whereby the emperor/sovereign enjoys the loyalty and devotion of his people because of his wisdom and benevolence. Hobbes's Leviathan would end civil wars and bring law and order to his kingdom, and the people would thus accept him unquestioningly.

But Hobbes conceded that while a Leviathan may end the state of nature within the kingdom or state, the problem of the state of nature persisting between national Leviathans remained. *Leviathan* is not a prescription for world peace, only national peace. And thus, the problem presents itself anew. Must nation states perpetually be in a war of all against all? Must their nature be to seek power at all cost? Having, in theory at least, resolved the issue of national peace, can we resolve the issue of international peace? It is important to concede at the outset that the link between the national Leviathan and the global Leviathan is not intrinsic to Hobbes's thinking. The link is through analogy. Hobbes provides a structure and a discourse. It is the burden of this book, to apply the Hobbesian structure convincingly to the international order.

## HEDLEY BULL'S ANARCHICAL SOCIETY

Published in 1977,[5] Hedley Bull's book is a search for order in what he saw as the natural state of anarchy in international relations. How could this anarchy be kept at bay? Bull posits three possibilities.[6] He lived through one such possibility at the end of WWII. The rhetoric of post-war institution building was clearly Kantian, and can quickly be discerned in the multilateral constitutive instruments of the day: the Charter ("to live together in peace with one another as neighbors"); the Universal Declaration of Human Rights ("it is essential to promote the development of friendly relations between nations"); the Statute of the Council of Europe ("convinced that the pursuit of peace based upon justice and international co-operation is vital for the preservation of human society and civilization"); and the Constitution of UNESCO ("the wide diffusion of culture, and the education of humanity for justice and liberty and peace are indispensable to the dignity of man and constitute a sacred duty which all the nations must fulfil in a spirit of mutual assistance and concern"). The Europeans took matters further and established a Grotian society of nations, which, again in Bull's lifetime, developed from a Coal and Steel Community, to a Common Market, and then to the European Economic Community. Soon after his death it became the European Union. But the overriding post-War development that Bull witnessed was the Cold War, a Hobbesian expression of realism that established high-level order by virtue of the doctrine of mutually assured destruction, while the balance of the world continued to deal with a natural state of insecurity. In Bull's estimation, the world was not as envisaged by Immanuel Kant or Hugo Grotius but was, sadly, true to Thomas Hobbes.

Hedley Bull died in 1985. He did not witness Gorbachev's failed attempt to rescue the Soviet Union through the doctrines of *glasnost* and *perestroika*. He did not know the world would pass through a Kantian moment epitomized by the massive coalition under UN authority to evict Saddam Hussein from Kuwait. He did not study the transition from order through mutually assured destruction to order through benign hegemonic stability under American auspices. And, having seen the chaos of the Cultural Revolution, Bull would have been surprised to learn that a mere generation later, China would realistically aspire to superpower status. Needless to say, Bull could not anticipate the reckless war of choice in Iraq that would squander America's soft power nor the Trump presidency by which the United States would abdicate from world leadership.

This is where current CIA Director William J. Burns's previous observation blends in. Having witnessed the vandalism committed by the Trump Administration against the Federal bureaucracy, and the damage to his beloved State Department in particular; having seen the cancerous doubt injected in all of America's key alliances; having seen American foreign policy turned into a personal transactional process where authoritarian figures dominate; Burns lamented that "we have drifted into one of those rare periods of transition, with American dominance in the rearview mirror, and a more anarchical order looming dimly beyond."[7]

The anarchy Burns is referring to is not the *bellum omnium contra omnes*, the war of all against all, that haunted Hobbes in the seventeenth century. This "war" is among nation states and not individuals and it need not necessarily take the form of international bellicosity. It is not only a reversion to the state of nature, but a relentless path of states against nature. It is not only about hot wars, but also about destructive competition between nations. The substantive chapters will identify and describe the Hobbesian behavior of nations in numerous fields. Armed with this evidence, the concluding chapter will go beyond the concept of anarchy to argue that the international Hobbesianism of the twenty-first century is the absence of effective cooperation in dealing with existential threats.

What is lacking is the social contract on a global scale to work together under guidance from a Leviathan. What is lacking is successful collective action transcending paralyzing game theory problems of free riders and veto players. What is lacking is rational action under benign leadership. Bull and Burns agree that the United Nations is not that leader. Bull writes rather dismissively that "I have also been influenced by the feeling that the United Nations, because of the great mass of documentation it engenders, has been overstudied, and that this tends to deflect scholarly attention away from sources of international order that are more fundamental."[8] Burns is a little more diplomatic in noting that "international institutions are beginning to break—paralyzed by too much bureaucracy, too little investment, and intense major-power rivalry."[9] But both Bull and Burns were talking about the UN of their day, the UN we know only too well, UN 2.0. This book imagines to a new and different UN.

## A NEW LEVIATHAN

Since the time of Thomas Hobbes, the world has been through the industrial revolution, colonialism, imperialism, world wars (hot and cold), globalization and the digital revolution. Great thinkers from Immanuel Kant to Jürgen Habermas have contemplated the possibility of world peace. Political leaders from Woodrow Wilson to Franklin Roosevelt have striven to establish the international architecture to bring about world peace. The theoretical basis for world peace has been seen in democracy or capitalism or a mix of both in "the end of history." Others wish to create utopia on Earth by a return to obscurantist religious visions. This book is intended as a contribution to the field of positing beneficial international architecture, though it is neither utopia nor even world peace that is being sought but rather the more modest idea espoused by Dag Hammarskjöld, the Secretary-General of the UN, who famously said that the United Nations "was not created to take mankind to heaven, but to save humanity from hell."[10] To rescue us from hell, we need the United Nations to become the Leviathan among the world's sovereigns.

Nearly four centuries have elapsed since Hobbes wrote his book. A twenty-first century Leviathan will not look like the version imagined in the seventeenth century. And an international Leviathan will be fundamentally different from Hobbes's national model. The international Leviathan cannot aspire to have a monopoly of the use of force. Sorry, no black helicopters patrolling downtown Savannah! Yet the world needs an international Leviathan now, just as Hobbes argued his nation needed one then. We simply can no longer rely on muddling through. The United Nations is hardly that Leviathan, but it can become so. An international Leviathan must lead by the force of persuasion, by moral authority, and by the overriding obligation to defend the planet from its immediate anthropogenic threat. This book will show how the UN can become that Leviathan. In doing so, it will draw from the novelty in the Hobbes philosophy. There needs to be a social contract on a global scale.

Is there an alternative to global Leviathan politics? We live in a world of competition between nation states based on a tenuous set of rules that are currently weakening to the point of near irrelevance. Were a "nation-first" philosophy to take hold in many countries around the world, those rules, held together by weak international architecture, based on moral suasion, and lightly underpinned by the United States as benign hegemon, would evaporate. The world would lurch quickly towards an all against all disorder. That is the current trajectory. And that is why the sub-title of this book refers to the "post-American world." This is not necessarily a commentary on American strength and capacity, but rather a description of the final days of the global architectural design bestowed on the world by the United States at the end of WWII. But even if this now tenuous design were to be maintained a while longer, though often disrespected or ignored, the best-case scenario is one of muddling through with borderline competence and effectiveness. This may have been sufficient in pre-anthropogenic times, but it is clearly insufficient today. The world needs the leadership and direction that a Leviathan can bring.

But why the UN? Is there another candidate. There may have been a time in the immediate post-Cold War period when it would have been plausible to propose the United States as the prospective Leviathan. It then had the military and moral authority possibly to discharge this onerous responsibility. But nobody could propose that solution today with a straight face. The endless wars in the Middle East have sapped America's capacities and willpower. And the 2016 Presidential election outcome demonstrated the existence of sufficient domestic opposition to this role as to preclude the United States from asserting global leadership. The American withdrawal under Trump from, in turn, the Iran nuclear deal, the Paris Climate Change accord, the Human Rights Council, and the World Health Organization has even punctured the more modest Clinton Administration claim of America as the indispensable nation. This is another sense in which we live in a post-American world regardless of post-Trump attempts to put Humpty-Dumpty together again.

If not the United States, perhaps another nation state which is also a civilization, China, can take its place. It is certainly a pretender to the throne.

But China is disqualified as a candidate for the status of benign Leviathan both as a nation state and as a civilization. As a state, China's Leninism is disqualifying. It puts the interests of the party above all else. And, as I have argued elsewhere,[11] a Leninist government running a capitalist economy is necessarily corrupt. It fits completely within the Klitgaard formula,[12] whereby C = M + D – A (Corruption equals monopoly plus discretion minus accountability.) As a civilization, China believes in hierarchy radiating from the middle in which it considers it is situated. It lacks the universalist philosophies of the United Nations, or for that matter, the United States. The nations of the world would be organized in a series of tributary relationships with the Middle Kingdom in which the interests of the former would always be in thrall to the needs of the latter. No, we need to look elsewhere for a Leviathan.

Should we create a new Leviathan? It would be foolish and ahistorical to believe that we can successfully design a new Leviathan from scratch. The world has spent one hundred years working on the design of the League of Nations and its successor, the United Nations. We have made many mistakes and learned many lessons along the way. We need to build on this history, not ignore it. Even if the evidence points to deep internal resistance to change from within the UN and its Member States, the logical step would be to build a UN 3.0, drawing on the positives from the current UN 2.0 and ditching the negative features. I do not hazard this thought casually because I recognize the practical benefits of continuity. But the reality to date has been that the UN is incapable of achieving significant reform.

## WHAT'S RIGHT AND WHAT'S WRONG WITH THE UN?

One of the leading figures proposing reasoned reforms is Thomas Weiss, whose 2016 book, *What's Wrong with the United Nations and How to Fix It*, put forward a series of reforms to the practices and management of the UN.[13] I place this book in the "nudge" literature. The proposed reforms were hardly radical. They would not transform the UN but rather nudge it in more sensible and productive directions in an iterative process. Another worthy publication that fits in the nudge category is the weighty 2016 report by the Independent Commission on Multilateralism chaired by former Australian Prime Minister Kevin Rudd.[14] It enjoins the international community to resuscitate the UN. But the UN seems resistant even to nudges. The most significant reform since the turn of the millennium is the holding of the Universal Periodic Review of each Member State's human rights record. And even this step is simply a streamlining and improvement of previous practices and can hardly be said to have had a significant positive impact on the world's human rights record. So, we may well need a UN 3.0, but it will remain a UN, by whatever name.

Whether "fixing" the UN or rebuilding it, the first step is a sober analysis of its strengths and weaknesses. Curiously, there is one answer to both questions: Member States (the *majuscules* come from the UN Charter). The Member States sustain the UN with their assessed contributions, their voluntary contributions, and their peacekeepers. They provide the resources essential for the organization to maintain itself. They often supply the senior officials staffing the upper reaches of the Secretariat. But the Member States are also the UN's greatest weakness. They use the UN for their own narrow purposes, they stymie the UN from having its own perspectives and if something goes awry, they turn the UN into their very own whipping boy. The major challenge, therefore, is to find ways to maximize the strengths and minimize the weaknesses inherent in the current situation of Member State domination of the UN.

Drawing on the Charter, the term employed above has been "Member States," but this is clearly a misnomer for the true representation at the UN. It is not Member States that sit in the organization's august chambers, but representatives of their governments. And there lies the nub of the problem—governments. Governments represented at the UN run the gamut of regime types from totalitarian to liberal democratic, passing through other categories such as authoritarian, military, personalistic and pseudo-democratic. One could further sub-divide these categories into narco-governments, criminal gang governments, corrupt governments, governments as a family business, puppet governments, and powerless governments of collapsed states. It is their representatives who run the UN! What is needed is a UN where the influence of these governments is diluted to the point where the UN is no longer their plaything. We need a Leviathan UN that will reverse the playbook and have influence over governments and their actions.

All organizations need leadership. This is true of corporations, schools, militaries, and international organizations. Among the first steps to be taken in any reform process is the need to ensure proper leadership. The UN, by definition, does not have it. That is because the selection of the Secretary-General (S-G) of the UN is effectively decided by five countries, the five permanent members of the UN Security Council (P5). These five countries aspire to world political quintopoly. Given the declining relevance of France and the United Kingdom, it might be more accurate to think of this group as the world troika. They reject any competition to their power and privileges. They ensure that no such threat can come from the organization they control, the UN, and one of their means of ensuring that the UN will remain quiescent and constrained is through their power to appoint, and crucially, reappoint the Secretary-General.

The usual formula is to select a bland former foreign minister, ensure that he (it has always been a "he") does nothing against their interests or beyond their wishes in his first five-year term by being coy about his reappointment, and upon reappointment, turn him into a lame duck a couple of years before the end of his second term. In a ten-year period, this might leave a small window of three years for activism. I served under Ban Ki-moon and he fitted the formula perfectly. Not only was he bland in public (though a kind and engaging man in private), but he also had the additional attribute of speaking unintelligible English and even worse French. I heard a story about the French delegation, that has as one of its roles to maximize the use of French at the UN, pleading with S-G Ban to stick to English. He behaved suitably moderately for his first five years and upon his reappointment, launched several initiatives which were easily thwarted by the Member States. (I will have more to say about some of those initiatives in the Globalization chapter.) Accepting his lame duck status graciously, he spent the last couple of years of his term unsuccessfully scheming to become President of South Korea, but being on the conservative side of Korean politics which went into freefall with the impeachment and conviction of the corrupt conservative President Park Geun-hye, his prospects dissolved.

The case of S-G Ban is not unusual in UN history. The United States and the Soviet Union were pleased to have Kurt Waldheim of Austria as S-G because they could keep him in check by the threat of blackmail over his secret Nazi history, no doubt well known to both countries. Javier Pérez de Cuéllar of Peru arrived as a compromise candidate, served two uneventful terms, and left no impression on the organization thus meeting the needs of the P5 admirably. Boutros Boutros-Ghali of Egypt on the other hand, had intellectual gravitas, big ideas and a commendable independence which caused the United States to veto his second term. After the Boutros-Ghali kerfuffle,[15] the P5 thought they had better appoint a bland UN bureaucrat, and as Africa's first S-G had only lasted one term, they chose Kofi Annan of Ghana. It was a strange choice in the sense that Annan had been in charge of UN peacekeeping operations when they suffered two of their most galling reverses in Somalia and Rwanda, but the P5 no doubt gambled that this would make him even more meek. They were wrong. Annan's loyalty was to the UN and his presentation skills were pleasing to the publics of the world. Annan demonstrated the capacity of a S-G to speak over the heads of the governments of the world directly to their people. Annan demonstrated his independence when he called out the Bush Administration for invading and occupying Iraq contrary to international law. The Bush Administration's retaliation was vicious.[16] It is thus understandable that the P5 would choose as Annan's successor, a person whose English was incomprehensible. The current S-G, António Guterres of Portugal, has only just completed his do-nothing first term, so it is too early to pronounce judgement, but the fact that he gained the job through a sweetheart staffing deal with Russia causes reflection.

Is there another way to endow the UN with true leadership? I will outline a method of doing so by diluting the influence of governments and ending the monopoly of the P5 in the appointment process. The proposed method is to make the appointment tripartite by including business and civil society in the decision making. The chapter on The General Assemblies will spell out how this can be accomplished and the benefits it will bring. The proposal may sound shockingly radical but, in fact, there is a clear precedent for such an approach in the tripartite appointment of the Director-General of the International Labour Organization, a specialized agency of the UN. One of the curious strengths of the radical sounding proposals throughout this book is that in so many cases, they have an embryonic existence in current practice. It would also require a clipping of the veto power held by the P5. Chapter 5 spells this out and the concluding chapter contains a play-by-play process to achieve it.

Changing the appointment process to make the S-G a true leader is only one of many steps to renew the Secretariat of the UN. Boutros-Ghali was once asked by a journalist "how many people work at the UN?" After a moment's thought, his response was "about half." In my experience, that is a generous fraction. There are competent and dedicated members of the UN Secretariat with whom I had the honor to serve, but they must carry the full load. Too many others cannot be so described. The UN pays excellent salaries, so how did this situation come to be? The answer once again is the machinations of Member States and their government representatives. One of the first steps a strong S-G would take is discard one of the two current staff appointment criteria. Article 101(3) of the UN Charter states:

> The paramount consideration in the employment of the staff and in the determination of the conditions of service shall be the necessity of securing the highest standards of efficiency, competence, and integrity. Due regard shall be paid to the importance of recruiting the staff on as wide a geographical basis as possible.

The reality is that the second sentence has supplanted the first, the rider has taken the reins. The first sentence requires a value judgement, the second a passport. Add to this the lobbying and scheming of national missions to the UN and it will come as no surprise that the simple fact of nationality trumps the difficult judgement about efficiency, competence, and integrity. The notion of employment of staff on as wide a geographical basis as possible is in its worst light, a crass division of spoils, and in its best light, an attempt to earn international legitimacy. My argument is that the UN Secretariat must earn its legitimacy by performance not by the array of passports held by its members. These and other changes will be unpacked in the chapter on the Secretary-General and the Secretariat (the *majuscules* again come from the Charter.)

## A VISION OF THE UN AS LEVIATHAN

As previously noted, a modern international Leviathan must lead by the force of persuasion, by moral authority, and by the overriding obligation to defend the planet from its immediate anthropogenic threat. As also noted, this Leviathan must arise through a global social contract. A social contract does not mean unanimity. Crooks, deniers, and gadflies will not disappear, but they must decisively be placed in a small and irrelevant category of irrational eccentrics. The mainstream of national opinion around the world must resolutely accept the reality that human activity has triggered catastrophic climate change requiring painfully concrete mitigating action. Upon coming to that realization, people will call for an international Leviathan.

However cogent the reports of the UN Intergovernmental Panel on Climate Change may be, they have not persuaded beyond the intellectual elites and young people terrified for their futures. The balance of the population will, regrettably, only be convinced by the ever-increasing fierceness of climate change-induced wild weather. When hundreds of millions of climate change refugees scramble across borders, when islands disappear, when a billion people can find no food, when half of Miami is under water, when large tracts of Australia and other dry places become uninhabitable, people will want action. Even those not in the direct path of tragedies will feel the wrath of climate change when insurance, if available, becomes unaffordable, when low lying property loses its value and when food supply chains become tenuous. Sadly, it will be too late by then to reverse climate change, but it will not be too late to mitigate its effects and make societies more resilient to its threats. That is when the global social contract will form. It will not take too long.

The UN Leviathan will use its convening power to bring together key actors in governments and beyond. The UN Leviathan will use its moral authority to require adequate responses. The UN Leviathan will use its legal authority to require certain conduct and to castigate uncooperative participants. The UN Leviathan will defend the health of the planet to the best of its considerable ability. Today's UN can do none of these things as it lacks independence, willpower, and capacity. The aspirational vision of the UN as Leviathan must find ways to endow the new UN with each of these qualities.

Independence seems an unattainable goal but, in fact, it is the least difficult of the three to achieve. Ending the current reality of making the UN financially dependent on Member States is an essential early step. Yes, Member States are members of a club and must pay club fees, but this will not be the

UN's only source of income. Accordingly, Member States, and in particular the host country, will not be able to use this source of funding as a sword of Damocles. James Tobin suggested a currency transaction tax to fund the UN in 1972.[17] France has made its tax on airline travel in favor of the UN work effectively.[18] We live in an age of almost unfettered globalization, so it is not difficult to imagine the ease with which to carve a tiny fraction of a percentage on the revenues it generates to fund international organizations. Beyond currencies and airline travel, the logic of globalization is the need to have a tax on internationally traded goods to fund the regulation of globalization that is so sorely lacking today. A global social contract would establish the taxation base for the UN and its specialized agencies. Independence would flow from assured financing. The concluding chapter will provide some numbers to flesh out this step.

The willpower to use its new-found independence may be more difficult. One of the things that surprised me when I worked at the UN was how subservient Secretariat members were to national delegates even though the Secretariat's independence was supposedly defended by the Charter. Article 100 calls on the Secretariat not to take instructions from delegations and for delegations not to issue such instructions. The article is not currently being respected.

The reality is that the General Assembly's control of the budget is the cudgel used to control the Secretariat. Incidentally, all programs controlled by the General Assembly are, by definition, lowest common denominator programs. Innovation and impact usually come from programs supported by voluntary contributions. Another form of control comes from the insidious way some delegations involve themselves in personnel appointment and promotion issues. They do this sometimes for reasons of national prestige and sometimes because of personal connections, and I have even heard of cases where the members of a delegation successfully placing one of their nationals in the Secretariat, get a cut of that new employee's attractive salary.

There is a culture of Secretariat subservience to delegations in the UN. It begins with the S-G being subservient to the P5 and runs right through the organization. The theoretical independence of the Secretariat established by the Charter has not been effective. Tobin taxes establishing financial independence should be effective, but the Secretariat culture would have to change. To achieve that outcome, a large number of Secretariat members would need to be pensioned out of the organization. Their replacements would be appointed solely "on the basis of the highest standards of efficiency, competence, and integrity."

This step would also help with the capacity issue by having all UN staff, rather than only "half," working effectively. But that is only the beginning. The UN as Leviathan would require a far larger budget even if it stopped doing a lot of useless busy work in support of the General Assembly and concentrated on actions with impact. The budget for the UN in 2020 was $3 billion.[19] The budget request for the State Department for 2020 was $40 billion.[20]. Yes, they do different things. But the comparison is nevertheless indicative of how underfunded the UN is. A Leviathan needs a proper budget.

## PEACE AND SECURITY

The peace and security chapter does not offer any kind of magic wand. Humanity has always lived with insecurity and will continue to do so. The aim of a security Leviathan would be to limit the insecurity as much as possible. The chapter attempts to understand the contextual relevance of the UN Security Council. It has an undoubted centrality in the UN system, but it is not the central player in the global security system. That player has been the United States in a *Pax Americana* system. Europeans do not look to the UN for their security, they look to the North Atlantic Treaty Organization (NATO). East Asians do not look to the UN for their security, they look to the United States. Latin America continues to exist in the shadow of the Monroe doctrine. In this system, the UN is responsible for the tenuous security of the remaining "stragglers and strugglers" around the world. But the *pax Americana* system is coming to an end. It was sickened by the reckless Iraq adventure, and it has been all but killed off by Trump. It cannot be resurrected. The coalition in opposition to Putin's criminal attack on Ukraine built by the Biden Administration may be its last hurrah.

I argue that the Security Council will enjoy a new prominence in the post–*Pax Americana* world. It will not provide the supposed security that the various American alliance treaties promise, but it will be the forum of a new "concert of powers." It will be the forum where the major powers will practice deconfliction strategies. It will continue to be a cozy forum for its permanent members (P5) and an uncomfortable place for its elected members. The P5 have little interest in reforming this body. But new practices may be forced on them and one of these weakens the veto power. The chapter argues for a far broader definition of "procedural matters" on which no veto is possible, in effect leaving the veto power only in relation to Chapter VII action.

The chapter asks whether there is a force for positive disruption of the Security Council. The pretenders to the status of permanence, even without a veto, are unlikely to ever graduate from their pretention. Germany and Japan have become pacifists, a quality not on the job requirements. India will be blocked by Pakistan and even if it can surmount this hurdle, it is difficult seeing it overcome China's objections. Other candidates have far fewer qualities than these three. The ten elected members of the Security Council (E10) all learn the same lesson—the election is the highpoint of the adventure because, after that, it only goes from bad to worse. They are kept in a purgatorial state of breathless busyness and minimal influence. They never have and never will disrupt the P5.

The only person or institution than can be a force for disruption through action and exhortation is the Secretary-General of the UN. But, of course, not the current version or any successor selected and constrained in the current manner. A financially independent S-G, not held hostage to the P5, could finally grow into the role envisaged under the Charter. Once again, the seeds of a system are apparent. The independent S-G is foreseen in Article 99 of the Charter. That article describes him as having "opinions." It has occasionally been acted on, most recently in S-G Guterres's call for a global ceasefire during the COVID-19 pandemic,[21] and his description of the Russian war against Ukraine as "absurd,"[22] but rarely effectively. As described above, the office of S-G is effectively constrained under the current arrangements.

One suggestion made in this chapter is for the S-G to be given limited enforcement capacity. Once again, this radical sounding idea exists in embryonic form. The Charter envisaged an organization with forces at its disposal in Article 43. That process never got off the ground. But the need for the S-G to have his own uniformed team was sufficiently pressing that, without any basis in the Charter but with the grudging acceptance of the troop contributing states, the S-G turned the small UN Truce Supervision Organization, based in Jerusalem, into his military team. The chapter ties these together and describes a powerful S-G able to deploy his considerable moral suasion and backed by his own division of well-armed troops. These troops do not undertake the enforcement role of the Security Council under Chapter VII of the Charter, nor do they take on the role of peacekeeping. But they give the S-G the capacity to deal with "spoilers." They turn the S-G from a Secretary into a General.

## DEMOCRACY AND HUMAN RIGHTS

The chapter on democracy and human rights begins with a discussion of the origins of these concepts in the modern world. One way of doing so is to compare Karel Vasak's three generations of human rights with Samuel Huntington's three waves of democratization. There are similarities and divergences. Vasak's generations, as the concept implies, are offspring of their predecessors. They are linked and connected and share the overarching philosophy of being inherent, inalienable, and interdependent. Huntington's three waves, on the other hand, seem disconnected and lack historical coherence, with the third wave lacking any sort of general explanation. The chapter attempts an explanation of the three waves as responses to the defeat, in turn, of absolutism, fascism and communism.

The UN adopted human rights as one of its pillars and purposes but, at the insistence of the Soviet Union, ignored democracy. This was the normal state of affairs throughout the Cold War. But at its conclusion, a significant change occurred. The 1993 Vienna Conference on Human Rights adopted a new concept to rehabilitate democracy. The concept is that democracy, human rights, and development are "mutually reinforcing."[23] Accordingly, the UN came to see democracy in instrumental terms as a means through which to achieve its human rights and development objectives. Democracy became an accepted subject for polite conversation at the UN. The challenge was how to support it in a Westphalian world.

The chapter details many of the achievements of the international community in the promotion and protection of human rights. States were given new obligations to report on the situation in their country, to respond to criticisms from experts and civil society representatives, and to abide by decisions of authoritative bodies. Individuals were given new means of asserting and defending their rights, through complaints mechanisms and even juridical processes. New mechanisms were established such as special rapporteurs, expert bodies to hear complaints, and a new International Criminal Court. Sovereignty was not defeated but it was being constrained.

There were achievements in the field of democracy promotion as well. International election observation became a norm, with refusal to cooperate leading to a presumption of corruption. A growing list of international organizations made the practice of democracy a condition of membership. Several of these organizations developed procedures and penalties when unconstitutional changes of government occurred. Given its instrumental value, the UN Security Council took practical steps to promote democracy in its nation building mandates for peacekeeping missions. Two of these, most recently in Côte d'Ivoire, gave the Secretary-General's Special Representative the power to certify the election results.

Even in a Westphalian world, a UN Leviathan can be designed to have a telling influence in support of democracy and human rights. As on previous issues, the ideas to do so have already been invented. They now need to be brought to scale. The chapter investigates the establishment of a UN Court of Human Rights that will determine the existence of systemic violations by national governments. And, drawing on the Côte d'Ivoire precedent, the chapter proposes that the currently quiescent UN Electoral Assistance Division be turned into a powerful certifying authority for *all* national elections—North or South, East or West, rich or poor.

## DEVELOPMENT AND GLOBALIZATION

The development chapter, shockingly entitled "Against the Sustainable Development Goals!" begins with a diatribe against government-centric development. The diatribe is prolix, examining history, looking at several geographic regions, drawing on the development literature, and providing examples. It tries to tackle two specific myths: that government planning is the best means of economic development; and that development is synonymous with infrastructure. It traces the history of "systematic planning supported by legal compulsion" from the colonial days to the Soviet Gosplan method, through to the East Asian "developmental state," and finally to today's top-down Belt and Road Initiative, described as the crown on the head of the Chinese authoritarian colossus. Given such a checkered history, it is remarkable that this idea became the centerpiece of the OECD members' official development assistance and the model for African governments.

But there were other voices and other ideas, and they became influential with the publication of Amartya Sen's *Development as Freedom*. The new ideas put people at the heart of the development process. Development, its proponents argued, should be about developing people's capabilities, and protecting their human rights. Economic development would follow, including the construction of infrastructure in a bottom-up process of debate, contestation, and taxation.

Once this distinction is understood, the role of the UN becomes clear. To begin with, the UN is weak on project delivery. It is too timid, bureaucratic, and risk averse. It should get out of the project delivery business and instead concentrate on the business in which it has strengths—the ratification, espousal, and defense of norms. The Leviathan UN should use the resources at its disposal, its moral authority, its independently raised budget, and its brand. The UN would seem to be diminished by not having as many people in the field, driving around in four-wheel-drive vehicles and living and working in air-conditioned homes and offices. But the on-the-ground tasks are better accomplished by others, usually local businesses, and local civil society, supported by the international community. Indeed, the chapter explains a mechanism for this result to be achieved. The UN will become the Leviathan because of its moral stature. It can then deploy that stature and its budget in support of human development processes and programs.

The result in the change of attitude towards the concept of development from authoritarian top-down to a far more democratic bottom-up approach, will be to achieve restorative governance. The term is borrowed from the criminal justice field and broadened to apply to a far wider range of processes and services provided by a government. It is described as "the science of restoring and developing social capital, social discipline, emotional well-being and civic participation through participatory learning and decision-making."[24] That should be the tool used by the UN Leviathan in the field of development.

The following chapter deals with the related phenomenon of globalization. The chapter may be summarized in its heading—globalization needs governance. The first part of the chapter provides a long and perhaps tedious list of all the different mechanisms used to govern globalization. There are treaties, summits, intergovernmental expert fora, multi-stakeholder partnerships, commercial mechanisms, sector specific arrangements, and civil society-constructed structures. They demonstrate the need for governance. Some work well, others less so. The UN is a key player in many of these governance structures. But it needs to do much better.

Prior to examining how the UN can improve its involvement, the chapter asks the "why?" question. Why do we need to govern globalization? Two broad responses are provided. Drawing on the work of Thomas Piketty, the first response is that capitalism is inevitably leading to ever greater rates of inequality. The results will ultimately be untenable, and history has shown, as Walter Scheidel demonstrates, that large-scale war, transformative revolution, destructive pandemics or state collapse may be the only means of reversing the trend. We need to find a better way. The second reason is that globalization has created a bifurcated economy of those plugged in and those left out. It is creating a new cleavage in domestic politics. We have seen that new political cleavage in operation in the *gilets jaunes* phenomenon in France, the Brexit vote in the UK, and Trump's election in 2016. Globalization needs to be governed to soften its effect on those not directly plugged in.

The UN Leviathan of the twenty-first century will not take on these tasks directly. This book does not argue in favor of world government. Instead, it will influence the outcome using three processes. The principle of subsidiarity aims to ensure that decisions are taken as closely as possible to the citizen. It is already employed in the European Union to determine which decisions should be taken at the continental, national, provincial, or local level. We need to add global at the head of that list to provide the correct division of governance responsibility. The technique of certification is defined as "the validation of actors, their performances, and their claims by authorities."[25] The UN needs to become the certifying authority for various governance schemes, existing and proposed. The final quality added by the Leviathan is legitimacy. Based on its moral authority, popular acceptance and effective performance, the United Nations Leviathan would have the legitimacy to rule on the subsidiarity division of responsibility and to certify the actions of others. Thus, can globalization *sauvage* be tamed.

## TACKLING CLIMATE CHANGE

This short chapter does not attempt to rehearse the scale of the problem. The UN has done that through the Intergovernmental Panel on Climate Change. The chapter demonstrates how Hobbesian has become the international response to climate change. The rhetoric of cooperation is overwhelmed by the reality of national governments adopting short-term policies for marginal economic advantage to the detriment of the global commons.

The chapter focuses on the role the UN Leviathan should play. No single entity can hope to successfully deal with a problem of this magnitude. It will take enormous efforts from many sectors of society. The UN Leviathan is an important actor and beyond continuing its work of gathering and disseminating information on global warming, there are several new steps that are unpacked in the chapter.

One of the most successful tools ever developed by the UN is the Human Development Index. It is basically a name and shame index wrapped up in caring language. The UN needs a sharp name and shame tool for climate change. The good news is that it need not invent one. The Climate Change Performance Index already exists, has fifteen years behind it, and is reputable. It needs to be expanded beyond the current crop of countries, though they account for 90% of the problem, and then given UN branding. Hopefully, it will have the same impact on public opinion as has the Human Development Index. Incidentally, the United States comes dead last in the Climate Change Performance index.

The chapter has a discussion of the concepts of free speech, fraudulent misrepresentation, and international criminal law, including the origins of the concept of crimes against humanity. Individuals may express whatever opinions they wish including climate change denial. But what if these views are expressed by a person in corporate or government authority who knows them to be wrong but benefits materially from that climate change denial? We are now in the domestic law field of fraud. On the global plane, we need to turn to international criminal law. The UN Leviathan needs to designate willful climate change denial by a person in authority as a crime against humanity. The designation, though difficult to justify on precedential grounds, has the considerable advantage of being literally correct.

Finally, the chapter reviews the entire strategy of dealing with global climate change. We have placed far too much faith in governments. Yet, even the best of them determine policy through a short-term calculus imposed by the next election. Relying on governments has simply not worked. We need a new strategy, and the chapter spells out what it calls the Davos gambit. For many, the corporate world has a reputation for greed and dodgy behavior.

And, like governments, it deals with short-term deadlines like quarterly reports and annual general meetings. But much of the corporate world, and certainly the world's two largest industries, insurance and pensions, necessarily take a longer-term perspective. Global warming is bad for business. The corporate world must be shamed, cajoled, and flattered into becoming the champion of climate change mitigation. This strategy holds more promise than relying on governments and their empty slogans. The corporate world has the power of trade and investment. These need to be harnessed for the greater good.

## ONE BILLION REFUGEES

The next chapter employs the term "refugee" in a far broader way than the current definition which is based on the early Cold War realities and codified in the 1951 Refugee Convention. The current definition requires an individual to flee across an international border because of a well-founded fear of persecution for a limited set of reasons. The archetype the drafters had in mind was the idealistic freedom-loving young person refusing to live under communist rule and fleeing to the West. The rule established was that such a person could not be sent back. All well and good. But we are living in a different world with different needs.

The germ of the concept we need to draw from the 1951 definition is the reasonableness of escape. But it need not necessarily be escape from political persecution. It might be escape from a chaotic failed state, escape from a natural disaster, or escape from an anthropogenic disaster. A study by the United Nations University estimates that in the second half of this century, there could be one billion people seeking such escapes.[26] Even half or a quarter of that number would overwhelm the current capacities and could trigger international conflict.

Not even a Leviathan can "solve" a problem of this magnitude. But it will take a Leviathan to manage it so as not to destabilize the rest of the world. The response to a mini version of this crisis, the one million refugees who flooded into Europe in 2015, demonstrated the essentially Hobbesian response of national governments. The three options for dealing with people reasonably seeking refuge are care in the place of first escape, return once it is reasonable to do so and resettlement in a third country. The chapter will examine each of these and plot the role of the UN Leviathan in their execution.

## MORE PANDEMICS

When I began writing this book, pandemics were not at the forefront of my research. Even though there was criticism of the response to the 2014–16 Ebola outbreak, the general view was that the world health system seemed capable of handling things. COVID-19 overturned that calculus. It demonstrated the weakness of the multilateral system and the selfishness of national governments. It has convinced me that the world needs a global health Leviathan.

The World Health Organization (WHO) is not that Leviathan. The chapter determines that it is very much a creation of the twentieth century, a timid hostage of governments with little courage to take an independent stand. The major evidence of the incapacities of the organization is particularly eloquent—the world has established new bodies to do the work that the WHO used to do. Both Gavi, the Vaccine Alliance, and the Global Fund to Fight AIDS, Tuberculosis and Malaria (Global Fund) have been established this century to vaccinate children and deal with the three diseases. They have become the brains of the process and UN entities such as the WHO and UNICEF are basically contracted suppliers, though they discharge important quality control and delivery jobs, respectively.

The revolution was not triggered by a government or a UN official, but by Bill Gates. He is at the tip of the spear of the many non-state actors that play a critical role in the global health system. Gates brings with him many private sector values such as competition, bargaining, evidence-based decisions, efficiency, higher volumes, and lower costs which have transformed the working methods of the global health system. Matching their importance in the funding and delivery processes, non-state actors have also become part of the governance structures of both Gavi and the Global Fund.

COVID-19 demonstrates the structural weakness in the global health system. China, for Leninist reasons, did not abide by its responsibility immediately to report a possible pandemic precursor event. And once the virus escaped Wuhan and began to devastate vulnerable populations in country after country, the governments of the world began to behave in a Hobbesian manner of blame all against all. The assumptions about how a global health system works were all stripped away. The WHO became a hostage in the feud between China and the United States. Countries competed and refused to cooperate in fighting the pandemic. The realization dawned that the system in fact relied on a benign national hegemon for its success. That hegemon has abdicated and so we now need a Leviathan.

Bill Gates is not the Leviathan. As noted, the United States abdicated its role. China is an unacceptable replacement. The best response is to turn the

WHO into the Leviathan we need. The chapter lists the four things that are required of a UN global health Leviathan: independent funding; tripartite World Health Assembly governance; focused legal and enforcement powers; and competent staff.

Each of these can be achieved, and as is the case for this and many other proposals, a precedent exists. The WHO already has the power to legislate international health regulations, it is simply a matter of utilizing that power more broadly. And the UN Security Council has already determined that a pandemic can be a threat to international peace and security under Chapter VII of the Charter. A tripartite World Health Assembly, including powerful industry representatives, would develop further enforcement measures. We now look back calmly on the terrifying Ebola outbreak. The COVID-19 outbreak has dwarfed the Ebola fear. Will the next pandemic make us look back calmly at COVID-19?

## A VISION, NOT A ROADMAP

As noted in the opening paragraph, the United Nations as Leviathan is not a description but an aspiration. It is a vision for which there is no roadmap. This will be criticized. What is the point of aspiring to something which is unacceptable to the filibuster-enabled United States Senate or to the Kremlin dictator-for-life? Why point to a better future but refuse to tell the reader how to get there? I feel the weight of the criticism, but it is misplaced. There is no roadmap to the future. The analogy does not hold, a roadmap can only be drawn for an existing geography. The immediate future may well benefit from a plan, a strategy, a campaign. But the longer-term future can only be envisioned, it cannot be plotted. If people want this future vision, they will have to fight for it.

I make one exception to this approach. Because the veto power in the UNSC as currently exercised stands as a roadblock to any progress in making the UN a more relevant and effective institution, the concluding chapter plots a path for a significant restriction in the use of the veto. The veto should only be available for decisions under Chapter VII of the Charter. All other decisions should be seen as procedural. Basically, the international community must gang up on the permanent members of the Security Council and formally reinterpret the Charter. The chapter plots how.

The concluding chapter attempts to tie together some of the ideas in this book. Because Tobin taxation forms a fundamental foundation for the vision of the UN as Leviathan, some of the principles underpinning it will be discussed. It needs to be progressive, not regressive, taxation. It needs to fall on the shoulders of those who can carry the weight. And it needs to be able to be collected. It is not new money but rather a zero-sum game. It will lead to a major battle with governments, perhaps even the fundamental battle.

The issue of a reformed UN versus a UN 3.0 needs to be grappled with. The term "reform" has lost salience through overuse. The literal meaning is worth recalling, to form anew. Black letter lawyers will argue that the only way to do so is with a root and branch rewriting of the Charter which would then have to be ratified by the necessary qualified majority including the five permanent members of the Security Council. There are several amendments to the Charter, including in relation to the size of the Security Council which have been adopted in this way. But this method of reform is the exception, not the rule. Most of the important innovations at the UN came about through practice, rather than through amendment. This is how peacekeeping was developed. This is how the entire development agenda was pursued. This is how the various human rights protections were instituted. A series of resolutions by the General Assembly and the Security Council could do the trick. But if that is not forthcoming, the difficult fallback option is not simply to renew, but to restart and build a UN 3.0. The big difference between the time of the San Francisco conference and today is that governments no longer hold a monopoly on decision making.

The concluding chapter will also try to situate this book in the political science literature. I am not an advocate of a world government. I simply cannot envisage it. When it is portrayed in fiction, like the science fiction movie *The Fifth Element*, it is a Weberian institution with massive military might. A world government attempting to hold preponderant force terrifies me. The UN Leviathan is not a world government, but it may deliver some of the positives expected of a government. It will lead. It will develop norms and rules. It will speak for "we the peoples." It will also accuse and castigate, and it may prosecute and convict. It is envisionable in a way that world government is not. Accordingly, while I see this book as part of the cannon of cosmopolitanism, the term "world governance" replaces "world government."

## A CONFESSION

I occasionally fall victim to despair. The evidence of toxic climate change, the current Anthropocene extinctions, aggressive wars of choice, growing levels of inequality, and continuing injustice in so many parts of the world, is being met by a shrug of inaction. We should not be too surprised when we examine the current crop of global leaders; there was until recently a "moron"[27] in the White House, and there remains a ruthless megalomaniac in Zhōngnánhǎi, and a murderous amoral opportunist in the Kremlin. This is not a recipe for the sort of global cooperation that is currently required. I sometimes tell myself not to worry because I will be dead soon, so it is not my problem.

But there is another perspective. We are living through a hinge in history. The post-WWII global architecture guaranteed by the United States is no longer fit for purpose and the guarantee is no longer bankable. We need to invent the next phase of international and inter-human relations. We are armed with knowledge and communication tools. We should see this as a hopeful time when we can seize the future. Drifting to calamity is one option. This book proposes a different option whereby our choice is between a Hobbesian future and his Leviathan solution. We all must do whatever we can for as long as we can, to respond. I am now a scholar, so this is what I can do. Hopefully, it will be one of many influences leading to a global social contract in favor of change and the establishment of the UN Leviathan we need.

## NOTES

1. The Project Gutenberg EBook of Leviathan, by Thomas Hobbes, https://www.gutenberg.org/files/3207/3207-h/3207-h.htm
2. Lou Marinoff, "Thomas Hobbes: A grim portrait of human nature." *The Times Literary Supplement*, 11 January 2019.
3. Max Weber, "Politics as a Vocation." 1918. From H.H. Gerth and C. Wright Mills (Translated and edited), *From Max Weber: Essays in Sociology*, 77128, (New York: Oxford University Press, 1946).
4. UN Charter, Article 4(1)
5. Hedley Bull, *The Anarchical Society: A Study of Order in World Politics*. (London: Macmillan Press, 1977)
6. Ibid., 23
7. William J Burns, "The United States Needs a New Foreign Policy," *The Atlantic*, July 14, 2020.
8. Bull, op. cit., 17
9. Burns, op. cit.
10. Press Release S-G/382. "Address by Secretary-General Dag Hammarskjöld at University of California Convocation, Berkeley, California." May 13. 1954.
11. Roland Rich, *Democracy in Crisis: Why, Where, How to Respond*. (Boulder Co.: Lynne Rienner Publishers, 2017), Chapter 5.
12. Robert Klitgaard, "International Cooperation Against Corruption," *Finance and Development*, March 1998, 3–6
13. Thomas Weiss, *What's Wrong with the United Nations and How to Fix It*. (Cambridge: Polity Press, 2016).
14. Kevin Rudd, "UN 2030: Rebuilding Order in a Fragmenting World," Chair's Report, Independent Commission on Multilateralism, 2016. https://asiasociety.org/sites/default/files/I/IPI-ICM-UN-2030-Chairs-Report2FINAL.pdf

15. Boutros Boutros-Ghali, *Unvanquished—a U.S. – U.N. Saga,* (New York: Random House, 1999).

16. Kofi Annan, with Nader Mousavizadeh, *Interventions—A Life in War and Peace*, (New York: Penguin Press, 2012).

17. James Tobin, "A Proposal for International Monetary Reform," *Eastern Economic Journal*, vol. 4, Jul/Oct. 1978, 153–159.

18. FCC Aviation. n.d. "French Solidarity Tax." https://www.fccaviation.com/regulation/france/solidarity-tax

19. UN News, 2019, "General Assembly approves $3 billion UN budget for 2020," https://news.un.org/en/story/2019/12/1054431

20. US Department of State, "Department of State and USAID FY 2020 Budget Request." March 11, 2019. https://www.state.gov/department-of-state-and-usaid-fy-2020-budget-request/. This figure includes USAID.

21. United Nations, "Now is the Time for a Collective Push for Peace and Reconciliation," 23 March 2020, https://www.un.org/en/globalceasefire

22. United Nations, "Time to negotiate end to 'unwinnable' war in Ukraine, Guterres declares," 22 March 2022, https://news.un.org/en/story/2022/03/1114392

23. World Conference on Human Rights, "Vienna Declaration and Programme of Action." Vienna, 25 June 1993. https://www.ohchr.org/en/professionalinterest/pages/vienna.aspx, paras. 8, 74

24. Ted Wachtel, "Governance and the use of authority: encompassing diverse definitions of 'Restorative.'" *European Forum for Restorative Justice*. September Newsletter Volume 17(3), 2016, 8

25. Sidney Tarrow, *The New Transnational Activism*. (Cambridge University Press, 2006). 194.

26. Nidhi Nagabhatla, Panthea Pouramin, Rupal Brahmbhatt, Cameron Fioret, Talia Glickman, K. Bruce Newbold, Vladimir Smakhtin. "Water and Migration: A Global Overview," *UNU-INWEH Report Series*, Issue 10, 2020.

27. Adam K.Raymond, "Report: Tillerson Called Trump a 'Moron' for Comparing War to Renovating a Restaurant." *New York Magazine*, October 4, 2017. http://nymag.com/intelligencer/2017/10/report-tillerson-called-trump-a-moron.html?gtm=top

# *Chapter 2*

# First Person Singular

As this book is about a vision of the future, the reader is entitled to know who is perceiving it. A vision can visit anybody. But it might be the more compelling if that somebody had some experience and knowledge of the subject. This chapter sets out the case in favor of the author's credibility. To make the case, this chapter will adopt the concept of the three United Nations drawn from the UN Intellectual History Project.[1] The point of this story is to note that the author is one of a small handful of people to have been a member of each of the three UNs.

The First UN is the UN of Member States, all 193 of them. It is what the President of the 63rd General Assembly, Father Miguel d'Escoto Brockmann of Nicaragua, liked to call the G193.[2] It is the UN of the General Assembly and the Security Council. It is the UN of foreign ministers, permanent missions, and foreign ministry headquarters in capital cities. It is this UN that the public naturally sees as *the* UN. The Second UN is the UN of Secretariats, the total number of whom around the world, including those working in specialized agencies, comes to about 38,000.[3] The Third UN is the UN of non-state actors who work with or through the UN. It includes individuals, civil society organizations, philanthropists, academic institutions, and perhaps even private sector institutions working under the banner of corporate social responsibility.

I am one of a very small set of people to have had the privilege to be part of each of the three United Nations. I served in the Australian foreign ministry for 23 years and represented Australia in various UN conferences and assemblies in Geneva, New York, Paris, and Vienna. I also served at headquarters in Canberra as Assistant Secretary for International Organizations overseeing Australia's involvement in the UN. I was subsequently a member of the Secretariat in New York for seven years serving as Head of the UN Democracy Fund and, for the final four years, concurrently as Director of the UN Office for Partnerships. And I have also been an academic, leading the Centre for Democratic Institutions at the Australian National University for seven years in which time I published a book about the UN.[4] Currently I am the Director of the MA Program in Political Science—United Nations and Global Policy Studies at Rutgers University, New Jersey. I will draw on these various experiences in this chapter.

## THE FIRST UN

It is not difficult to be harshly critical about the first UN. Then Secretary-General Ban Ki-moon once lashed out at the Security Council for its inaction during the Syrian war describing it as a "shameful symbol of the international community's divisions and failure."[5] Indeed, there is a disquieting uniformity in the criticisms coming from both the right and the left, though the reasoning differs. The American right accuses the UN of being ineffective and is suspicious of UN attempts to regulate American conduct. The European left accuses the UN of being ineffective and subservient to its political masters, the first of which is the United States. Whether the critics realize it or not, these lines of criticism are aimed at the first UN, the Member States of the UN. This is the Madison Square Garden argument famously made by Richard Holbrooke in his attack on irrational criticism of the institution: "Blaming 'the United Nations' for what happens inside the talk palaces on the East River is like blaming Madison Square Garden for the New York Knicks."[6]

Having been a member of delegations to UN conferences and assemblies and later having witnessed the work of those delegations, it is not difficult to point to the problems. The most obvious criticism is their narrow focus on immediate national interests. There are very few climate change deniers among UN delegations, yet it took a decade to achieve a non-binding UN action agenda to deal with a problem that poses an existential threat to humanity. The reason is that delegations, and the Foreign Ministries that instruct them, and the governments in which those ministries form part, are motivated by narrow short-term national or even partisan interests. The astounding argument I heard from a delegate from the sub-Continent went along these lines: "the West has been polluting the planet for decades to become wealthy, now it's our turn to pollute the planet and get rich."

At least that argument had an (ultimately self-defeating) economic premise. Far too often, delegates at the UN take positions for the narrowest political reasons. European countries, whether EU members or simply hopeful candidates, will fall in line with EU policies regardless of what they might actually think of them. Some Africans will oppose the application of international criminal law because an African may be prosecuted. As for the global South as a whole, it is as if we were still living through the era of colonization, because this is the issue that continues to motivate the Group of 77 (now with 134 members.) Its undoubted continuing influence demonstrates the victory of politics over reality. Even Australian delegations would normally be instructed to choose national interest over international principles where these were assessed to come into conflict, the exception being those rare times when a progressive government is confidently in power and gives preference to reasons of international solidarity.

Yet, it is these same delegations, instructed by ministries that form part of national governments that are also largely responsible for the many achievements of the UN. The hundreds of multilateral treaties, the impressive human rights canon, the dozens of peacekeeping forces, and the achievements in eradicating diseases, all were debated, agreed, and largely funded by the First UN.

It is a sign of the success of the system that we take many of these rules and systems for granted. But it is nevertheless a significant body of work. When candidate states join the European Union, they need to catch up to the *acquis communautaire*. The *acquis* (French, meaning that which has been acquired) is the huge body of laws, common rights and obligations that is binding on all the EU member states. The UN *acquis* is equally formidable.

As noted, the UN *acquis* includes the field of peacekeeping. While it is necessary and useful to criticize UN peacekeeping, it would be untenable to make a case that the world would be a better place without it. There have been 71 peacekeeping missions of which over a dozen remain active and in which 125,000 people serve, the large majority of whom are soldiers.[7] An example of the reality of international solidarity is the provenance of these soldiers; they come from 121 countries.[8]

As a small cog in Australia's delegation to the Third UN Conference on the Law of the Sea in the late 1970s and early 80s, I saw the best of the First UN. Perhaps it was because of the technical nature of the subject matter, and no doubt also because the tyranny of geography imposed certain positions on participating nations that overwhelmed any allegiance to ideology, but whatever the underlying reasons, the debates at UNCLOS 3 were far more on point than point scoring. The conference pioneered some innovative approaches. The package deal approach meant that the whole of the text had to be accepted or rejected, reservations were not permitted thus denying countries the right to pick and choose those parts of the text to which they agreed to be bound. Taking a lead from the 1972 Stockholm conference on the environment, civil society organizations were invited to participate in the deliberations. It would have been easily defensible to argue that as a treaty making conference among nations, non-state actors had no place at the table. But under the astute leadership of Tommy Koh of Singapore, the decision was taken to allow them in. The conference benefitted from their expertise and from the uncomfortable knowledge that the diplomatic deal-making going on was being watched by "outsiders." And the conference adopted and defined a concept which may yet have a deep meaning in the future when it declared that the area of the seabed beyond national jurisdiction is the "common heritage of mankind." Perhaps in the years to come the international community may wish to revisit this concept and consider whether the air we breathe, the forests that generate it and the soil in which our crops are grown are also part of the common heritage of humankind.

I experienced the ethical discomfort that members of the First UN dread—instructions contrary to one's principles. Turning the clock forward a couple of decades from those Law of the Sea days, I found myself as head of the International Organizations branch of the foreign ministry. One of the issues in my in-tray concerned the (then) draft Declaration on the Rights of Indigenous Peoples (it was adopted by the UN General Assembly in 2007). Up to the election of a conservative government in 1996, Australia had been cautiously in favor of the process and open to the text of the document but, thereafter, the government attitude was closer to one of hostility. I was to lead the Australian delegation to the Geneva negotiations armed with a set of instructions from the new government with which I profoundly disagreed. No, I did not resign. But prior to the first session in Geneva, I called for a meeting with the civil society representatives of the Australian indigenous community and told them the best I could do for them was to be honest and explain that the government's position had changed. During any negotiation, it is a tactical decision as to how active a delegation should be and, on this occasion, the Australian delegation spent much of the time quietly reviewing the issues. One of my instructions, however, was to support the position of the Australian states in our federal system and a senior official of Western Australia formed part of the delegation. It so happened that this state government had made a heartfelt apology to its indigenous people, a step the conservative federal government would refuse to contemplate for its entire decade-long time in office. Following my instructions to support our state governments, I read this apology to the indigenous people into the conference record in plangent tones. I suspect that many delegates did not quite understand the significance of the word "Western" and saw it as an apology from "Australia."

I would leave the ministry soon thereafter. Not bitter and twisted, as can happen, but rather chasing the opportunity to head Australia's new democracy institute at the Australian National University. Accordingly, I would in a small way become part of the Third UN before moving on to the Second UN and later returning to the Third UN.

## THE SECOND UN

In 2007, after a rigorous selection process, I eagerly took on the job of heading the UN Democracy Fund in New York, and thus became a member of the Second UN. I was under no illusion as to the quality of my new colleagues, after all, during my job interview one of the panel members fell asleep! But I was delighted to encounter so many dedicated and competent men and women in the Secretariat. The question that hung over all of us concerned our role. Were we the mere cyphers of the Member States forever awaiting their detailed instructions, or did we have some notion of an independent obligation to advance the UN agenda and meet its goals?

Many members of the Secretariat to a greater or lesser degree adopt the former posture. They are in thrall to the delegations and in particular that from their own country. They wait (mostly in vain) for clear instructions from the General Assembly. They adopt a tried and tested Soviet idea, that if they never take any initiative they cannot possibly get into trouble. What struck me as odd about this posture is that unless one is caught with one's hand in the cash register, the UN does not know how to discipline a poorly performing staff member and so there is no trouble to get into! I and many others took a different approach. It flows naturally from Article 99 of the Charter: "The Secretary-General may bring to the attention of the Security Council any matter which *in his opinion* may threaten the maintenance of international peace and security" (italic added).

The Charter foresees a Secretary-General with his or (hopefully before too long) her own opinions. And as the staff members of that Secretary-General, it also follows that we would support that Secretary-General when he exercises his opinions. Indeed Article 100 of the Charter makes it clear that the Secretariat should "not seek or receive instructions from any government" and that Member States shall "not seek to influence them." While our professional loyalty must be to the Secretary-General, the ultimate loyalty of all staff members must be to "we the peoples" who bestowed the mandate on both the states and the Secretariat.

This is not to downplay the fundamental role of the First UN. Acting on the mandate they have through the Charter, their job is to ratify, bring into force, and enforce the international community's norms, rules, and principles. The Second UN supports them in that role. The dilemma arises when a Member State ignores or does not comply with this *acquis*. Two former Secretaries-General, Boutros Boutros-Ghali and Kofi Annan, found out to their cost what happened when they called out the United States as not in conformity with the rules it had helped establish. Boutros-Ghali provides a step-by-step account of how he was denied a second term after he acted independently and thus fell out of step with the US.[9] Kofi Annan also relates how he had to withstand "a barrage of attacks against me" when he declared the invasion of Iraq to be illegal.[10] A more detailed account is contained in the following chapter.

I certainly did not face that level of attack when in charge of the UN Democracy Fund (UNDEF), but I take it as a sign that I was doing my job effectively that more than a few delegations were deeply displeased with my leadership. When I took over, UNDEF was under interim leadership and had made some good progress in establishing itself. But it followed a common trait within the Second UN—risk aversion. It avoided the risk of offending Member States; it avoided the risk of supporting "unknown" entities; and it avoided the risk of getting its UN colleagues off-side by the simple expedient of directing some of the flow of funds to UN agencies. This path would clearly lead to a tame product. So, we decided to manage these risks instead of simply running away from them. UNDEF became a funder of local civil society in the global South with very few projects going to the well-known NGOs from donor countries. UNDEF slowly but surely shut off funding to other UN agencies unless this was the only way to fund an NGO on the ground. And UNDEF, while never wishing to be needlessly provocative, selected grant recipients without consulting the Member States in whose territory the project would be delivered. If a delegation were unhappy with our choice, it could tell UNDEF not to fund the project on its territory and UNDEF would have no choice except to comply. But, as I told each of the complaining Ambassadors in turn, that process would not be confidential, and I would report it to our Board and thus the episode could be expected to enter the public domain. I think it is a sign that the project selection was in fact supportive of democratization that the countries that complained included Belarus, Nicaragua, and Venezuela. The UNDEF Board was dominated by its major funders and in particular the two largest funders at that time, the United States and India. The Board supported the process UNDEF had developed allowing it to continue its work.

One of my proudest achievements at the UN was to be part of the small Secretariat team that drafted the Secretary-General's Guidance Note on Democracy.[11] While it is true that the norm making role is very much in the hands of the First UN, the Secretary-General can inject himself in the process by way of providing instructions to his staff. These guidance notes set forth the Secretary-General's perspectives on how Secretariat members should deal with various issues.[12] I recall, at the high-level staff meeting in which Ban Ki-moon approved the Guidance Note, clearing with him our intention to publish the text. He readily agreed, fully aware of its normative character.

The Guidance Note on democracy sets out a position on various issues on which Member States would never be able to reach consensus:

- It takes a position on the relationship between democracy and development, by saying the latter "is more likely to take hold if people are given a genuine say in their own governance"
- It puts the emphasis on internal threats to democracy ("coups") rather than external threats
- While privileging local ownership, it does so only within the context of internationally agreed norms and principles, thus rejecting cultural relativism
- It stakes out an important position in describing democracy as "a reflection of self-determination"
- It acknowledges the indispensable role of a free press, an active civil society, and a multi-party system.

The Second UN can be an important force of international progress under the leadership of a courageous Secretary-General. But it remains a bureaucracy and it is unlikely to be the source of many new ideas and innovations. For that one must turn to the Third UN.

## THE THIRD UN

The Third UN comprises all those civil society actors, non-government organizations and individuals who interact with the UN in various ways. Weiss thinks of these groups as knowledge networks or epistemic communities.[13] Indeed, the framers of the Charter already had in mind a Third UN, without adopting this terminology, when the Charter empowers the Economic and Social Council to make arrangements for consultations with non-government organizations in Article 71. The Third UN is thus also an "original" part of the UN.

I wish to suggest two sub-categories within the Third UN not discussed in the original Weiss formulation: The Third UN can be in either a formal or an informal relationship with the UN. From the outset, the UN understood its own limitations. National interest would invariably drive the policy positions of the First UN and despite some occasional flashes of independence, the Second UN would normally simply service the needs of the First UN. This may be a necessary requirement of *realpolitik*, but it is rarely a path to innovation and new ideas. For that reason, the UN accepted the need to appoint independent outside experts to think through key ideas and present recommendations for consideration by the First UN. Some of the key successes of the UN system have come through this means.

An early example of a formal association with the Third UN was the establishment of the International Comparison Program as a means of comparing the economies of UN Member States. The concept of purchasing power parity (PPP) had been known for some time and incisively theorized in the early twentieth century but it only became a necessary part of the international architecture when the UN Statistical Division and the World Bank, beginning in 1967, decided to launch an ongoing economic comparison process requiring solid comparative data. A partnership was born with the University of Pennsylvania where Professor Alan Heston and his colleagues produced the necessary world PPP tables on which the UN's comparative analysis rested.[14]

The "outside commission" method was pioneered in 1968 by the President of the World Bank, Robert McNamara, who asked Lester Pearson, former Prime Minister of Canada and Nobel Peace Prize laureate, to form a Commission to undertake a study of the consequences of twenty years of development assistance.[15] This was followed up in the 1980s by the Independent Commission on International Development Issues, chaired by former German Chancellor Willy Brandt, which set the goal of a 0.7% ratio of official development assistance to gross national product.[16]

Another telling example of a formal partnership with the Third UN is the creation of one of the UN's greatest contributions, the Human Development Index. In the late 1980s, the Administrator of UNDP sought out a noted Pakistani economist, Mahbub ul Haq, to advise on ways of measuring progress other than through the blunt national income per capita means. Mahbub ul-Haq based his ideas on Amartya Sen's capabilities theory and invited Sen to help design the new index.[17] Sen initially demurred arguing that any attempt to encapsulate such a vast array of issues into a single figure was "crude and inelegant."[18] But he subsequently joined the design team and the result has been not only an innovation in measurement but a new way of conceptualizing development, a subject that will be unpacked in a later chapter.

A good example of a continuing formal role for the Third UN can be seen in the special procedures of the Human Rights Council, whereby independent human rights experts have mandates to report on thematic or country-specific human rights issues. There are 44 thematic and 12 country mandates, as well as several commissions of enquiry.[19] The experts mandated to investigate these issues are independent and do not represent their countries of nationality or their employers (often academic bodies). They are unpaid though they receive allowances for expenses incurred. Member States usually cooperate with the experts but there have certainly been cases when experts have been refused entry to a country in question. It is their independence and expertise that lend credibility to the reports of these experts, and this allows the First UN to take appropriate action based on their recommendations.

A broader and deeper iteration of the formal Third UN mechanism can be seen in the work of the Intergovernmental Panel on Climate Change. Though it is an intergovernmental panel and thus formally forms part of the First UN, its work draws on hundreds of scientists who write and peer review its reports at the request of the IPCC.[20]

The key to the distinction between the formal and informal status within the Third UN turns on whether or not the involvement of the outsider is formally requested by the UN or its entities. Where an individual Member State takes the initiative, it should not be seen strictly as part of the formal Third UN. In 2000, Canada established the International Commission on Intervention and State Sovereignty chaired by my former boss Gareth Evans and his Algerian colleague Mohamed Sahnoun. It led in remarkably quick time to the UN General Assembly in 2005 adopting the doctrine of the responsibility to protect. It represents a leading example of the work of the Third UN and perhaps can be seen to fall into a semi-formal category as it was an initiative of a Member State aiming to contribute to the UN normative canon.

The informal Third UN includes those thousands of NGOs which are accredited to ECOSOC or cooperate with other parts of the UN system. It was my great privilege as Executive Head of UNDEF to expand the numbers in this category through the funding of civil society projects around the world. Applications have been received from some 30,000 civil society organization the vast majority of which come from the global South and almost 800 of which have been funded. To a lesser or greater degree, they have become part of the Third UN.

The Third UN also includes thousands of academics all around the world who study, teach, and publish on the topics associated with the UN. Various parts can be said to have formal, semi-formal and informal status. The UN University in Tokyo and the University for Peace in San José, Costa Rica, were both established by resolutions of the UN General Assembly, the former in 1972 and the latter in 1980, and thus fall into the category of "at the request" of the UN. But they must both find their own funding and they act as independent institutions. The Academic Council on the United Nations System (ACUNS) is probably best seen as a semi-formal body. It was founded in 1987 to stimulate and support research and teaching on the role of the United Nations.

The rest of the academic world teaching about and studying the UN, including the UN Intellectual History Project based at the Graduate Center of the City University of New York from which the concept of the Three UNs is borrowed, is part of the informal Third UN where I now happily find myself once again. I was first in this category in 2004 when publishing *The UN Role in Promoting Democracy: Between Ideals and Reality* with United Nations University Press. This publication provides a strong example of the value of the Third UN. The book had thoughtful essays by noted academics such as Tom Farer, Laurence Whitehead and Edward Newman; technical contributions on UN transition authorities by Simon Chesterman, post-conflict elections by Ben Reilly and UN Security Council Mandates by Roland Rich; insider accounts of the work of the UN Electoral Assistance Division by Robin Ludwig and of UNDP by Richard Ponzio; and case studies of Namibia (Henning Melber), Cambodia (Sorpong Peou), Kosovo (Ylber Hysa), Timor Leste (Tanya Hohe) and Afghanistan (Amin Saikal). It thus provides a learned perspective that neither the First nor the Second UN have the independence or vocation to produce. With so many developments in this field in the fifteen years that have passed since its publication, it clearly needs a second volume! And the next iteration of my professional life was to migrate to academia, teaching half a dozen courses at Rutgers including one on the UN Security Council.

Should the Third UN be limited to academics, civil society and engaged individuals? Are there other categories that can also shelter within its span? Weiss initially rejected the idea of having any for-profit entity as part of the Third UN.[21] I agree that entities acting for profit do not fit. Thus, though consultants and contractors may add heft to the work of the UN, they remain part of the market. But I am inclined to be a little more flexible in the definition and, in discussion, Weiss agreed. I recently completed a consultancy for UNDP in Bhutan advising on non-state actors and philanthropy. UNDP met my expenses, but I of course did not ask for any fee or honorarium. Perhaps people in that position are called consultants but are not part of the market but rather, part of the Third UN.

Which leads to a question about corporations cooperating with the UN as part of their corporate social responsibility rather than their profit-making purpose. There is a vast amount of knowledge and expertise in the corporate world that the international community could surely employ to further the goals of the United Nations. Perhaps we should begin to welcome them as thought leaders in their fields of expertise. That is why in 2013, wearing my other hat as Executive Director of the UN Office for Partnerships I invited the UN Department of Economic and Social Affairs to join in hosting an ECOSOC event to discuss *The Solution Revolution*, a concept and book,[22] by Deloitte partners William Eggers and Paul Macmillan. The book argues that the solutions to the world's most pressing problems will only be found through dynamic partnerships of many sectors; public, private, civil society and academic. Deloitte is clearly part of the market economy but in relation to this research it might also have a foot in the Third UN.

I had previously partnered with Deloitte in a different field. The UN Democracy Fund had hundreds of projects around the world but only 5 professional staff members. We could not possibly monitor all these projects firsthand. Deloitte offered to help by inviting its many offices around the world to step in *pro bono* and visit a project to observe the passage of a pre-agreed milestone such as the holding of a training course or the convening of a meeting. While this might at times entail a half-day at another office in the same city, at other times it might require an eight-hour bus trip into the jungle to visit an indigenous community. We never paid Deloitte a fee, and they even met their own travel expenses, but that does not mean the company did not benefit from the arrangement. Staff surveys consistently showed that monitoring UNDEF projects was their favorite activity.

## HOW THEY FIT TOGETHER

The exact boundaries of each of the three UNs may be fuzzy and their inter-relationships may resist tight classification, but the concept remains valuable. Perhaps the best way of understanding those relationships is by borrowing the economic doctrine of comparative advantage. The First UN, speaking as it does for the world's governments, clearly has the advantage of authority and access to resources. It ratifies and enforces the world's normative principles. The Second UN has the advantages of continuity, proximity, and occasionally, expertise. As a permanent Secretariat it provides a good counterweight to the First UN's delegations that change personnel every few years. The Second UN also acts as a bridge between the First and Third UNs. But it is the Third UN which generates innovation and new ideas and is therefore indispensable to the UN "project."

The concept of the three UNs remains valuable to understand the concept of the UN Leviathan. Placing the First UN in its context demonstrates its importance but also its limitations. As noted above, the UN Leviathan must maximize the benefits from its Member States while minimizing the limitations these same Member States wish to place on the UN independence and competence. Succeeding chapters will demonstrate how this can be achieved.

## NOTES

1. Thomas G.Wiess, Tatiana Carayannis and Richard Jolly, "The 'Third' United Nations," *Global Governance* 15, 2009, 123–142.

2. Rain Barrel Communications. 2017. "Rain Barrel Remembers Miguel d'Escoto," https://www.rainbarrelcommunications.com/the-flow/rain-barrel-remembers-miguel-descoto

3. United Nations General Assembly. 2019. "Composition of the Secretariat: staff demographics: Report of the Secretary-General." A/74/82, 22 April 2019. Compare for example with the 100,000 employees of the US Department of Agriculture.

4. Edward Newman and Roland Rich, *The UN Role in Promoting Democracy: Between Ideals and Reality*, (Tokyo: United Nations University Press, 2004).

5. UN News Center, "At Security Council, Ban and UN special envoy outline 'way forward' on political solution for war-torn Syria." 29 July 2015 http://www.un.org/apps/news/story.asp?NewsID=51523#.VjzRzPmrTWI

6. Derek Chollet and Samantha Power, *The Unquiet American,* (New York: Public Affairs, 2012), 257. And here we are a decade later and the Knicks are still stinking up the joint!

7. United Nations Peacekeeping, *Peacekeeping Fact Sheet.* 30 November 2021. https://peacekeeping.un.org/sites/default/files/peacekeeping_missions_factsheet_246_nov2021_en.pdf

8. Ibid.

9. Boutros Boutros-Ghali, *Unvanquished: A US-UN Saga*, (New York: Random House, 1999).

10. Kofi Annan with Nader Mousavizadeh, *Interventions: A Life in War and Peace*, (New York: Penguin Press, 2012), 357.

11. United Nations. n.d. "Guidance Note of the Secretary-General on Democracy." https://www.un.org/en/pdfs/FINAL%20Guidance%20Note%20on%20Democracy.pdf

12. Apart from Democracy, other Guidance Notes deal with subjects such as Rule of Law; Transitional Justice; Statelessness; Racial Discrimination; Justice for Children; and Reparations for Conflict-Related Sexual Violence.

13. Weiss et al., op. cit., 131

14. UN Department for Economic and Social Information and Policy Analysis, Statistical Division, *World Comparison of Real Gross Domestic Product and Purchasing Power, 1985 Phase V of the International Comparison Programme*. Introduction, http://unstats.un.org/unsd/methods/icp/gdp/gdp01_htm.htm#_2

15. World Bank. Commission on International Development, *The UNESCO Courier: a window open on the world.* XXIII. 2. 1970, 4–14. https://unesdoc.unesco.org/ark:/48223/pf0000056743

16. Share the World's Resources, "The Brandt Report: A Summary." 2006. http://www.sharing.org/information-centre/reports/brandt-report-summary

17. Amartya Sen, *Human Development Report 2010, 20th Anniversary Edition, The Real Wealth of Nations: Pathways to Human Development.* "Introduction," 2010. http://hdr.undp.org/sites/default/files/reports/270/hdr_2010_en_complete_reprint.pdf

18. Comments by Amartya Sen at the launch of the 2011 Human Development Report, UNDP, NY.

19. Office of the High Commissioner for Human Rights. 2015. *Special Procedures of the Human Rights Council* http://www.ohchr.org/EN/HRBodies/SP/Pages/Welcomepage.aspx

20. Intergovernmental Panel on Climate Change. n.d. "Procedures" https://www.ipcc.ch/documentation/procedures/

21. Weiss et al., op. cit., 128.

22. William D Eggers and Paul Macmillan, *The Solution Revolution: How Business, Government, and Social Enterprises Are Teaming Up to Solve Society's Toughest Problems*. (Boston: Harvard Business Review Press, 2013).

# *Chapter 3*

# The General Assemblies

Why is the title of this chapter in the plural? Because the United Nations General Assembly is not fit for purpose. Wholesale changes are required both to the Assembly and its purpose. Furthermore, a general assembly of governments is not a sufficiently representative body to be able to speak for the world community. For reasons of representativeness and effectiveness, the world needs several assemblies.

## WHAT IS WRONG WITH THE GENERAL ASSEMBLY?

Chapter IV of the Charter deals with the powers of the General Assembly (UNGA). Curiously, the subject on which there are the most words in this chapter is international peace. But that is the subject on which the UNGA has the least effective power. Its powers have trigger verbs such as "consider" and "discuss" but the Chapter makes clear that the UNGA is subservient to the Security Council. Article 12 even makes clear that while the Security Council is dealing with an issue, the UNGA "shall not make any recommendation with regard to that dispute or situation." The UNGA has tried to assert authority in the peace and security field through the Uniting for Peace process which the UN describes as follows:

> General Assembly resolution 377(V) is known as the Uniting for Peace resolution. Adopted in 1950, the resolution resolves that if the Security Council, because of lack of unanimity of the permanent members, fails to exercise its primary responsibility to act as required to maintain international peace and security . . . , the General Assembly shall consider the matter immediately with the view to making recommendations to Members . . . in order to restore international peace and security. If not in session, the General Assembly may meet using the mechanism of the emergency special session. To date, 10 emergency special sessions have been convened.[1]

The first emergency special session of the UNGA was held in 1956 on the topic of the Suez crisis and the most recent was in 2018 on the "Illegal Israeli actions in Occupied East Jerusalem and the rest of the Occupied Palestinian Territory."[2] Of the other eight special sessions, several have focused on the Middle East dispute while others have dealt with Namibia, Hungary, Lebanon, Democratic Republic of Congo and Afghanistan.[3] The above quote does not take into account developments in 2022 when, on February 28, the twelfth special session was held to discuss Russia's invasion of Ukraine and resulted in an overwhelming 141 votes in favor of a resolution demanding Russia's unconditional withdrawal, with only four countries (Belarus, Eritrea, North Korea and Syria) joining Russia in voting no.[4] The special sessions are useful for drawing attention to issues and allowing members of the UNGA to express outrage, but they do not produce the sort of results for which the Security Council is empowered under Chapter VII. The UNGA may discuss any question within the scope of the Charter. The Charter suggests that the UNGA focus on international cooperation in the political, economic, social, cultural and health fields; the development and codification of international law; and the international trusteeship system.

The one issue where the UNGA has a decisive role is the budget of the UN. Article 17 gives it that exclusive power, mirroring the role of a directly elected lower house in a parliamentary system. And it also has the power to apportion the mandatory contributions to the budget according to a scale of assessments worked out by one of its committees, the Committee on Contributions. There is a separate formula for the peacekeeping budget:

> The General Assembly apportions peacekeeping expenses based on a special scale of assessments under a complex formula that Member States themselves have established. This formula takes into account, among other things, the relative economic wealth of Member States, with the five permanent members of the Security Council required to pay a larger share because of their special responsibility for the maintenance of international peace and security.[5]

In the reconceived UN, the peacekeeping budget should primarily remain the burden of governments with enhanced responsibility shouldered by the permanent members. The responsibility of the UNGA for the regular budget of the UN should also continue to be met by Member States. But the budget would be split in two. The regular budget would cover the costs of meetings and the cost of drafting, translating, and disseminating the publications those meetings have requested. It would continue to cover the cost to the UN of its role as the depository of treaties. In other words, all the costs of servicing the needs of Member States should continue to be paid by those states.

Then there would be an action budget of the UN 3.0 which would be determined by the S-G and approved by the General Assemblies. That would be collected through various Tobin taxes. There will be more said on Tobin taxation in succeeding chapters. The basic idea is that it is a tax on globalization. It will be collected without the intermediation of governments but directly from airlines, shipping companies, and banks. It will be substantial. Though collected from commercial entities, ultimately the tax is passed on to consumers. The concluding chapter demonstrates how a cost of an average of $25 per year ultimately paid by urban consumers would provide the UN with an annual budget of more than $100 billion. One way of looking at this tax on globalization is that it will provide the world with a means of tackling global problems as well as providing a global social safety net.

Beyond its current decisive responsibility for the regular budget, the General Assembly has the power to discuss anything and decide nothing. Even when the UNGA currently decides the budget, it is constrained by various parameters. On the supply side, the Geneva Group of major contributors to the UN budget places limits on budget growth and monitors waste and overlap.[6] This is a legitimate weapon of budgetary oversight. The United States pursues an illegitimate practice of withholding contributions even though it has a treaty obligation to pay them. On the demand side, there is the tyranny of the previous budget, which means that only the slightest alterations are possible as every budget line has its own constituency. When I discussed the work of the General Assembly with a UN colleague who was responsible for servicing its needs, he used the analogy of a Christmas tree; everybody comes along with their own baubles and hooks them to the tree. Budget lines often relate to these baubles. The implication is that there is no coherence to the work of the UNGA.

The UNGA can discuss anything, and often reality impinges on the UNGA agenda requiring the body to pronounce on issues of economic crisis, looming conflict, or pandemics. But reality ultimately only has a limited influence on the UNGA because it has forged a path on which it is determined to proceed. That path is the main raison d'être of the UNGA, and it is the never-ending battle against . . . colonialism!

Some might consider that the age of decolonization is long over, that the battles have been fought and won, that the world has moved on, though it is true that colonialism has left many negative legacies. But for the UNGA, fighting colonialism remains the overarching theme, its mission, its glue. The enemy has morphed from the handful of colonizers, to all the wealthy countries of the global North. The alliance marshalled to fight these demons is the Group of 77 (G-77) which was established in 1964 by seventy-seven developing countries and although the members of the G-77 have increased to 134 countries, the original name was retained due to its historic significance.[7] At the very least, the G-77 is a veto player at the UN and no resolution or budgetary decision can be taken without its approval. It is also the agenda setter and often the key decision maker at the UN. The word "colonialism" is not mentioned in any of its founding documents, but that is the link that holds together the countries. Looking at the original 77 members, only Thailand had never been colonized, largely because its able kings had learned how to accommodate and play its two formidable colonial neighbors, the French and British empires, against each other. And colonialism remains the link between the members because, while ostensibly the organization is about developing countries, several of the current G77 members are now in the wealthy camp. The sad reality of the UNGA is that it is not a deliberative assembly because delegates arrive at the debates with fixed and unchangeable voting intentions. Compromise can occur with the aim of achieving a resolution by consensus, but where views are irreconcilable, the G-77 stick together come what may.

## New Caledonia

There are very few occasions when the vote of the G-77 is split, but I was involved in one such incident concerning the question of New Caledonia. I was the UN section head in the Australian foreign ministry when political events in the French territory of New Caledonia turned violent in the mid-1980s.[8] The indigenous Melanesian people of the island organized themselves and sought to gain political power, but they were outnumbered by the settlers from France. Paris relied on this form of imposed majoritarianism to ignore the indigenous demands, leading to clashes between the two groups. The other Melanesian countries of the region including Papua New Guinea and Vanuatu were outraged and demanded that Australia "do something." We concluded that bilateral representations to France would be ineffective and that the only way to influence the situation was through the United Nations.

The UN Charter was drafted at a time when colonial empires continued to be asserted. The United States may have wished to put an end to this situation, but it did not achieve that outcome in the Charter which continued, from its predecessor, in Article 73, the notion of trusteeship over territories "whose peoples have not yet attained a full measure of self-government." It was only in the 1960s with the primacy of the G-77 that the organization turned resolutely against colonialism. One institution established by the UNGA in 1961 was The Special Committee on the Situation with regard to the implementation of the Declaration on the Granting of Independence of Colonial Countries and Peoples, also known as the Special Committee on

Decolonization, or the Committee of 24 (C-24). New Caledonia was on the original United Nations list of Non-Self-Governing Territories from 1946 to 1947, but France argued that it was maintaining the principles of the Charter with respect to the inhabitants of the territory, and it came off the list. The Australian initiative in response to regional demands, was to have New Caledonia reinscribed on the C-24 list and thus require France to report on its administration of the territory to the UN and be subject to UN supervision and recommendations.

I recall the discussions in the foreign ministry and with our delegation in New York on the prospects of success. The delegation pointed out that France, a permanent member of the Security Council, was a formidable adversary and that the campaign would need to be fought tooth and nail. The Europe division chimed in that Australia had a vast range of interests with France and it was not clear how these would be affected in any retaliation. The Pacific division argued that Australia had no choice but to take the lead as none of our Pacific neighbors had commensurate resources or diplomatic reach. I was proud that the final decision by the Labor Party government rested not on interests but on principle. The Kanak people of New Caledonia were our neighbors, and they were being mistreated. We had the capacity to take action and we had no alternative but to do so. The subsequent action took place in 1986 at the 41st General Assembly.

In seeking reinscription, Australia and its allies had an enormous advantage—we were fighting for decolonization. Whatever sophistry the French employed to dress up their case, they were fighting for colonialism. In fact, it was surprising that the French were able to muster as much support as they did. The vote on UNGA/RES/41/41A was 89 in favor of reinscription, 24 against with 34 abstentions and 12 failing to vote. The 89 votes came primarily from G-77 members. The 'no' votes came primarily from France's former colonies in Africa and from some of its neighbors in Europe. The United States and Canada registered cowardly abstentions. We congratulated the delegation heartily, but I know they were disappointed not to have achieved 100 votes in favor. While France downplayed the significance of the vote, politics in New Caledonia changed thereafter and a serious dialogue between the French government and the Kanak community ensued. The UN continues to monitor events in New Caledonia.

Thirty-three years later, my pride in the Australian government's opposition to colonialism turned into anger and humiliation. Australia was led by a conservative government in 2019 when another important decolonization issue came before the UN. The UK once had a vast empire, but the decolonization era left it with only fragments. The story of one of these fragments, the Chagos Archipelago in the Indian Ocean is told by Philippe Sands who was a legal adviser to the government of Mauritius.[9] In June 2017, the UN General Assembly was asked to vote on a resolution to seek from the International Court of Justice (ICJ), an advisory opinion on whether the Chagos Islands remained part of Mauritius. The archipelago had been excised from Mauritius in 1965 by the UK colonial administration and renamed the British Indian Ocean Territory. Between 1968 and 2003, the entire population of around two thousand inhabitants was rounded up and sent to other places. One result was the leasing of one of the islands, Diego Garcia, to the United States as a military base. The General Assembly voted overwhelmingly to seek the Advisory Opinion and, the following year, thirteen of the fourteen judges of the ICJ held that Mauritius retained sovereignty over the archipelago and that the UK must "end its unlawful occupation as rapidly as possible." The United States judge claimed the court did not have jurisdiction. In May 2019, the issue came back to the General Assembly to endorse the ICJ opinion. Once again, the vote was overwhelming, with only four countries voting "no" with the UK: Hungary, Israel, the Maldives . . . and Australia! Damn the principles, vote on short-term interests. Pathetic.

## Partnerships

The New Caledonia vote was an exception. Usually, G-77 solidarity holds, and it was the deciding reason for the failure of an initiative proposed by the Secretary-General. Between 2010 and 2014, I was concurrently Executive Head of the UN Democracy Fund and acting Executive Director for the body of which it formed a part, the UN Office for Partnerships. In that period, the then Secretary-General, Ban Ki-moon, was in his second term. In other words, he was finally free to take initiatives without fear of displeasing the P5 and other Member States. One of his big-ticket initiatives was to restructure the Secretariat to establish an Under-Secretary General for Partnerships and supporting team. For that, however, he needed UNGA budgetary approval.

"Partnerships" has become the latest buzz word from the development assistance fraternity. It means different things to different actors. For one of its principal boosters, the United States Agency for International Development, it is focused on public-private partnerships for development and the Agency maintains an extensive database of examples.[10] For the Organisation for Economic Cooperation and Development (OECD), "partnership" is seen as the solution to the admitted failings of official development assistance. From the inception of the OECD's Development Assistance Committee's (DAC) dialogue on aid effectiveness which led to the 2005 Paris Declaration, the idea of partnerships has grown in importance. At the third meeting of this dialogue process in Busan in 2011, together with the United Nations Development Program (UNDP), the Global Partnership for Effective Development Co-operation (GPEDC) was established, to become the major coordinator in delivering the 2030 Sustainable Development Goals.[11] While USAID focuses on public-private partnerships, the DAC has a more extensive definition encompassing governments, civil society, private sector actors, international organizations and trade unions. But however broadly or narrowly it is understood, "partnerships" remains a buzz word.

The reason there is a focus on partnerships flows from the realization that governments alone cannot deliver on their development promises. They must work with other actors at home and abroad. The private sector and the philanthropic foundations have enormous resources. Civil society and trade unions have reach deep into the community. Effective development strategies require cooperation with these sectors. But, of course, that was not the way some government delegations at the UN saw things.

For what it is worth, I argued against the S-G's initiative at internal meetings, making the point that we already had an "Office for Partnerships" and that we could achieve much of what the S-G sought by simply beefing up that office through modest taxation of the many initiatives we undertook with private sector actors. Continuity, I pointed out, would not require seeking the blessing of the UNGA. But the S-G's counter argument was that to place the partnership flag firmly on the UN map required a more robust and formal adoption of the partnership idea, a result achievable through the creation of the Under-Secretary-General post. Unspoken was the reality that Mr. Ban was trying to bolster his legacy by requiring such formal steps.

It follows from the OECD's embrace of the partnership idea, that its members were already on board. The key, as always, was to persuade the global South, the G-77. An intense round of lobbying followed, focused on the African countries. Development assistance remains a significant part of their development plans and many understood, having participated in the DAC discussions, that the future had to include the private sector. We thought we were making good progress, but we were suddenly confronted by an adamant opponent. The Brazilian delegation, reflecting the politics of the Lula/Rousseff government, succeeded in torpedoing the S-G's initiative. It is not unusual at the UN and in other political fora for discussions to focus on tangential formal issues and not the underlying reasoning. And so, we began a two-year process of chasing our tails in various committee meetings and informal discussions. The actual reason for Brazil's opposition was never broached. Yet, it should have been because it is substantive and not without merit. Brazil was concerned that privileging the partnership process would invite many powerful actors, from the Gates Foundation to Coca-Cola, into the UN domain. This would ultimately diminish the power of delegations (of governments). The UNGA may engage in days of discussion over a program worth several million dollars, but Bill Gates can sign a check in a few minutes. Delegations would be shown to be rather empty vessels. Brazil was right to blow the whistle, but it did not have the courage to discuss the true nature of the problem for fear of laying bare the UNGA's limitations.

But we had Africa's support! Brazil only had a few diehard Bolivarian fellow travelers like Cuba, Venezuela and Bolivia supporting its position. Surely the S-G would win this battle. No chance. Brazil played its trump card, G-77 solidarity, telling the Africans to get in line, which they duly did. The UNGA subsequently killed the proposal by a thousand small delays, postponements, and further discussions, until Mr. Ban's term came to an end, and it was then allowed to die a natural death. Not only is G-77 a veto player, but by claiming G-77 solidarity, every sub-group of the G-77 is also a veto player. No wonder any good idea gets vetoed.

As things stand, the government delegations basically share among themselves the veto power to block UN resolutions and activities. The Charter, in Article 71, envisaged a situation whereby ECOSOC would consult with civil society actors. But to be admitted into the ranks of civil society organizations with consultative status requires an applicant to run the gauntlet established by an ECOSOC committee. A telling study of the work of the committee was conducted by Simone Vromen.[12] Once again, the G77 is the key veto player in the process, having delegated its veto powers to a few of the more active delegations. Cuba has been on the Committee since its inception, and it is aided and abetted by China and Pakistan. Over the years, many applicants active in the field of human rights have been blocked from acquiring status, particularly if the applicant's field of concern is gay and lesbian rights.[13] The criteria for blocking an applicant are spelled out in ECOSOC Resolution 1996/31, Article 57(a) of which includes as a reason to refuse admission "politically motivated acts against Member States of the United Nations."[14] The system is there to protect governments from criticism by civil society within the UN processes. While human rights groups have been a known target of the G77 operatives, groups that support democracy have also been blocked. This has happened to the National Democratic Institute for International Affairs, most recently in 2019.[15] The Konrad Adenauer Stiftung, another democracy group and a major deliverer of German ODA, was also blocked by Cuba who "asserted that the declared purpose of the organization revealed a flagrant interference in the internal affairs of Cuba."[16] This sounds sufficiently categorical to conclude the matter. But Germany then quietly entered into bilateral negotiations with Cuba, and Cuba subsequently lifted its objection. Clearly, Cuba had a business plan!

## A UNITED NATIONS GENERAL ASSEMBLY OF EXECUTIVE BRANCHES OF GOVERNMENT (UNGAX)

The first point that needs to be made is that the parent institution remains the United Nations. It is a Westphalian institution reflecting the division of the world into nations, just as the UNGA does now and the UNGAX will later. The reason is more practical than principle. The Westphalian world exists and will continue to do so until a military, environmental or pandemic cataclysm tears it apart. And it is not only because I do not want to envision such a cataclysm that I stick to the known world structure, but it is impossible to envisage the post-cataclysmic future in any plausible way that allows for a description of global architecture. Further, are there alternatives? We could go to the artificial UN Regional Groups where the Asian group begins in Yemen and ends in Samoa! Or where Australia and New Zealand are in Europe, and a quaint entity known as the East Europe group continues to exist, though several of its members are in the European Union with others clamoring to get in. Worst still, we could turn the scholarly clock back a century to the time of Arnold Toynbee and see the world in civilizational terms thus bringing Huntington's dystopia that much closer. Or perhaps, follow the Bretton Woods institutions' model and rank nations by power and assign representation commensurately. In a sense, we already have such a ranking in the UN system through the Committee on Contributions' formula to divide assessed contributions to the regular budget by a process of comparing national economies. Such a ranking is, frankly, unnecessary because a nation's influence will by and large follow that ranking regardless of formal representative structures. So, when it comes to the Executive Branches of Government, there is little alternative but to stick with the nation state system we already have, recognizing that sovereignty is a variable, not a constant, and that in substance, every nation is having its sovereignty hollowed out to a greater or lesser degree.

Inertia is a powerful force in international relations. UNGAX can be expected to work much the same way as UNGA does today. The same delegates meeting in the same fora finding new ways to pick at the wound of North/South relations. To shake up the system, there needs to be a competitor. That will be one of the most significant roles to be played by the other general assemblies to be established in UN 3.0.

## A UNITED NATIONS GENERAL ASSEMBLY OF CIVIL SOCIETY (UNGAC)

It follows from the vision of the Secretary-General being appointed by a tripartite decision of governments, civil society, and business, spelled out in the next chapter, that each of these sectors should have its own General Assembly. The one for executive branches of governments already exists. But two further assemblies will need to be established: the UN General Assembly of Civil Society (UNGAC) and the UN General Assembly of Business (UNGAB)

There is no compelling reason to stick with the Westphalian system when it comes to the UNGAC or UNGAB. These sectors think global and act local. National boundaries cannot resist the spread of ideas. And in our globalized world, boundaries are negligible impediments to business, finance, and investment. Just as it is best practice to have the different chambers of a bicameral system elected by different voting systems, it is also necessary for reasons of representativeness and effectiveness to have the other UN assemblies constituted by means different from the existing assembly. In addition, there is a practical reason why the nation state divide is inappropriate for civil society and business—the likelihood that authoritarian governments will stack "their" delegations with cronies, creating assemblies of GONGOs (government organized non-government organizations) and oligarchs linked to the political leaders. A nation state-based assembly would simply not reflect the reality of civil society. To find an alternative, it is worth again focusing on an existing institution and find ways of scaling it to global needs.

Best practice in this regard can be found in the national legal regime for not-for-profit civil society organizations in the Philippines, established, of course, in the post-Marcos and pre-Duterte years. CSOs enjoy both tax exemption and donation tax deductibility. Most importantly, the sector has achieved a status accepted by the government of self-regulation to certify those that may benefit from this tax advantage. To achieve this result, in 1999, six of the country's largest national NGO networks[17] organized the Philippine Council for NGO Certification, or PCNC.[18] PCNC draws its legal authority from its agreement with the Department of Finance to undertake the certification role, and it has now expanded its goal to promoting professionalism, accountability and transparency within the NGO/CSO movement.

The lesson to be drawn from this example is the benefit of self-regulation for coherence and legitimacy. Self-regulation at the national level is difficult to translate to the global level. Difficult, but not impossible. Following the Philippine precedent, there would be a need to enlist a steering committee of fifteen or so major civil society organizations. That steering committee would then establish criteria for membership of the UNGAC as well as an application, review, and selection process. Mirroring the membership of UNGAX, UNGAC would have the same number of members, currently 193.

## The Steering Committee

A formula would be devised to establish the steering committee. It is an important decision given the power the committee will have to set in place the building blocks of the initial system. UNGAC could vary the rules along the way, so it is important that the initial assembly be independent, representative, and broad in its expertise. There will always be a danger of governments and business seeking to influence this process.

My formula is partly based on strength, partly thematic and partly geographic. Strength can be determined by budget, longevity, and reach. The themes needing coverage mirror the pillars of the United Nations, peace, development, and human rights. Because development means sustainable development, the environment is also a theme. Geography does not mean every square kilometer of the Earth is represented. While there are many worthwhile civil society groups in China and Russia, as members of UNGAC, they would be under intolerable pressure from their authoritarian national leaders. Provenance is important. For example, there are several worthy groups working on Latin American issues, but with addresses in Washington. Preference needs to go to local groups. With these factors in mind, if the UNGAC steering group were to be appointed in 2022, I would select the following:

**Table 3.1: Proposed Composition of the Initial Steering Committee.**

| *Name* | *Headquarters* | *Theme* | *Strength* |
|---|---|---|---|
| Red Cross | Switzerland | Peace | $2b budget, vintage |
| Greenpeace | The Netherlands | Environment | 3m members |
| Oxfam | UK | Development | £1b budget |
| Amnesty International | UK | Human Rights | Global reach |
| CIVICUS | South Africa | Civil Society | Global reach |
| Médecins Sans Frontières | France | Peace, Health | Global reach |
| International Crisis Group | Belgium | Peace | Global reach |
| Mercy Corp | USA | Development | Global reach |
| Techo | Chile | Development, Youth | Latin America |
| BRAC | Bangladesh | Development | 100k employees, Asia |
| Forum Asia | Thailand | Human Rights, Asia | Covers ASEAN |
| NGO Caribbean D. F. | Trinidad Tobago | Development | Covers Caribbean |
| Action Aid | South Africa | Development | Covers Africa |
| People in Need | Czech Republic | Human Rights | Covers East Europe |
| PIANGO | Fiji | Development | Covers Pacific Islands |

The cost of the convocation process as well as the cost of holding the UNGAC sessions would be met by the participants through a formula. Because the three assemblies would share premises, staff, and services, there would be a large percentage of common costs. The formula would weigh capacity to pay in determining the division of costs between the three assemblies, just as the Committee on Contributions does today between Member States. Given that civil society is by definition comprised of not-for-profit organizations, it would be invidious to require them to carry equal costs. The work of the steering committee would be to convoke the inaugural UNGAC. I believe the best way to carry out this task is to establish a set of criteria and then to call for applications from civil society on the basis of a relatively simple on-line process.

I established and managed just such a process at the UN Democracy Fund, and we received about two thousand applications a year from civil society organizations. The process was governed by a number of principles. It was free to apply. It was not onerous to apply. Every application was reviewed by expert analysts. Every year, about 250 of the 2,000 applications stood out from the rest because of the strength of the ideas behind the projects they were proposing to deliver. The tough part of the job, which generally fell on my shoulders, was to select 50 of the 250 for funding. The key criteria I employed were innovation and likely impact together with the reality that beneficiaries needed to come from countries most in need. I used to explain to the UNDEF Board that there was no known science that would allow the "best" projects to be selected, but that given the breadth of application and the rigorous selection process, one could be confident that excellent proposals had been selected.

Clearly, compromises had to be made. At UNDEF, given our tiny staff, we only accepted applications in one of the two UN working languages, English or French. They were submitted in about an 80/20 split. The English language applications were often a syntactic mess. But English is a forgiving language, as any *lingua franca* needs to be, and we could discern the ideas being presented quite readily. The applications in French were invariably grammatically perfect! The spelling, declensions, and syntax all in place. It spurred a mental image of all those French nuns, teaching in all those African classrooms, never satisfied with anything but the correct answer. But perfect grammar, and all those "cependant," "malgré tout" and "néamoins," does not necessarily add up to good ideas. UNDEF rewarded ideas, not grammar. It would not be feasible to deal with applications for UNGAC membership in all languages, but it would be unfair to restrict them to the two working languages. Sticking with UN practice, the UNGAC would be conducted in the six official languages of the UN, as, in any case, participants would need to participate in discussions in one of those languages. Accordingly, the applications should be restricted to the six official languages of the UN (Arabic, English, French, Mandarin, Russian and Spanish).

And we had issues with corrupt national officials. Grants were given directly to local civil society organizations who were selected on a competitive and meritocratic basis without seeking the views of the government of the country concerned. But once the decision was made, those governments were informed as a courtesy. Some objected point-blank. Others tried to finesse a way forward. An important part of my job was to find the best outcomes in these situations. Once selected, the civil society organization would draft a project document explaining in detail how the money would be spent. I received a phone call from a selected CSO in Kinshasa. They wanted advice on a budgetary matter. The foreign ministry had been in touch and advised that the Democratic Republic of Congo delegation in New York would be instructed to block the grant from UNDEF unless the local CSO paid the individual from the foreign ministry $20,000. How should this $20,000 be budgeted, they asked. I explained that bribes and ransom money could not be paid from UNDEF funds, and I further advised the CSO to call this bluff. We heard no more from that DRC government official.

The selection criteria employed by the Steering Committee would probably be similar to the set of conditions used for its own selection—strength, theme, and reach. But perhaps an additional criterion would be in order—courage. Because it is important for all civil society to be represented, participation from semi-authoritarian countries would be essential. When selecting applicants from such countries, the courage to be independent of government threats or blandishments would be a key criterion.

## The Work of UNGAC

Generally, all three Assemblies would tackle the issues on the global agenda dealing with peace, sustainable development, and human rights and democracy. The UNGAC would provide a civil society perspective on these issues. These would balance the views of the other Assemblies because they would adopt a bottom-up perspective. Civil society would undoubtedly examine threats to peace from a human security perspective by examining the impact of decisions on affected people. Civil society would look at sustainable development issues from a household perspective rather than a national planning perspective by asking how households will be able to obtain clean water, primary education, healthcare, and safe and affordable cooking fuel or cookstoves. Civil society would be particularly attuned to the requirement for the promotion and protection of human rights and democracy as these constitute their ultimate protections.

But that does not mean that civil society would ignore big picture issues. In my experience, civil society is the most coherent voice on issues such as global warming because it is the sector least interested in short-term gains and windfalls. I experienced this firsthand some years back when I led the Australian delegation to a conference on protection of the marine environment at the International Maritime Organization, whose headquarters is on the Thames in London. Outside the conference, Greenpeace was holding a demonstration to highlight its concerns. There were banners, chants and even paragliding off Lambeth Bridge. We, the delegates, shrugged this off as simply a fund-raising stunt. But inside the conference, Greenpeace had an observer delegation which could not be shrugged off because of its mastery of the issues and of the science behind the issues. The Greenpeace delegation would call out the obfuscation and dissimulations of the government delegations (including my own!). Civil society understands the individual and the household, but it also has a solid purchase on global issues.

Participants at the UNGAC would also need to pursue aspects of the agenda particular to that sector. There is no more important issue for them than the current plague of harassment against civil society in many parts of the world. This calls for a response that can be described as norm entrepreneurship in defense of civil society. A solid start has been made by a pair of civil society organizations with their Defending Civil Society Report of 2012.[19] In later years, CIVICUS continued the process with annual State of Civil Society Reports.[20] The 2012 Report proposes a series of rights required by civil society to safeguard its work. The UNGAC should adopt as one of its first tasks, the discussion and translation of the following seven principles into binding treaty form on behalf of civil society organizations (CSOs):

- The Right of Entry; an element of the freedom of association to ensure civil society groups can be established free of onerous or arbitrary government registration processes
- The Right to Operate Free from Unwarranted Government Interference; allowing CSOs a necessary degree of privacy in their internal affairs
- The Right to Free Expression; to be enjoyed and protected by law both as individuals and as CSOs
- The Right to Communicate and Cooperate; including at the international level through the Internet and social media

- The Right to Freedom of Peaceful Assembly; free of onerous government requirements going beyond reasonable safety rules; and protected by the government from counter demonstrators
- The Right to Seek and Secure Resources; from legal sources, individual, corporate or government, domestic or international
- The State Duty to Protect; by providing an enabling, apolitical, and respectful legal environment

Another key requirement of the UNGAC is to approve the appointment of the Secretary-General. As will be unpacked in chapter 4, the appointment process would be tripartite as opposed to the current system of horse trading by the P5 until they come to a lowest common denominator decision. The UNGAC would need to determine its procedures for participating in this negotiation. This will not be easy. Civil society is not particularly adept at disciplining its members, delegating authority, and supporting compromise outcomes, yet these are the factors that would have to be adapted to enable the UNGAC leadership to participate nimbly and effectively in the negotiating process. What needs to be borne in mind is that there is no science to predict which candidate will do the best job. The key is that whichever candidate is selected, she will not be in thrall to governments and thus will be able to do the job independently.

## A UNITED NATIONS GENERAL ASSEMBLY OF BUSINESS (UNGAB)

Why do we need a United Nations General Assembly of Business (UNGAB)? Because the business sector has become more powerful than the government sector. Because the business sector has capacity and resources beyond that of the government sector. Because in our globalized world, we cannot solve global problems without the cooperation and participation of the business sector. Accordingly, it must have a voice in global governance.

It could be argued that the business sector already has a voice through its lobbying of governments. But this is an indirect and suspicious *sotto voce*. It is not the purpose of this monograph to deal with the perils of domestic lobbying. But by having its own voice at the international level, the need to lobby governments will be commensurately reduced.

Some will argue that business and government will simply work hand in hand. But we are already seeing many businesses take a far more responsible position than some governments on issues like climate change.[21] And we are also seeing many businesses embrace the concept of corporate social responsibility under pressure from their boards, shareholders, employees and customers.[22] There is even some evidence that ethical investment has reached a tipping point around the world.[23] The UNGAB will bring a distinctive, important, and hopefully, globally responsible voice. A final criticism may be that we already have such a voice, at Davos. Yes, but the Davos meeting is a private endeavor lacking the necessary formality and legitimacy of the United Nations. The three Assemblies are needed to balance each other. There is no reason, however, why the Davos voice should not influence the UNGAB outcomes.

Establishing the UNGAB is in some ways simpler than establishing the UNGAC, but in other ways more complex. The simplicity comes from the fact that there is a common metric—money. This allows for all sorts of rankings to be established based on market size or profit size or share value. But let us not forget what Bob Dylan taught us—money doesn't talk, it swears![24] Money is one metric, but not the only one. Other values include corporate good citizenship, long-term sustainability, and contribution to society. This suggests to me that the UNGAB needs to have not only the behemoths of finance, technology, and industry but also the philanthropic foundations spawned by those self-same behemoths.

Nationality is a particularly tricky issue when dealing with these behemoths. The largest corporations will usually be global. The location of headquarters may be a guide to nationality, but the race-to-the-bottom tax havens may detract from that identification. The point is that, just as with civil society, the UNGAB will not be Westphalian. Just as with the UNGAC, the process to convoke the UNGAB should be through the appointment of a steering committee that would establish the rules for membership of the UNGAB, which would also mirror the size of UNGAX. The initial participants would be selected through an application process mirroring that of UNGAC though with different criteria reflecting the core values being sought.

In applying the criteria, it is necessary to exclude corporations addicted to the carbon economy. They are ineligible because they do not have long-term sustainability and they are a net burden on society. Another caveat is that just as UNGAC is not open to GONGOs, the UNGAB should not be open to state-owned or state-controlled companies. This makes it difficult to select companies from authoritarian countries like China and Russia. Nor can corporations controlling sovereign funds be members. China is in the embryonic state of developing philanthropic foundations given the recent green light to "new philanthropy" by President Xi Jinping, but it is far too early to consider these as independent of party or government.[25] The UNGAB needs to provide a contradistinctive view to that provided by Executive Branches. If selected in 2022, the steering committee might look as follows:

**Table 3.2: Proposed Composition of Initial Steering Committee.**

| *Name* | *Headquarters* | *Sector* | *Strength* |
|---|---|---|---|
| JP Morgan Chase | New York | Finance | Size, reach, influence |
| Hong Kong and Shanghai Bank | Hong Kong | Finance | Size, reach, influence |
| Deloitte | Tokyo, New York | Accounting | Size, reach, influence |
| Alibaba | Beijing | Technology | Size, reach, influence |
| Alphabet | Palo Alto, USA | Technology | Size, reach, influence |
| SAP | Walldorf, FRG | Technology | Size, reach, influence |
| Apple | Cupertino, USA | Tech, Manufacturing | Size, reach, influence |
| Unilever | Rotterdam | Manufacturing | Size, reach, influence |
| General Electric | Boston | Manufacturing | Size, reach, influence |
| Christian Dior | Paris | Manufacturing | Size, reach, influence |
| Gates Foundation | Seattle | Health, development | Major player in field |
| Mo Ibrahim Foundation | London | Governance | Major player in Africa |
| Wyss Foundation | Washington | Environment | Major player in field |
| European Foundations Centre | Brussels | Development, Human Rights | Represents European philanthropies |
| Sasakawa Foundation | Tokyo | Peace | Among largest in Asia |

The costs of the convocation and subsequent conduct of the UNGAB would be based on the cost sharing formula, taking note of this chamber's capacity to pay. Within the assembly, it would be met by a levy on the business community to be designed and enforced by the business community itself. One idea to limit costs and duplication would be to use the United Nations Global Compact Secretariat as the UNGAB Secretariat and perhaps also as a vehicle to fund other activities. The Global Compact was a fine idea, inspired by John Ruggie,[26] that has not been sufficiently utilized by the business community. The UNGAB structure would present an opportunity to strengthen this entity, increase its role and give it a relevance it currently lacks.

Many people, especially on the left side of politics, are deeply suspicious of the business sector. These suspicions are not without foundation. Many businesses have behaved in ways that do not benefit society. But, if we accept the market as the means of organizing the production and distribution of necessary goods and services, we must also accept the essentiality of the business sector. There is no point tarring all businesses with the same amoral profits-at-all-cost brush. At the same time, one needs to be wary of the corrupting influence of the profit motive. One hope is that giving the business sector some responsibility for global governance will act as a factor encouraging globally responsible conduct. Another factor is that it will respond best to self-regulation. But the final factor must be public participation. Individual investors, shareholders, employees, and customers must be involved in the process. Governance issues cannot simply be delegated to corporate leaders. Individual activism is as important in the business sector as it is in the government and civil society sectors.

The United Nations cannot become the Leviathan we need without the cooperation of the market. The business sector needs to be brought into the fold and it needs to buy into the work of the United Nations. The UNGAB is the formal means for achieving those ends. While there will not be a Chapter VII for the business community, there are powerful enforcement tools in its hands. The flow and direction of trade and investment are those powerful tools. Ultimately, these tools may be the key to gaining broad compliance with the UN goals and norms.

## A UNITED NATIONS PARLIAMENTARY ASSEMBLY?

There has been a campaign for several years for the General Assembly to be paralleled by a UN Parliamentary Assembly which "in the long run, once its members are all democratically elected, could be developed into a world parliament which . . . may be able to adopt universally binding regulations."[27] I am unenthusiastic about this idea. Many doubt that democracy can be effectively scaled up to the global level. The idea sounds utopian, which rings danger bells: fear those who proclaim the path to utopia as it invariably leads to dystopia. We need not even utilize a thought experiment to try to understand what a UN Parliamentary Assembly would look like; we have a living example in the form of the Inter-Parliamentary Union which asserts:

> The IPU is the global organization of national parliaments. We promote democratic governance, institutions and values, working with parliaments and parliamentarians to articulate and respond to the needs and aspirations of the people. We work for peace, democracy, human rights, gender equality, youth empowerment and sustainable development through political dialogue, cooperation and parliamentary action.[28]

So, the first issue is why should we reinvent this wheel? The IPU has been around since 1889, it has held more than 140 of its own Assemblies. It works closely with the UN in several ways. And many national delegations to the UN General Assembly already include parliamentarians. All the strengths of a UN Parliamentary Assembly are pretty much reflected in the current work of the IPU. And many of the likely weaknesses of the proposed UN Parliamentary Assembly are already reflected in the problems suffered by the IPU. The IPU is the global organization of national parliaments with 179 Member Parliaments from the 193 UN Member States in the world.[29] Some of those parliaments are democratically elected, most are not. Most of the world's parliaments are either rubber stamps for their executives (a polite term for dictators and strong men) or show pieces with little power or impact. The IPU has commendably adopted democracy as its goal and its vision is "a world where every voice counts, where democracy and parliaments are at the service of the people for peace and development."[30] But the reality is far from the vision. Nevertheless, the IPU should continue its work towards that vision and need not be hindered by the proposed competing institution of a UN Parliamentary Assembly.

## THE THREE ASSEMBLIES

What would the decision-making process look like when the UN moves from a relatively simple single assembly to the more complex three assemblies? One of the developments in recent decades is that most UNGA decisions have been taken by consensus, with only the most contentious attracting a vote. Consensus is a useful institution in that it forces compromise and agreement, but that agreement may be in favor of weak lowest common denominator positions. It is likely that the consensus culture would continue among the three assemblies, but there still needs to be a process to determine decisions where consensus is not possible. And as will be outlined in subsequent chapters, these decisions will not be subject to veto by the permanent members of the Security Council because the veto will be limited to decisions under Chapter VII of the Charter.

One option is to require all decisions to have a majority of each chamber. This would make each chamber a veto player. But that would stifle decision making. The world would be in the same situation from which it currently suffers of having any cluster in the G-77 play the group solidarity card and thus trigger the automatic majority of UNGAX. For a more workable solution, I would borrow from the amendment procedure of the Australian federal constitution and require a majority of delegates and a majority of chambers. As the size of UNGAX will dictate the size of UNGAC and UNGAB, then, based on the current membership, each chamber would have 193 delegations and a majority would be 290 of the 579. In addition, two of the chambers would also need a majority in favor of the proposition. This establishes a dynamic among both the chambers and their individual delegations. There are no veto players as any chamber can be outvoted by the other two. But if the delegations of one chamber adamantly opposed a proposition and no votes in favor were gained from that chamber, the other two chambers would, in effect, need to vote by difficult 75% majorities to carry the proposition. That would be a rare occurrence.

What sort of decisions would the three assemblies take? Perhaps the most important is the appointment of the Secretary-General. Ideally, she would be appointed by consensus. But even if it came to a vote, the S-G would have the support of the majority of delegations and the majority of chambers and would no longer be subject to the P5 veto. That is a recipe for a far more independent and assertive S-G which is one of the key requirements of the UN 3.0.

The three assemblies would also take decisions on the broad direction of the budget. Obviously, we need to get away from the current method of securing funding for one's own baubles on the Christmas tree. At the same time, the S-G cannot alone decide on spending the huge budget that taxing globalization will generate. A middle ground is required. I would borrow from Westminster practice of having the S-G determine the budget and then having the three assemblies approve it on an up-or-down vote. While the UN is currently toying with an annual budget, there would be less churn by going back to a biennial budget. But the S-G would be given discretion to move a certain percentage of funds between different areas of expenditure if the circumstances, as explained to the three assemblies, so dictate. If we followed through on Westminster practice, a rejection of a budget would probably lead to the resignation of the S-G.

Finally, the three assemblies would grapple with normative issues. The three assemblies would not have treaty making power. As things stand, this remains a matter for nation states. Over time, the three assemblies could examine this position. But, at the outset at least, the decision making would be on the "soft law" of passing normative resolutions, development goals, and the occasional name and shame process. I would foresee far fewer resolutions being adopted but for far greater impact.

## NOTES

1. Dag Hammarskjöld Library. n.d. "What is the Uniting for Peace resolution?" http://ask.un.org/faq/177134

2. Dag Hammarskjöld Library. n. d. "Resolutions adopted by the General Assembly - Emergency Special Sessions." http://research.un.org/en/docs/ga/quick/emergency

3. Ibid.

4. United Nations, "General Assembly resolution demands end to Russian offensive in Ukraine," 2 March 2022, https://news.un.org/en/story/2022/03/1113152

5. United Nations Peacekeeping. n.d. "How are we Funded." https://peacekeeping.un.org/en/how-we-are-funded

6. Gunther Altenburg, "The Geneva Group," *A Concise Encyclopedia of the United Nations*, https://archive.org/details/UNEncyclopedia/page/n5/mode/2up, 198–9

7. The Group of 77. n.d. "About the Group of 77." https://www.g77.org/doc/

8. David A. Chappell "The Noumea Accord: Decolonization without Independence in New Caledonia?" *Pacific Affairs*, Vol. 72, No. 3 (Autumn) 1999, 373–391.

9. Philippe Sands, "Britain's Colonial Legacy on Trial at The Hague." *The New York Review of Books* June 23, 2020.

10. USAID, "New Partnership Initiatives," 2021. https://www.usaid.gov/npi

11. Global Partnership for Effective Development Cooperation. "GPEDC at a Glance." 2020. https://www.effectivecooperation.org/content/gpedc-glance-0

12. Simone Vromen, "The Council Committee on NGOs An analysis of the reports of the Council Committee on NGOs between 2005 and 2015." *Utrecht Law Review*, Volume 13, Issue 1, 2017, 82–98.

13. Ibid., 91

14. NGO related Resolution 1996/31. https://www.un.org/esa/coordination/ngo/pdf/res96-31.pdf

15. United Nations Meetings Coverage and Press Releases, "Non-Governmental Organizations Committee Recommends 11 Groups for Consultative Status, Defers Action on 85 in Fourth Day of Resumed Session." 2019. https://www.un.org/press/en/2019/ecosoc6992.doc.htm

16. ECOSOC, "Report of the Committee on Non-Governmental Organizations on its 2018 resumed session," 11 June 2018. E/2018/32 (Part II).

17. The Association of Foundations, the League of Corporate Foundations, The Philippine Business for Social Progress, the Bishops-Businessmen's Conference for Human Development, the Caucus of Development NGO Networks and the National Council for Social Development Foundations.

18. Fely I. Soledad, "The Philippine Council for NGO Certification," *The International Journal of Not-for-Profit Law*. Vol. 3, Issue 2, Dec. 2001.

19. International Center for Not-for-Profit Law and World Movement for Democracy Secretariat, *Defending Civil Society*, second edition, June 2012. https://www.icnl.org/resources/research/ijnl/defending-civil-society-2

20. Civicus, "2019 State of Civil Society Report." https://www.civicus.org/index.php/state-of-civil-society-report-2019

21. General Electric Press Release, "GE Releases Position on Climate Change: Calls for Accelerated Deployment of Renewables & Gas Power To Drive Impactful, Faster Decarbonization." 2020. https://www.ge.com/news/press-releases/ge-releases-position-on-climate-change-calls-for-accelerated-deployment-of-1

22. Blackstone, "An Integrated Approach to ESG." https://www.blackstone.com/our-impact/corporate-social-responsibility/overview

23. Gillian Tett, "Ethical investing has reached a tipping point: Environmental, social and governance considerations are finally moving into the mainstream," *Financial Times*, 18 June 2019.

24. Lyrics from Bob Dylan "It's Alright, Ma (I'm Only Bleeding)."

25. Elizabeth Crane, "China's New Philanthropy: A New Form of Revolution?," lecture, Douglass Campus, Rutgers University, 10 March 2020.

26. John Ruggie, *Constructing the World Polity: essays on international institutionalization*, (London: Routledge, 2002).

27. UNPA Campaign. n.d. “The proposal of a UN Parliamentary Assembly.” https://en.unpacampaign.org/proposal/
28. Inter-Parliamentary Union. n.d. “About Us.” https://www.ipu.org/about-us
29. Inter-Parliamentary Union. n.d. “Members.” https://www.ipu.org/about-ipu/members
30. Inter-Parliamentary Union. n.d. “About Us.” https://www.ipu.org/about-us

# *Chapter 4*

# The Secretary-General and the Secretariat

Sadly, those who love the organization are condemned to be its most trenchant critics. And that criticism must go beyond the behavior of the Member States. We need to begin with the Secretariat and its leader, the Secretary-General. I had worked in a large law firm and in a national foreign ministry before I joined the UN, so I was able to compare the culture of each institution. The law firm and the ministry were not dissimilar in that they both had highly competitive environments, both valued competence above all else, and both erred in the direction of work in the work/life balance. The main difference was that the law firm had a clear metric for measurement—billing clients, while the foreign ministry had a more tenuous metric—the satisfaction of the Minister. The atmosphere at the UN was far more polite and collegial in that the backstabbing was invariably conducted surreptitiously. The culture was more oral than written, thus favoring big talkers rather than thoughtful writers. The metric of success was fitting in. In hindsight, the law firm and the ministry strived for excellence, the UN was comfortable with mediocrity.

This chapter will examine the structure of the Secretariat and in particular the relevance of nationality and its impact. It will then turn to the head of the Secretariat, the Secretary-General.

## THE SECRETARIAT

Like so much about the UN, the sub-section of the Charter on the appointment of staff is a compromise:

> 101.3 The paramount consideration in the employment of the staff and in the determination of the conditions of service shall be the necessity of securing the highest standards of efficiency, competence, and integrity. Due regard shall be

> paid to the importance of recruiting the staff on as wide a geographical basis as possible.

The contending ideas were, on the one hand, that the staff should be of the highest competence, or, on the other, that they should come from Member States through geographic and demographic equity. Both ideas were incorporated in the Charter. The issue of competence was thought to be dominant, so it is described as the "paramount consideration" while geographic equity is simply to be given due regard. In reality, the opposite has occurred.

It was probably inevitable that some form of even representation of Member States would become the primary consideration. The UN Joint Inspection Unit provides an excellent summary of the development of the system of "equitable geographic distribution."[1] In the early days of the UN it was a simple calculation based on the assessed contribution to the organization, but it eventually became a rather complicated formula:

> 40 per cent of the posts are allotted via the membership factor, 5 per cent via the population factor, and 55 per cent in proportion to the scale of the assessments of Member States. The posts calculated via each factor are then added and result in a number of posts constituting the midpoint of the desirable range (15 per cent upward and downward from the midpoint).

Meanwhile, "the highest standards of efficiency, competence, and integrity" boils down to a threshold of having a higher university degree and then being assessed by a committee. In other words, equitable geographic distribution is a mathematical formula while competence is a value judgement. Member States have made sure that the math wins. It should be noted that this formula only applies to regular Secretariat posts paid by the regular budget and does not apply to the greater number of posts in peacekeeping missions and in offices funded by voluntary contributions. But the posts in the key policy sectors of the Secretariat are regular budget posts and these are the posts of most interest to Member States.

What is the rationale behind equitable geographic distribution? Many people would see this as an expression of fairness, a conclusion suggested by employing the term "equitable." Fairness is, however, an elastic notion as can be discerned from the decades of contestation about affirmative action policies. Fairness to candidates from Moldova, a country below quota, is unfairness to a disappointed candidate from India, a country above quota. Because of its elasticity, fairness is an unreliable rationale.

An early UN General Assembly resolution on the composition of the Secretariat expresses another version of the rationale at the core of the principle of geographical distribution:

> in view of its international character and in order to avoid undue predominance of national practices, the policies and administrative methods of the Secretariat should reflect, and profit to the highest degree from, assets of the various cultures and the technical competence of all Member nations.[2]

There seems to be a contradiction or at least a contradistinction in the listed reasons for the policy—the need to "avoid undue predominance of national practices" and the need to "profit . . . from, assets of the various cultures and the technical competence of all Member nations." So, let us parse this sentence to understand its intent. It means, let us not have too many Westerners running the UN. This sentiment is understandable at the time given the membership of the UN in 1947 when 14 of the 57 members or almost 25%, came from Western countries and the Secretary-General was from Norway.[3] Today, the formal figure is closer to 15% (29 of 193 Member States are from the West European and Others Group[4]) but the reality is that eleven of the 23 members of the East Europe Group are members of the European Union, and several more are candidates for and aspirants to membership bringing the total to around 44, or 23%. The rationale therefore remains not to have the UN run like a Western institution and to ensure that the countries of the global South (the G77 group at the UN, numbering 134 countries[5]) are represented in the Secretariat proportional to their significant political influence in the General Assembly.

The explanation that Member States push to have their nationals in the Secretariat as a means of enhancing their political influence runs contrary to the specific terms of the Charter. Article 101 of the Charter states:

> In the performance of their duties the Secretary-General and the staff shall not seek or receive instructions from any government or from any other authority external to the Organization. They shall refrain from any action which might reflect on their position as international officials responsible only to the Organization.

Each Member of the United Nations undertakes to respect the exclusively international character of the responsibilities of the Secretary-General and the staff and not to seek to influence them in the discharge of their responsibilities.

Has this article been respected? In the breach! Many Secretariat members respect this provision and give their allegiance solely to the international organization they serve. I put myself in this category. Some Secretariat members try to straddle the needs of the UN with the policies of their countries of citizenship, sometimes for reasons of national loyalty and sometimes in the hope of personal advancement through lobbying by their country's UN delegation. And quite a few Secretariat members see themselves as representatives of their countries and extensions of their national delegations. A similar breakdown exists among Member States meaning that some delegations will try to achieve their objectives by way of instructions to their nationals in the Secretariat.

This taxonomy goes some way to explain why delegations are active in personnel issues, appointments, promotions, and placements. It might simply be an issue of national pride but that strikes me as an unsatisfactory explanation in the realist world of UN politics. For some delegations, it might be a means of making money by supporting a candidate in return for a cut of their future salary, given that a mid-level UN official will earn three of four times the official salaries of some ambassadors. Another likely explanation for most delegations who involve themselves in this process is to maximize the influence of the country in the UN. This is clearly the objective of the P5, the five permanent members of the UN Security Council.

Since the inception of the UN, the P5 have adopted the informal practice of precluding the option of having one of their nationals as Secretary-General of the UN. This should not be seen as a voluntary sacrifice by high-minded nations. Each P5 member would happily monopolize the post if it could get away with it. After all, the United States monopolizes the position of President of the World Bank because the voting structure allows for that result. The US bought off the Europeans by guaranteeing their monopoly of the position of Managing Director of the International Monetary Fund. The reason for the P5 self-denial at the UN is best explained as a realization of the inevitability of mutual preventive vetoes. To compensate themselves for this supposed self-sacrifice, the P5 monopolize all the major Under Secretary-General positions heading key UN departments. No, this is not for national pride but for national interests. Is it any surprise that other Member States follow the P5 example and seek Secretariat positions for their own national interests?

The underlying rationale, therefore, of the staffing quota system at the UN is not about fairness, equity, or equality of opportunity, it is about a division of the spoils by Member States. Member States see securing Secretariat positions at the UN for their nationals as a perk of sovereignty. And it follows, that the use made of those Secretariat positions is also subject to the sovereign decision making of Member States even though they each promised as parties to the UN Charter that they would "not to seek to influence them in the discharge of their responsibilities." The best known use of the UN for national interest purposes was by the Soviet Union and it is exhaustively outlined in a 1985 Senate report on the subject.[6] It was also the subject of detailed inside analysis in the book by a famous defector, Arkady Shevchenko.[7] It is highly likely that the practice continues to be employed by Russia today though the only public evidence points to the use of positions in the Russian delegation to the UN as covers for spies.[8] In February 2022, the United States expelled twelve members of the Russian mission to the UN for involvement in espionage.[9] Russia is surely not alone in using UN delegation and Secretariat positions for its spies or to pursue other national interests.

This recitation of the way Member States think they "own" the UN Secretariat would be moot if it was working with "efficiency, competence, and integrity." But clearly it is not. We know this, in the form of a snide joke, from a former Secretary-General of the UN. Asked by a journalist the question "how many people work at the UN?," Boutros Boutros-Ghali acidly replied, "about half."[10] From my personal experience I would consider that a generous fraction. In my interview for the UN job, one of the members of the UN selection committee slept through most of the proceedings, though, in his defense, he did not snore. There are many excellent members of the UN Secretariat but there are also many time servers. The categories do not correspond to any geographic or cultural grouping. In my view, the reason we have a Secretariat half filled with duds is the equitable geographic distribution rule. Not because of any civilizational explanation but because it relegates the "paramount" consideration of efficiency, competence, and integrity to a proforma examination of having a higher degree and the requisite number of years of experience. Once this rather facile threshold has been reached, it is up to the Member States to engage in their mischief.

I have left for last the final rationale for the equitable geographic distribution rule, that it enhances the legitimacy of the UN. The argument goes that the UN is an organization of all the countries of the world, so its Secretariat must reflect that reality. This representation gives the UN a legitimacy it would not otherwise have. Let us review this argument by looking at the practice of an analogous institution, the federal nation. Do federal nations engage in a type of *numerus clausus* that ensures each federal unit is proportionally represented in the national bureaucracy? They may take note of and try to correct major regional or racial discrepancies, but they do not fall back on distribution formulae to ensure every federal unit has a proportional number of civil servants. That would end up with a situation where the next American Ambassador to Berlin must come from North Dakota! Yet their bureaucracies do not lack legitimacy because they gain performance legitimacy if they deliver efficiently on the government's programs and policies.

That is what we should be aiming for at the UN. We want the UN to gain legitimacy through performance not through an artificial distribution rule that relegates performance to a secondary requirement. We need to break the link between the Secretariat and the member states and select a Secretariat for meritocratic reasons alone. We need to get Member States out of the selection process altogether and reject the notion that any jobs at the UN "belong" to a particular country. Sorry United States, you cannot forever retain the position of Under Secretary-General for Political Affairs. Sorry Russia, you cannot keep hold of the position of Under Secretary-General for Security Council Affairs. Sorry China, you cannot forever place your loyal apparatchicks in the position of Under Secretary-General for Economic and Social Affairs. Let all positions be decided on merit and capacity.

"Next year will be the last of my mandate," Zeid Ra'ad Hussein, UN High Commissioner for Human Rights, wrote in an email to staff. "After reflection, I have decided not to seek a second four-year term. To do so, in the current geopolitical context, might involve bending a knee in supplication; muting a statement of advocacy; lessening the independence and integrity of my voice—which is your voice."[11] This is a rare but eloquent statement of the lack of independence of the Secretariat. Admittedly, the issue of human rights is one of the most sensitive dealt with by the UN. But it is exactly on sensitive issues that the UN needs to speak out, rather than on issues where a consensus already exists.

## THE SECRETARY-GENERAL

All positions? Should that not include the Secretary-General (S-G) position? The Charter does not provide a list of qualifications for the position. The practice has been established that the S-G must not be a national of the P5 and that the concept of equitable geographic distribution should continue to apply, but this time in relation not to Member States but to the geographic groups that act as voting blocs for UN elections. There have been four S-Gs from the West European and Other Group; two each from the Asia and Africa groups; one from the Latin America and Caribbean Group; and none from the Eastern Europe group. There was a concerted attempt in 2016 to appoint a woman. One excellent candidate was Irina Bukova, the Director-General of UNESCO, from Bulgaria and therefore from the Eastern European group and thus allowing the organization to complete the geographic sweep as well as having the first woman as S-G. But the US was suspicious of anybody who had spent their formative years in a communist system, and so, the P5 went for the former Portuguese Prime Minister and UN High Commissioner for Refugees, António Guterres.

That the process of appointment is unsatisfactory is clear to one and all. There is a campaign called One for 7 Billion, comprising some 750 civil society organisations with a combined reach of more than 170 million people worldwide, calling for an inclusive and merit-based selection process that offers the best chance to find the most effective Secretary-General.[12] The demands of the campaign are, however, quite modest. Apart from having the candidates address the General Assembly, the basic requirement is that the

Security Council put forward two names to the General Assembly. But this still leaves plenty of room for P5 mischief.

Until the Guterres appointment, the process was opaque taking place within the confines of discussions among the P5 and then blessed by the General Assembly. In the case of the most recent appointment, the President of the General Assembly at the time, Peter Thomson of Fiji, invited candidates nominated by Member States to address the Assembly in a sort of campaign speech. Thereafter, the process returned to its opaque roots, taking place within the confines of discussions among the P5 and then blessed by the General Assembly. *Le plus ça change.*

All nine S-Gs have had their qualities, but they have also had weaknesses. The list begins with Trygve Lie of Norway who was made ineffectual by the wrangling over the Korean war and stepped down soon after being voted a second term by the General Assembly. Then came Dag Hammarskjöld of Sweden who is the only S-G to die in office, killed in a plane crash while flying to ceasefire negotiations in the Congo, thus ending a promising and activist period. The Cold War had set in deeply by the time of Hammarskjöld's death and the next S-G was from a country that was part of the Non-Aligned Movement (NAM). U Thant, the Burmese Permanent Representative to the UN, had served as the secretary of the formative NAM Bandung conference in 1955. U Thant was followed by Kurt Waldheim, an Austrian diplomat who would later become President of Austria. There is a strong suspicion that, knowing of his undisclosed service as an intelligence officer in the Wehrmacht in Greece during WWII, the United States and the Soviet Union were pleased to have him as a compromised S-G who could be manipulated by those who knew his secret. Then came Javier Pérez de Cuéllar, a rather colorless Peruvian diplomat.

It was now Africa's turn. The regional organization, the Organization for African Unity (OAU, today transformed into the African Union, AU) could not agree on a sub-Saharan candidate and, with the strong support of France, whose President François Mitterrand was a close friend, Egypt's Deputy Foreign Minister Boutros Boutros-Ghali was appointed. The norm was to serve two terms, but Boutros-Ghali was denied a second term because he fell out with the United States. In his first term, he demonstrated a surprising independence which alarmed the Clinton Administration. It was surprising because the practice before and since is that S-Gs do nothing controversial in their first terms so as to be allowed to serve a second term. As the first S-G after the Cold War, Boutros-Ghali considered he did not have the luxury of inactivity in a suddenly more relevant UN. He was activist and independent and demonstrated that he was uncontrollable by the then sole superpower. He gives his version of the events in his book *Unvanquished*,[13] which, no doubt intentionally, can also be read as UN Vanquished.

Why has the African S-G been denied a second term, asked the African delegates? And so, another African, a senior official from the Secretariat, Kofi Annan of Ghana, was appointed and duly completed two terms. His first term earned him a Nobel Peace Prize for his rousing rhetoric for human rights and development. His second term saw him in the crosshairs of the Bush Administration after he called the invasion of Iraq contrary to international law. He was a captivating speaker and he found ways to speak to "we the peoples" directly rather than through the intercession of their governments. His voice was his major asset and in a psychosomatic reaction to the onslaught from the United States, he lost his voice for several months.[14]

Alarmed at the way Annan had been able to bypass governments and speak directly and effectively to their people, the P5 decided that his successor should lack that skill. Ban Ki-moon, who was my boss in my seven years at the UN, was a hard-working, energetic, and considerate man. But he was incomprehensible. Speaking one-on-one, his English was fine but once he tried to read his speeches in public, the audience would tune out after a couple of mangled sentences. The French delegation, which insists all candidates for the post must speak both UN working languages, after hearing Ban mangling his French, pleaded with him to stick to English.

I was surprised at the selection of Guterres as S-G. He was not a woman. He was not from a country in the Eastern European group. And he was an activist High Commissioner for Refugees. The Americans were unhappy with all the other candidates, some of whom had served their formative professional years under Soviet domination, but why did the Russians accept Guterres? The answer was whispered to me from former colleagues in the Secretariat. In return for Russian support for his selection, Guterres appointed Vladimir Ivanovich Voronkov of Russia as Under-Secretary-General of the newly created United Nations Counter-Terrorism Office, established by the General Assembly on 15 June 2017, with the appointment coming a mere six days after Guterres took office. In other words, standard operating procedures have resumed.

Some of the key words from preceding paragraphs are ineffectual, compromised, colorless, and incomprehensible. These are the qualities sought by the P5. A couple of S-Gs did not conform to these requirements and they had to be sacked or harried. Is it any wonder that the Secretariat is in a mess given the compromised position of the boss? Just as it is necessary to break the link between the Secretariat and the Member States, so it is necessary to find a new way to appoint the S-G which will sever the puppet-master powers of the P5.

The UN is surprisingly precedent bound in the way it behaves. Its leadership is comforted by the existence of a previous decision that will underpin a difficult new decision. It is a sign of both institutional stability and institutional timidity. It should therefore come as a comfort that the proposed new way of selecting a S-G has a strong precedent in the UN family.

According to the rules of the International Labour Organization (ILO),[15] nominations for the position of Director-General may be submitted by any member of the Governing Body which comprises 28 governments, 14 representatives of employer organizations and 14 representatives of worker organizations. Unethical practices such as promises, favors, gifts provided by, or in support of, candidates for the post of Director-General are prohibited. Candidates address the Governing Body and are then elected by a majority vote. In other words, the P5 does not have a monopoly over this issue, neither do the ten States of chief industrial importance which have permanent seats on the Governing Body; and, indeed, employers and workers voting as a bloc could in theory frustrate the wishes of governments.

Can we invent a new system for the election of the S-G that generally follows this precedent? The ILO is a specialized agency dealing with the world of work, but the UN is the overarching agency dealing with peace, development, and human rights. It needs a broader coalition of interests. In the previous chapter, the structure of the three assemblies was mapped out. They are co-equals, and each would therefore be involved in the selection of the S-G. The three assemblies, the Executive Assembly of which include the five permanent members, would be the decision makers. It may require a tripartite selection committee to whittle down the list of candidates to two or three to make the voting process manageable. The P5 would not be able to use the veto in the process. This change of practice would be secured by a reinterpretation of the Charter mapped out step by step in the final chapter.

The mechanism for decision making by the three Assemblies was spelled out in the previous chapter. Decisions would be taken by a majority of delegates (of the three assemblies) and a majority of assemblies. How the politics of the process would play out is difficult to predict. Those who see the world in thrall to a neo-liberal ideology would no doubt point the finger at governments and business acting in cahoots. But the interests of these two sectors do not always coincide and the addition of the philanthropists in the business assembly could influence that sector's perspectives. Civil society could become the decisive sector in any falling out between the others. Having all three assemblies involved would provide the framework within which the informal discussions and negotiations would take place. The fact that no assembly could marshal a sufficient majority simply within its own ranks, means that there would be a need for compromise. Civil society may have to accept somebody with significant experience in the governance of international organizations—one cannot put a learner in the driver's seat of an eighteen-wheeler. Business may have to accept someone who has served in government and understands how to influence them. Governments may have to accept someone of talent and charisma though they have traditionally seen this as against their interests.

The next tweak of the system would need to be a new understanding of the rules concerning the second term. As things stand, S-Gs are effectively elected to a ten-year term with a reconfirmation process at mid-point. A corollary of this situation is that in the first five years, the S-G does nothing controversial that might jeopardize his second term. Is this a good way to run a railroad—do nothing for five years and then squeeze all the initiatives in that small window between reappointment and lame-duckery? The S-G should be able to act confidently from day one. This would no doubt lead to actions that would antagonize one or all three of the sectors, so a rule requiring reappointment by consensus would inevitably lead to either one term S-Gs or timid S-Gs. The required rule should be that the S-G is reappointed unless the trilateral method agrees to appoint a different candidate. Accordingly, not reappointing the S-G would have to be a trilateral decision with the alternative S-G already known.

The sweetheart deals would be gone. The nationality issue would be irrelevant. The P5 would retain their veto on Chapter VII resolutions but not for the appointment of the S-G. The world would seek a leader of unquestioned capacity and integrity. If the United Nations Leviathan existed today, the person who could naturally and popularly fill the S-G position would be someone like Barack Obama. Imagining Obama at the helm of the UN crystallizes the vision of an independent body armed with moral authority, dealing competently with the weighty issues being faced. If this simple mental exercise is all it takes for the vision to have credibility, then the vision cannot be so farfetched.

## PERFORMANCE LEGITIMACY

Having lost the superficial legitimacy of necessarily holding a wide range of passports, the Secretariat would need to build up its performance legitimacy. It would remain a Secretariat servicing the practical needs of the meetings of the assemblies and the Security Council, but this would become a subsidiary role. The Secretariat's major role will be delivering substantive results for "we the peoples." Succeeding chapters will spell out some of these roles such as certifying elections, indicting human rights offenders, governing globalization, managing the massive problem of climate change refugees, and organizing the response to climate change. Having a S-G of global credibility will be a major step in that process. But independent funding of these roles remains fundamental. The concluding chapter spells out how the UN will tax globalization to secure that funding, a concept pioneered by James Tobin.

Under merit appointment, will the UN be a sea of white faces? There are two answers to this question. First, there is nothing intrinsically or genetically that would predispose Europeans to be better at global governance than people from any other region. I saw this in the UN Secretariat where the competent people did not align with any one region. As noted above, the two most independent S-Gs came from Africa. I see it among my student cohort. Rutgers is among the most diverse universities in the world, and as a state university, it is relatively affordable for students from New Jersey. Many of my students are the first in their families to gain tertiary education. The high performing students come from a range of backgrounds. On this basis, there is no intrinsic factor in favor of white faces. But the second part of the response is that there may well be structural factors that point in one direction or another. To pursue an idealistic career path is a luxury afforded to the wealthy. To have the capacity for global governance, it helps to come from a family or society with universalist values. These are the sort of factors that may affect the diversity of the Secretariat. They are structural, not racial. Ultimately, the key is to provide the highest degree of competence and thus gain performance legitimacy.

A shake up of the Secretariat should be accompanied by a review of the proliferation of UN specialized agencies, offices, and funds. Specialization is to be encouraged, silo-ization is not. We currently have too little of the former and too much of the latter. One market-based corrective is that if the particular body is simply servicing the needs of Member States or even the tripartite membership, then those members will have to pay for the services directly, it should not come from the Tobin taxes. It would work like a normal conference: a quorum of countries would call for the meeting, the cost is determined, and a fee is set for participation. This should have the effect of scheduling fewer standing meetings in favor of more *ad hoc* meetings as the need arises. And it should mean that far fewer reports will be commissioned. In any case, the third UN of think tanks, civil society, and academics, is often more qualified to write reports on various situations and issues and the policy response options. It might cost members a little more, but why not build some contestability into the process by having two or three groups prepare reports.

There is also scope for rationalization. The UN lists 34 specialized UN bodies.[16] I do not wish to get bogged down in the details and the inevitable bureaucratic holy wars accompanying any reorganization, so these are simply initial ideas that might be worth considering. The UN Development Program (UNDP) owns that important word, development, while the UN Children's Fund (UNICEF) has the advantage of working on behalf of children. They both do similar things. UNDP is the larger and more effective body, and it acts as the UN's foreign service. UNICEF has the more powerful brand name. Why not combine the two and keep the best of both? There is both a World

Trade Organization (WTO) and a UN Conference on Trade and Development (UNCTAD). The latter is a mere shadow of the former in terms of influence and impact. But UNCTAD has an impressive research capacity focused on the needs of the developing world. So why not simply add that useful capacity to the WTO. Circumstances have caused the work of the UN Environment Program and the World Meteorological Organization to converge, with climate change the overriding preoccupation of both bodies. Should they maintain separate existences?

There is also much rationalization possible in the work methods of the General Assemblies. It is difficult for outsiders to believe, but the same issue presented in almost identical terms might be debated in four separate UN forums. It might be debated and voted on in the Human Rights Council, then again at the Economic and Social Council, once again in the Third Committee of the General Assembly, and finally one more time on the merry-go-round in the Plenary of the General Assembly. Even the government delegates, who live through this nonsense, understood that something had to be done, and so an informal practice developed of only dealing with old chestnut issues once a biennium. It is on the issue of work methods that we will see one of the benefits of the establishment of the other two assemblies, UNGAB and UNGAC. The business delegates will organize their work by adopting an efficiency metric and the civil society delegates a priority metric. If UNGAX wishes to spin its wheels discussing the same old issues *ad nauseum*, it will simply lose relevance.

I have been writing this book in the time of COVID-19, which is also the time of the Black Lives Matter movement. I am deeply sympathetic. I understand the importance of the consciousness raising and community organizing activities generated by the movement. But I am a policy wonk. So, I ask myself what policies can be adopted in response. In doing so, I am conscious of the reality that although a problem might be multi-faceted and complex, political leaders and the public do not have the stamina for a complex response. This is not a search for a silver bullet, but an acceptance of the reality that any policy response is relative and comparative, aiming to find the best policy with the greatest impact and the most certain capacity for delivery. Many would argue that providing reparations fits the bill. Perhaps. From a policy perspective, I fear there are too many difficulties in the selection and distribution process, and too much blowback. I am attracted to the Booker/Presley proposal for means tested baby bonds to help close the wealth gap.[17] But it will take a generation for the benefits to start kicking in. My single policy response with immediate impact: decriminalize drug use. All drugs, not just marijuana. Pass the issue to the medical community and take it away from the law enforcement community. There have been calls to "defund the police." This has a punitive connotation and lacks logic. What needs to happen is to "detask" the police—take away tasks they currently perform and give it to those who could perform it better. A corollary of detasking is commensurate defunding. End the absurd war on drugs that simply empowers vicious gangs all around the world. In pretty short order, the prison population would be halved, and gangs would be in the unenviable position of finding other sources of income. Does that mean society must tolerate opioid addiction? It already does because it is ineffectual in dealing with it. Maybe the medical community will do a better job of dealing with addiction than does the criminal justice system. Most addicts would rather line up at the pharmacy than steal or prostitute themselves to feed their habit. Of course, those societies with universal health care would do much better than those without. The United States has lived through this in the not-too-distant past. Remember prohibition? Alcohol is now legal and continues to cause considerable harm, but society has learned to tolerate it.

What has this got to do with the UN? There is a UN body that deals with drugs—the UN Office on Drugs and Crime (UNODC). It always annoyed me that UNODC merely hid behind those countries prosecuting the war on drugs and never had any original policy ideas on the matter. UNODC would simply argue that its job is to facilitate the operation of the United Nations Convention against Illicit Traffic in Narcotic Drugs and Psychotropic Substances of 1988. But by fulfilling this enabling role, UNODC provides international cover for the war on drugs. The war on drugs dates back to Richard Nixon in 1971. We have been fighting it for half a century with no possibility of victory. The paradigm is wrong, the analogy is misconstrued, the methodology has only increased violence and harm. A UN Leviathan would provide contestability to the dominant paradigm. A UN Leviathan would speak truth to power.

## NOTES

1. Joint Inspection Unit. 2012. "Staff recruitment in United Nations system organizations: a comparative analysis and benchmarking framework." JIU/NOTE/2012/3, Geneva.
2. United Nations General Assembly resolution 153 (II) 1947.
3. United Nations, "Growth in United Nations Membership." https://www.un.org/en/about-us/growth-in-un-membership
4. United Nations, "Regional groups of Member States." https://www.un.org/dgacm/en/content/regional-groups
5. The Group of 77,"The Member States of the Group of 77." https://www.g77.org/doc/members.html
6. Senate Select Committee on Intelligence, *Soviet Presence in the UN Secretariat*, Washington, May 1985. https://www.intelligence.senate.gov/sites/default/files/publications/9952.pdf

7. Arkady Shevchenko, *Breaking with Moscow*, (New York: Knopf, 1985.)
8. Colum Lynch, "The U.N.: Russia's den of spies," *Foreign Policy*, June 29, 2010.
9. Colum Lynch, "U.S. Expels 12 Alleged Russian Spies," *Foreign Policy*, February 28, 2022.
10. Obituary of Boutros Boutros-Ghali. *The Telegraph*, 16 February 2016.
11. Colum Lynch, "U.N. Human Rights Chief to Leave, Citing 'Appalling' Climate for Advocacy." *Foreign Policy*, December 20, 2017.
12. One for 7 Billion, https://www.1for7billion.org/
13. Boutros Boutros-Ghali, *Unvanquished: A U.S.-U.N. Saga*, (New York: Random House, 1999.)
14. James Traub, *The Best Intentions: Kofi Annan and the UN in the Era of American World Power*, (New York: Farrar, Strauss and Giroux, 2006). Chapter 15.
15. Annex III to the Compendium of rules applicable to the Governing Body of the International Labour Office adopted by the Governing Body at its 240th Session (May–June 1988) and amended at its 312th Session (November 2011)
16. United Nations, "UN System." https://www.un.org/en/about-us/un-system
17. Cory Booker, "Booker, Pressley Reintroduce 'Baby Bonds' Legislation to Combat Wealth Inequality," July 26, 2019, https://www.booker.senate.gov/news/press/booker-pressley-reintroduce-and-ldquobaby-bonds-and-rdquo-legislation-to-combat-wealth-inequality

# *Chapter 5*

# Peace and Security

The first line of the Covenant of the League of Nations is "to promote international co-operation and to achieve international peace and security."[1] The Charter of the United Nation begins with "we the peoples" expressing a determination "to save succeeding generations from the scourge of war."[2] Clearly, peace is the international community's foremost objective.

The drafters of the Covenant believed the raw memory of the Great War would dissuade the world from repeating this course of action. But they also established architecture to deal with breaches of the peace. The aggressor would be so designated, and all the nations of the world would unanimously "subject it to the severance of all trade or financial relations, the prohibition of all intercourse between their nationals and the nationals of the covenant-breaking State, and the prevention of all financial, commercial or personal intercourse between the nationals of the covenant-breaking State and the nationals of any other State."[3] It amounted to the international equivalent of shunning. The 1930s witnessed several cases of naked aggression. Most went unpunished though rhetoric was deployed in the League. But there was action taken against the Soviet Union which was expelled in 1939 for aggression towards Finland. And Japan withdrew in 1933 before it could be expelled. In general, however, the enforcement mechanism set out in the Covenant turned out to be too difficult to implement, or at least too difficult for member states to summon the commitment to implement.

## THE CENTRALITY OF THE SECURITY COUNCIL

The drafters of the Charter learned this lesson well. In place of unanimous shunning, the great powers would become guarantors of peace. The Charter system has worked far better than the Covenant system. Three quarters of a century after the new model was put in place, a third world war has been avoided. Yes, there was the Korean war in which the North's attempt to reunite the country by force led to a conflict supported by ideological rhetoric, in which one million were killed in action. Yes, there was the Vietnam war in which a struggle for national liberation was wrongly perceived as an ideological battle. And yes, there were many other conflicts around the world where the Cold War ideological enemies fought through surrogates. But the United States and the Soviet Union ensured that their mutual belligerence, heating up in places like Berlin, Turkey, and Cuba, did not escalate to full scale war.

Some argue that this long peace has little to do with the architecture of international institutions and much more to do with the reality of mutually assured destruction brought about by the enormous arsenals of nuclear weapons in the hands of the superpowers.[4] While that remains a powerful argument, it does not negate the utility of the international organizational architecture. The United Nations Security Council provides the great powers with a propaganda forum, a negotiating venue, and a safety net. It is the venue that demonstrates the *primus inter pares*, first among equals, place of the great powers in the world. Has it constrained their warlike conduct? It did not dissuade the British and French from launching their "police action" in the Suez. It did not stop the Chinese attack on Vietnam in 1979. It did not prevent the Soviet Union from invading Afghanistan or Russia from invading Ukraine. And it did not halt the United States from invading Iraq though the blessing of the Security Council was initially sought and withheld. But we can only guess counterfactually about the conduct it did in fact restrain. We cannot guess with any confidence what the world would look like without a UN Security Council. The extent of its benefits may be unknowable, but we can be quite certain that whatever are those benefits, they outweigh the negligible costs of maintaining the body.

Returning to the Covenant and the Charter, the circumstances of their creation merit recall. They were drafted after two cataclysmic wars. They would not have been drafted without these wars. Based on those precedents, the willpower to establish a new world security order would have to form in the wake of a third cataclysmic world tragedy. This is not unthinkable, though such a calamity is unlikely to take the form of a third world war given the positive track record of high-level restraint between superpowers. It could, however, flow from the destabilization of the great powers. Putin's attempt to reestablish the Soviet empire could lead to ruinous war in northern Eurasia. A revolution against the excesses of the Communist Party of China could take that country back to the warring states era. And, with hundreds of millions of weapons in private hands, a civil war in the United States could do even more harm than the first edition. We also need to think of the destabilization of the world order brought about by hundreds of millions of climate change refugees. It is these sorts of circumstances that could bring about the cataclysm causing a fundamental change in the architecture of the Security Council. They are not propitious circumstances. The maintenance of the current architecture would thus be a reflection of high-level peace and stability.

That is the unarticulated premise in the calls for reform, rather than reconstruction, of the Security Council. It is not my intention to summarize all the reform proposals but simply to say there are two major foci. The first deals with the size of the Council and the identification and privileges of the new members. The second deals with the possibility of placing limitations on the wielding of the veto by the permanent members. The proponents of reform are, with one interesting exception, those on the outside looking in. Thus, there are insistent calls for increasing the number of permanent members from putative candidates for that privilege such as Germany, Japan, and India. There are calls for increasing the size of the Council by a wide array of countries to reflect the increase in the size of membership. After all, the Council was enlarged from 11 to 15 in 1963 to reflect an increase of 62 in membership from 51 to 113, so, the argument goes, it should again be increased now that the membership has grown by a further 80 countries.[5] And, finally, there are calls by countries from the global South who complain about the lack of representativeness of the Security Council because parts of the world like Asia and Africa are underrepresented or even because whole religions such as Islam, Hinduism or Buddhism have no permanent place whereas four of the five permanent members are predominantly Christian.

Indeed, in one recent authoritative volume on the work of the Council,[6] there are two specific proposals for Council enlargement: Edward Luck argues for a Council of 20 with 15 elected members serving three-year terms and eligible for reelection once,[7] while Kishore Mahbubani posits a 7+7+7 formula whereby there would be seven permanent members including only China, Russia, and the US from the current batch, seven members rotating regularly among 28 designated next level powers and seven elected from the rest.[8] Both authors accept the political difficulties of achieving such an outcome. Luck's proposal is more modest and could possibly attract P5 support while triggering opposition from claimants to the status of permanent members. Mahbubani's interesting proposal would unleash the devil in the details in its attempt to identify the four new permanent members and the 28 next level candidates.

The logic of enlarging the Council is not compelling. It rests in part on national ego, and in part on that phrase that has so diminished the UN—"equitable geographic distribution." The key criterion should remain effectiveness. There may well be a good case for India becoming a non-veto wielding permanent member given its considerable contribution to peacekeeping, but the reality is that China will not allow this to happen. The case for Japan and Germany is weak. One of the great achievements of the post-WWII world has been the transformation of these two mighty societies with their warlike traditions into pacifists. But pacifism is not in the job requirements for permanent membership of the Security Council. France and the UK may no longer straddle the world as they did in colonial times, but they have a quality that is sorely needed. The electorates of these two countries accept the cost of great power status in treasure, and more importantly, in blood. Whereas the governments of Japan and Germany would surely collapse as soon as the body bags from Chapter VII enforcement operations start returning home, the people of France and the UK will accept that cost because they know that to maintain any semblance of great power status, they need fighting militaries prepared to do the tough enforcement jobs. Japan and Germany wish to buy their places on the Security Council with treasure, but the real need is for countries with competent militaries and publics prepared to accept the resultant cost in blood.

The second issue on the reform agenda is the P5 power of veto. It is generally understood that no new permanent members would gain the right of veto. The debate has turned on the ideas to limit veto use by the existing P5. One proposal has come from France, a P5 member. France has called on its fellow P5 members to "voluntarily and collectively pledge not to use the veto in case of recognized mass atrocities."[9] Another proposal has come from the Accountability, Coherence and Transparency (ACT) group of 25 middle powers writing: "The Code of Conduct calls upon all members of the UNSC—elected and permanent—to not vote against any credible draft resolution intended to prevent or halt mass atrocities."[10] And another notable proposal has come from a group of Elders comprising former statesmen and women with high gravitas who argue that "the P5 must not use their veto without explaining their decision and proposing an alternative plan in accordance with international law that can achieve the same goals."[11] None of these three proposals has effectively gained much ground, though the ACT group attracted 80 sponsors. They do demonstrate, however, that the idea of limiting the veto is being seriously considered.

As things stand, there may be deliberation, but the "reform" debate has not produced results. The P5 see no need for change and thus adopt a fundamentally passive aggressive attitude. Reform of the Council can come in either one of two ways; from inside or outside. From inside, means voluntary reform by the Council and in this respect, there have been some improvements and innovations in working methods.[12] The French idea of voluntary restraint in the use of the veto may yet find support. But any voluntary limits will be rejected if they are seen as impinging on basic national interests. That leads to a discussion of change by outside forces through amendment of the Charter. Proponents of Charter amendment would point to the 1963 episode when the Council membership was last increased as a precedent. But the increase in size from 11 to 15 with a consequential increase of the qualified majority from seven to nine votes, did not fundamentally affect the position or privileges of the P5, so they went along with it. The reality is, however, that Charter amendment to limit the veto is unlikely because the P5 hold a veto on this method. Chapter XVIII of the Charter requires any amendment to be ratified by two-thirds of the Members, "including all the permanent members" in effect establishing another veto power.

Any changes to the work methods of the Security Council will need to gain the support of the P5, however grudging. It is, however, not unthinkable that new practices could develop. After all, the Council developed the practice of allowing permanent members to cast abstentions *not* having the effect of a veto, even though the Article 27(3) of the Charter clearly requires "the *concurring* votes of the permanent members." The most promising means of limiting the scope of the veto power is to develop a new understanding of the term "procedural matter," on which no veto is possible but a majority of nine is required (Article 27(2)). The appointment of the Secretary-General should be a procedural matter. In fact, the cleanest argument would be that only action under Chapter VII is *not* procedural. The permanent members would thus retain the power of the veto for enforcement action, but not on any other issue. Their fundamental interests would be protected but they would lose their ability to frustrate non-enforcement action. All other resolutions, that is resolutions not requiring enforcement action, would be adopted by the qualified majority of nine affirmative votes, regardless of negative votes by any of the P5.

The UN 3.0 will thus retain a Security Council, probably looking much like today's version, but it will only be acceptable to the world community if the scope of the veto power is reduced. The proposal to broaden the general understanding of the definition of a procedural matter to all questions and decisions outside the scope of Chapter VII, is a simple and practical way of achieving significant change without attempting formal Charter amendment. I am emboldened in this proposal by the fact that, at the San Francisco conference in 1945, the Australian delegation put forward the same idea.[13] In the concluding chapter, I set out the mechanism whereby the UN can limit the use of the veto to Chapter VII situations.

## THE UNITED STATES AS GLOBAL SECURITY GUARANTOR

Let us not pretend that UN architecture alone can deal with the issues of global peace and security. Looking at 75 years of UN practice, the argument can be made that there are only two occasions when the UN Security Council authorized major military action to deal with an act of naked aggression. The first, the Korean war, was accidental insofar as the authorization for military action was given while the Soviet Union was committing the egregious miscalculation of boycotting the Council because of the question of who should hold the China seat. The second, the 1991 eviction of Saddam Hussein's forces from Kuwait based on a series of resolutions culminating in Resolution 678 that authorized all necessary means to be taken, is a far clearer example of the Security Council discharging its responsibilities to maintain peace and security as foreseen in the Charter. But, of course, the Kuwait operation occurred just as the Cold War was ending and was directed against a pariah leader who had committed naked aggression. In that sense, the circumstances for both uses of military force were exceptional.

This is not to deny the value of the invention of peacekeeping by the Security Council. The dozens of UN peacekeeping operations, and the hundreds of thousands of blue helmeted soldiers employed in their delivery, have played an important role in mediating conflicts, ending conflicts, and containing conflicts. But even the most ardent supporter of UN peacekeeping operations would not claim that this is the tool that has prevented World War III. We need to look beyond the UN Security Council to understand that result.

Mention has already been made of the concept of mutually assured destruction and the nuclear standoff. But we need to see this phenomenon within the context of a larger paradigm, the provision of global security provided by the United States, one aspect of which is the supposed nuclear umbrella sheltering its allies. Another is the resultant peace dividend benefiting many other countries as well. Looking in particular at the Western world, it is safe to argue that the primary vehicle of national defense is not to place one's hopes in the vagaries of Security Council collective security, but rather to rely on treaties of alliance with the United States. This has come to be known as *Pax Americana* and follows Charles Kindelberger's hegemonic stability theory.[14]

In this context, Kenneth Anderson provides a quaint but telling division of the world benefiting from the United States as the "parallel provider of security":

> So, the world can be divided into a series of clubs with respect to the parallel provider of security. The gold-plated, first-class club is the one that operates under the full benefit of the US security guarantee—not just NATO, but also Japan, Australia, South Korea, and a range of other industrialized, democratic allies. The next tier—business-class, so to speak—includes many states that are not so fully guaranteed in the sense that America would go to war for them, but still have an enormous security benefit in more passive ways, such as Latin American or Asian states in which the US presence reduces considerably the pressure to arm against one's neighbors. The third tier—coach—benefits from

> a lesser but still important range of passive public goods, such as the freedom and security of the seas.[15]

It follows from Anderson's taxonomy, that there are vast swathes of the planet not traveling on this aircraft. These are the marginal and failed states of Africa, parts of the Middle East, West and Central Asia, the Caucasus, Central America, parts of the Caribbean and parts of the South Pacific. It is in these areas that the Security Council provides security of last resort in much the same way as the International Monetary Fund is the lender of last resort in times of economic crises. The analogy with the IMF goes deeper. Just as the IMF attempts to tie its emergency assistance with conditions to improve the economic viability of the loan recipient, so has the Security Council crafted ever more elaborate mandates as part of its peacekeeping operations in an attempt to improve nation building aspects. The mandates go well beyond the narrow focus on ending or containing the conflict, and routinely contain other goals such as protecting civilians, promoting human rights, and safeguarding democratic institutions.[16]

The post-World War II architecture, whether of the San Francisco or Bretton Woods type, has morphed from a system of global security for which it was drafted, into a system trying to assist the global stragglers and strugglers. Of course, the world has learned to its cost that the effects of insecurity among the straggler societies is not quarantined within their borders but, rather, leaches out to the rest of the international community in the form of terrorism, piracy and trafficking of people, drugs and guns. So, to quibble with Anderson's analysis which sees this aspect of the international system's architecture as a form of altruism, the better argument is that it is a form of preventive security.

But it is not the major form of security on which the viable societies of the world rely. They rely on self-defense as their primary form of security, and many countries combine this with the American security guarantee. The Security Council form of security is for the "others."

Anderson's quaint taxonomy of reliance on the American security guarantee was written in 2009. How different the world looks a decade later! Rather than blithely rely on the various NATO, ANZUS and other such treaties of mutual cooperation and security, the President of France has said "What we are currently experiencing is the brain death of NATO" in reference to the perception of unreliability of the American guarantee.[17] Former President Trump may be idiosyncratic and inarticulate but his security perspective is close to the isolationist and America first concepts that have long existed in the American political discourse alongside the more engaged and internationalist "city on a hill" concepts. They cannot be ignored. Indeed, we should recall Brutus' "Friends, Romans, Countrymen" speech in Shakespeare's

*Julius Caesar* in which he opines that "The evil that men do lives after them. The good is oft interred with their bones."

We will have to live with what historians will describe as Trump's destruction of the *Pax Americana* system, so assiduously built by two post-WWII generations of American leaders. The alliance systems rest in part on physical attributes. There are solemn treaties which are periodically celebrated in flowery speeches. There may be a Secretariat with a Secretary-General with a joint command structure with clever acronyms. There are American forces stationed around the world, sometimes for symbolic effect and sometimes as a tripwire. There are strategies of interoperability, enhanced by training together, but, more tellingly, by buying expensive American kit. And there are all those payments of insurance premiums. The allies pay those premiums by fighting wars alongside the US. Australia has fought every war in which the US has been engaged for the last one hundred years. Canada has also paid its premiums which is why Prime Minister Trudeau was so enraged when President Trump justified tariffs on Canada for security reasons. He said Canada was America's "most steadfast ally" in war and peace, calling the tariffs "an affront to the . . . thousands of Canadians who have fought and died alongside American comrades-in-arms."[18]

But all those physical attributes of an alliance system, all those treaties, all that American equipment purchased, and all those allied deaths in combat, are secondary to the main requirement of any alliance, confidence. Allies must have confidence in each other. In particular, those allies traveling first class in the Anderson taxonomy, must have confidence that the United States will answer the call when their security is directly threatened. It is that confidence that Trump has shattered. And it is not clear that it can be reconstructed. The world has reached a Humpty Dumpty moment.

The strategic impact of this moment is made more acute by China's rise, peaceful and otherwise, and by the resurrection of Russia as an aggressive global military power. The Russian threat is more immediate but short-term. It would be easy to blame one person, Vladimir Putin, but the reality is that the Russian threat is also structural. Russia is not an economic power but rather resembles a state suffering from the resource curse. That resource has a definite life span. Psychologically, having been the other superpower for four decades, it is difficult for the Russian elite to accept a lesser status. It is almost as if the trigger for its return to global strategic prominence was President Obama's impolitic comment that Russia is merely a regional power.[19] This galvanized Putin and his supporters to prove Obama wrong. And Russia has the skills to follow up, as the world learned to its cost in Syria. Russia has a well-functioning intelligence community, showered with responsibility and resources by its former head, Putin. The major goal of the Russian intelligence community is to undermine democracy around the world, and it is doing a bang-up job. Russia also has military wherewithal. The Russian military-industrial sector continues to produce high quality kit, though the military itself is rather stretched and must lean on mercenaries. Nevertheless, in the short-term, Russia is a real threat. In the longer term, however, the weaknesses in Russia's economy and society will paralyze its capacity to project power.

The same cannot be said for China. China is flexing its economic muscles and will have the capacity to do so for the foreseeable future. China is only flexing its military muscles internally and at its peripheries. The big question for the international community is whether this state of affairs will last. Unlike Russia, which is accustomed to projecting its power abroad, near and far, China, as seen from its history, is not. China has never had an expeditionary military. China had the capacity to dominate the world in the fifteenth century when its fleet under Admiral Zheng He was unmatched in size and sophistication.[20] But the succeeding "emperor went so far as to ban the construction of any ocean-going ships and prohibit those that existed from being used for voyages beyond Chinese coastal waters."[21] China's strategy historically has been to dominate because of the superiority of its civilization. It prefers to extend its influence by the tributary system whereby others acknowledge China's superiority and tailor their policies to please China. But can the tributary system be recreated in the twenty-first century? Perhaps it can, especially if the US security guarantee turns out to be a paper tiger. It is painful for me to recognize that the test case will be Australia. Australia has had it both ways for the last several decades; its prosperity is tied to China while its security is tied to the United States. Australian governments have been avoiding this reality, but China has the capacity to make Australia choose. If Australia cannot rely on the United States' security guarantee, paying tribute to Beijing may not seem like such a bad option. As noted in the introduction, China is unqualified to succeed the United States as the hegemonic stabilizer. Its Leninist party will always put its interests above all else. And, civilizationally, China lacks the universalist norms and ideas that allowed the world to accept the US in this role. Indeed, the very expression "universal values" is banned from Chinese public discourse.[22]

The post-Humpty Dumpty world will be different from the one with which we have grown comfortable. Should the United States turn inward, it will lose many of the benefits of globalization. It is already crippling its prospects with its lack of investment in education. This does not mean that the United States will forfeit its military superiority. But the concern, bolstered by recent experience, is that the United States will use that military power capriciously. Simply being the most militarily powerful nation does not mean that others can rely on that power.

## A PERMANENT FORUM FOR A CONCERT OF POWERS

Where does this leave the United Nations Security Council? At the most basic level, it is the forum where the three powers referred to above are permanent members. Indeed, what we have learned from their practice on the Council is that despite their continuing ideological or strategic or economic competition, they often behave in a manner approaching collegiality. They behave collegially to safeguard their privileges. They behave collegially to maintain their exclusivity. They behave collegially to keep the elected ten members of the Council in their diminished place. In the post-Humpty Dumpty world, the Security Council may become a place of ever greater P5 collegiality.

It is not in the strategic interests of China, Russia, or the United States to go to war against each other. MAD continues to apply. It is in their strategic interests to work towards deconflicting situations which could trigger war between any of the three powers. A recent example of deconflicting tactics occurred in Syria where Russia and the United States maintained a dialogue to ensure that there were no accidental firefights between them. We can expect the Council to be a forum to continue that posture.

The collegiality is, however, likely to go further than assuring deconflicting tactics. It is likely to take on some of the properties of a concert of powers.[23] "Concert systems arise after major, counter-hegemonic wars and survive for about as long as the defeated hegemon is felt to represent a threat."[24] The classic example of employing such a concert is the Congress of Vienna in 1815 to shape Europe after the disruptions of the French revolution, the Napoleonic wars and the defeat of Napoleon. The 1945 meeting in Yalta between the (then) big three planned the post-WWII world. Similar meetings were held in Europe in 1989 and 1990 following the collapse of communist ideology. These meetings deal with far more than deconflicting tactics. They attempt to plan and shape international relations for the new era.

The Security Council has at times taken the look and role of a concert of powers. The rejection of the recolonization of the Suez Canal may be cited as an example. The expulsion of Saddam Hussein from Kuwait to safeguard the principle of sovereignty, may be another. And, though short-lived, the application of the doctrine of the responsibility to protect in Libya, may well be a further example. These examples are noteworthy because they did not directly engage the interests of the superpowers of the day. They were sufficiently distant from those direct interests to allow for a concert of powers to apply the relevant principles, as interpreted by those powers. Needless to say, when the principles did not suit any of the powers in a given situation, they were not applied.

This is likely to be the future role of the United Nations Security Council if it is be limited to that of a permanent forum for the major powers of the day.

That would be largely a continuation of existing practice. A cozy and collegial place for the great powers where their fundamental interests are not threatened. A useful place where they can discuss ways of avoiding direct conflict, often settling for battle by proxy forces. And occasionally, a place where some progress can be made, or risks taken to secure peace and security, as long as the cost is not too high, and the area is not of direct strategic concern.

We need to inject a word here about the status and role of France and the United Kingdom in the post-Brexit era. They are clearly the weak links among the P5. In a post-Brexit Europe, we can expect France to give its permanent seat a little more of a European coloration. France will deepen its consultations and briefings with its EU partners and speak for Europe . . . when this coincides with French interests. While the Europeans may grumble, they will accept the status quo. The European mentality is to look to NATO when confronting Russia, while looking primarily to the UN when dealing with Africa. France has the keenest interest in Africa and so the current situation will change little. One indirect benefit for Europeans is that the status bestowed on France by its permanent membership of the Security Council helps to balance the growing power of Germany in Europe which was previously also countervailed by the presence of the United Kingdom.

The United Kingdom is in a far weaker position. It is likely to become little more than England within a decade or so of Brexit. The first hurdle will then be the question of succession. There are two precedents. The international community was happy to see Russia succeed to the UN seat formerly held by the Soviet Union. Russia was the core Republic in the Soviet Union and Moscow is and was the capital of both entities. Furthermore, it made sense to maintain Russian disarmament commitments entered into by the Soviet Union and for Russia to be the continuing state in respect of the nuclear non-proliferation regime. But in a not dissimilar geographic situation, the international community did not accept that Serbia (then called the Federal Republic of Yugoslavia) was the continuity of the Socialist Federal Republic of Yugoslavia, the state once ruled by Tito. Serbia was not the core of the country which far more resembled a partnership of nationalities, and the international community did not wish to reward Serbia's aggression.[25] Serbia had to seek membership of the UN anew, just like the other former republics in the federation. It is likely that the international community would follow the Russian precedent in England's case, largely because of P5 solidarity and to not open the door to wholesale changes to the Council. Permanent membership of the Security Council will be the most prized possession left for England from the self-perceived glories of the colonial period. It will be the last indicator of English greatness when the economy inevitably falters, and social unrest deepens. England will work hard to retain that status. It has inertia on its side, always a prized commodity in international relations. But that will be insufficient. England will try to earn its continuing place on the Security Council by volunteering for ever more difficult military missions sanctioned by the Security Council. In that sense the working-class Brexit voters will get what they wanted, a return to the good old days—the days when their sons were used as cannon fodder.

But the concert of powers formula will not resolve most conflict situations around the world. Indeed, the Security Council as a concert of powers is a formula for high level security accompanied by low level conflict and churn, occasionally drawing Chapter VII action, but more often than not ignored behind a wall of pious rhetoric.

## IS THERE A FORCE FOR POSITIVE DISRUPTION?

Among the arguments for enlargement of the Council are the ideas of more equitable geographic distribution and for a better reflection of the current realities. An argument that is rarely articulated, because it would be so difficult to demonstrate, is that an enlarged Council would work better. Why would a council with 15 or 16 non-veto wielding members work better than a Council with only 10? After all, if there are strong ideas for actions in favor of peace and security, they can find their way to the Council through non-members in the normal course of multilateral diplomacy. There might be a case for a larger Council to share the significant workload of managing so many sanctions regimes and other initiatives requiring the monitoring of reporting by Members States. But any such bureaucratic benefits would be outweighed by the more unwieldly and inefficient management of a Council of 20 or 21.

The reality is that the current elected 10 members suffer from the deep frustration of being treated as amateurs among the P5 pros. Increasing the size of the Council will not change the circumstances that bring about this frustration. The experiences of newly elected members of the Council follow similar patterns. If election to the Council has been contested, an invariable occurrence in the West Europe and Others Group and a growing phenomenon in the Asia group, then the day of election in the General Assembly becomes the high point of membership. It is all downhill from there. Having beefed up the permanent mission to the UN with new staff at considerable expense to the foreign ministry budget, the new member takes its seat and begins a steep learning curve. There is at least one draft resolution per week to be debated, negotiated, and adopted. Many, such as extending the duration of a peacekeeping force, are relatively routine. Many others are agonizingly difficult and require wrenching decisions to be made at headquarters upon the advice of the mission. One need only recall the famous second Iraq resolution in 2003 that caused such consternation to the E10, knowing as they did that a refusal to accept the reckless American lead, could well cause bilateral repercussions. And as we subsequently learned, the diplomats representing the E10 were subject to possible *kompromat* investigations by the American and British intelligence services.[26]

Aside from such political problems, the new members will soon be inundated with other work. There are 16 peacekeeping operations to keep abreast of, each with difficult problems of mandate creep, host country belligerence, troop contributing country nervousness, budget overruns and, inevitably, scathing media and civil society criticism. And there are over a dozen sanctions regimes to implement. With the advent of smart sanctions attempting to target the actual perpetrators rather than the whole nation, the work of the Council must be finely tuned with decisions taken individual by individual, corporation by corporation. And smart sanctions target not only recalcitrant governments, but also non-state actors such as terrorist groups. The work takes place not only in New York but also in capitals because these finely tuned sanctions require all member states to constantly keep up to date their domestic regulations targeting sanctioned individuals' travel and financial flows.

Each new elected member will be assigned the chairmanship of at least one of the sanctions committees. "For elected members of the Council from smaller states who chair two or more committees, the burden can be quite heavy."[27] While other members of the Council are represented on these committees by diplomats below the level of permanent representative, the chair is expected to be the Ambassador.[28] E10 Ambassadors quickly learn that there is precious little time to be proactive. Their time is filled simply with keeping up to speed.

A common initiative for an E10 country to undertake, is to take advantage of the one month in the two-year term when that country presides over the Council (it may be twice, depending on the vagaries of the next elections and the subsequent alphabetic order of newly elected members). This is often the occasion for the Minister for Foreign Affairs to descend on New York for the photo opportunity of chairing the Security Council. But merely presiding over a meeting is often considered insufficient for an ambitious minister. There needs to be a national initiative crowned by a resolution for the Minister to shepherd through and triumphantly announce. This means months of preliminary work by the mission pleading with the P5 to tolerate the process.

Little time and energy are left for the big issues. Observers of the UN were thus surprised by the success of three E10 members (Australia, Jordan, and Luxembourg) in 2014 in initiating and having adopted a resolution on humanitarian access in Syria.[29] But this is far more the exception than the rule. Indeed, when a similar resolution was attempted in December 2019 at the initiative of Belgium, Germany, and Kuwait, it was vetoed by Russia and China marking the end of UN relief action in Syria.[30] It follows, that the E10 cannot and will not be the disruptors of the Security Council. They will not be able to effectively speak truth to power. They will have little capacity or indeed inclination to lead the work of the Council. They will leave the ownership of the Council very much in the hands of the P5.

Is there another candidate for constructive disruptor? One of the burdens of this monograph is to look beyond governments for solutions. Yes, governments are indispensable, but the United Nations must avoid the closed shop situation where governments control all aspects of the organization's work. There are innumerable examples where governments will follow their own narrow short-term interests and ignore the interests of "we the peoples." While this so clearly applies to the issues of climate change and development, it applies no less to issues of peace and security.

There is only one other candidate for the job of positively disrupting the P5 oligopoly. The Secretary-General must step up! We have not seen many activist Secretaries-General. Those that tried to challenge a P5 member found it came with a cost. Boutros Boutros-Ghali was denied a second term after he acted independently and thus fell out of step with the Clinton Administration.[31] Kofi Annan also relates how he had to withstand "a barrage of attacks against me" from the Bush Administration when he declared the invasion of Iraq to be illegal.[32] Annan does not relate, however, that in consequence of the incessant attacks over his position and the UN's mismanagement of the Iraq Oil-for-Food program in which his son was involved, he lost his voice for several months at the time he needed it most to defend himself.[33] The episode shades from the psychosomatic to the metaphysical. It is as if Annan, having gotten into trouble by speaking truth to power, was now self-correcting by losing the capacity to speak at all. The one other Secretary-General who might be said to have acted independently was Dag Hammarskjöld, who tried to intervene personally in the Congo to mediate a conflict between UN forces and Katangan rebels. He died in a mysterious plane crash in 1961 on his fourth visit.[34]

These are not propitious examples for any future Secretary-General. As previously noted, the current system is designed to place a quietist diplomat in the position. The Boutros-Ghali and Annan examples serve as warnings to others, should they decide to buck the system. But this book envisages a whole new system, one where the UN is no longer reliant on Member States for its budget and one where the Secretary-General is selected through a tripartite process that governments cannot easily dominate and the P5 cannot veto. Under that system it may well be possible to have an independent

Secretary-General who is able and willing to speak truth to power and act accordingly.

In fact, as previously noted, this is the situation envisaged by the Charter. There are three little words in the Charter that highlight its intention that the Secretary-General be an independent actor and not merely a facilitator of the wishes of delegates. Article 99 states:

The Secretary-General may bring to the attention of the Security Council any matter which *in his opinion* may threaten the maintenance of international peace and security. (italics added)

The three little words are "in his opinion." This confirms the Charter's vision of the Secretary-General as an independent player in global affairs. The Member States, and in particular the P5, do all in their power to preclude this vision from becoming reality.

## SECRETARY OR GENERAL?

Member States led by the P5 tend to control the narrative concerning the work conducted by the Security Council.[35] They preside, they speak, they vote. And they brief the press. The Secretary-General is treated as little more than a note taker. But that masks the reality of who holds the expertise, who understands the trouble spots and who ultimately must deliver the day-to-day operations—the Secretary-General and his Secretariat.

The following table eloquently makes clear that most action resolutions adopted by the Council are based on detailed reports by the Secretary-General:[36]

**Table 5.1. Mandates with Nation Building Aspects in Peacekeeping Operations.**

| *Situation* | *Mandate* | *Year* | *S-G's Report* |
|---|---|---|---|
| Nambia | SCRs 431 & 435 | 1978 | S/12636 |
| Nambia (Implementation) | SCR 632 | 1989 | S/20412 |
| Western Sahara | SCR 690 | 1991 | S/22464 |
| El Salvador | SCRs 693 & 832 | 1991 and 1993 | S/22494 |
| Croatia | SCR 743 | 1992 | S/23592 |
| Cambodia | SCR 745 | 1992 | S/23613 |
| Angola | SCR 747 | 1992 | S/23671 |
| Mozambique | SCR 797 | 1992 | S/24982 |
| Somalia | SCR 814 | 1993 | S/25354 |
| Liberia | SCR 886 and SCR 1020 | 1993 and 1995 | S/26422 and S/1995/881 |
| Haiti | SCR 867 | 1993 | S/26490, S/26352 |
| Rwanda | SCR 997 | 1995 | S/1995/457 |
| Bosnia-Herzegovina | SCR 1035 | 1995 | S/1995/1031 |
| Croatia- Eastern Slavonia | SCR 1037 | 1996 | S/1995/1028 |

| *Situation* | *Mandate* | *Year* | *S-G's Report* |
|---|---|---|---|
| Angola (Consolidation) | SCR 1118 | 1997 | S/1997/438 |
| Central African Republic | SCR 1159 and SCR 1230 | 1998 and 1999 | S/1998/148 and S/1998/98 |
| Sierra Leone | SCR 1181 | 1998 | S/1998/486 |
| Kosovo | SCR 1244 | 1999 | S/1999/779 |
| East Timor | SCR 1273 and SCR 1410 | 1999 and 2002 | S/1999/1024 and S/2002/30 |
| Congo (DRC) | SCR 1291 | 2000 | S/2000/30 |
| Afghanistan | SCR 1378 | 2001 | S/2001/1157 |
| Liberia | SCR 1497 | 2003 | S/2003/875 |
| Haiti | SCR 1542 | 2004 | S/2004/698 |
| Burundi | SCR 1545 | 2004 | S/2004/682 |
| Timor-Leste | SCR 1677 and SCR 1704* | 2006 | S/2007/50* |
| Congo (DRC) | SCR 1925 | 2010 | S/2010/512 |
| Côte d'Ivoire | SCR 1933 | 2010 | S/2010/245 |
| South Sudan | SCR 1996 | 2011 | S/2011/678 |
| Mali | SCR 2100 | 2013 | S/2013/338 |
| Central African Republic | SCR 2149 | 2014 | S/2014/857 |

The point of the table comes through in column 4, to demonstrate the indispensable role of the Secretary-General and his Secretariat. The Security Council does not design these massive operations, though it might fiddle with the proposed design. It does not craft the mandate, though again it might broaden or narrow certain elements. It does not negotiate with the troop contributing countries, though it may add a nudge or two. It is the Secretariat that holds the expertise and that carries out the required mandate. In that sense, the Secretary-General is already the equivalent of the Chair of the Joint Chiefs of Staff, a general, not a secretary.

The vision of the UN being presented in this monograph, is a vision of a possible UN of the future, the UN that an increasingly Hobbesian world requires. Some aspects of the vision are sharply defined, others are hazier. The vision of the Secretary-General as General is in the latter category. But, as with other departures from the current unsatisfactory practice, the germ of the idea or the precedent by analogy exists in current theory or practice. In this case, the precedent is Article 43(1) of the Charter:

> All Members of the United Nations, in order to contribute to the maintenance of international peace and security, undertake to make available to the Security Council, on its call and in accordance with a special agreement or agreements, armed forces, assistance and facilities, including rights of passage, necessary for the purpose of maintaining international peace and security.

As we know, no agreements were ever concluded and no Article 43 armed forces ever existed, though the Military Staff Committee that was supposed to manage these forces continues to meet, decades after its existence was made futile. The UN invented a new concept some years after the Charter was drafted—peacekeeping. In some ways, UN peacekeeping has undertaken some of the tasks initially envisaged by Article 43 forces. And the Military Staff Committee has in effect been replaced by the Departments of Peacekeeping Operations and its companion Department of Field Support.

Form follows function. This may be an architectural truism, but it is also applicable to the way institutions mold themselves to fulfil the function required of them. The very first peacekeeping operation was the UN Truce Supervision Organization (UNTSO). In May 1948, the Security Council, in resolution 50 of that year, called for a cessation of hostilities in Palestine and decided that the truce should be supervised by the UN Mediator, with the assistance of a group of military observers. The first group of military observers became UNTSO.[37] Seven decades later, there is no truce to supervise, but UNTSO remains. The 150 or so military personnel have in effect become the Secretary-General's small military contingent whose members can be deployed anywhere and anytime to observe, advise or initiate.

These are the two germs of the idea that help form the proposition that follows. The original design of the UN envisaged that it would have standing armed forces. The Secretary-General often needs competent senior people in uniform to take on special tasks. Drawing on these two ideas, my admittedly vague vision, hampered by my limited knowledge of military operations, is that a powerful Secretary-General must be far more of a General. He must have his own troops. The Secretary-General needs to have a well-trained and well-armed military Division properly kitted out with appropriate transport and weapons. I leave it to others with more expertise to elaborate on the details.

But unlike the idea envisaged in Article 43, the Secretary-General's Division would not comprise troops from Member States. They would be individually recruited, and their allegiance would be to the UN. It is likely many of them will be former national soldiers. They would have an integrated command structure headed by the Secretary-General, but the troops would be under the immediate command of a two or three star general. Clearly, they would need to be based within easy reach of "where the action is" and certainly not in Geneva or New York. A base in a place like Djibouti would make sense.

Why does the Secretary-General need to command his own armed forces? For much the same reasons as the United Nations needs its own source of revenue, to liberate it from the stranglehold by governments in which it presently finds itself. The Secretary-General needs the capacity to take action in the security theatre. He needs it for reasons of independence and for reasons of prestige. Without his own forces, the Secretary-General is essentially a secretary, and thus a paper tiger.

But what sort of action would the Secretary-General's troops undertake? Not enforcement of Security Council resolutions. That would remain the responsibility of the Security Council. And not peacekeeping operations, as that would also remain within the purview of the Security Council. The best answer I can give at this stage is that the Secretary-General needs a force of some 15,000–20,000 troops to provide him with the capacity to deal effectively with spoilers.

In his 2013 book[38] *The End of Power*, Moisés Naím has a chapter entitled "Pentagons versus Pirates" in which he describes the problem of asymmetric warfare. Large armies are designed to fight other large armies. But their main role has become to fight spoilers. Spoilers can take many forms. They might be military factions, criminal gangs, terrorist groups or even messianic believers. The way news is reported conflates immediacy for intensity, so that these spoilers are given wide coverage thus encouraging their actions. As the name I have chosen to call them implies, their aim is to produce a negative result, to spoil somebody else's well laid plans. They need to be dealt with quickly and sternly.

The Secretary-General would use his forces primarily when the United Nations is challenged by spoilers. When UN officials are kidnapped or under fire; when UN teams are threatened; when UN missions are harassed. These are situations in which, were they to take place today, the UN must politely ask the government of the state in which the problem is occurring to take some form of action. Most governments would comply. But others may hesitate or prevaricate. Others still may not have the competence or wherewithal to take effective action. The UN cannot be held hostage to such situations and needs to have the capacity to take relieving action at the discretion of the Secretary-General.

There may well be analogous situations involving human rights defenders or emergency relief deliverers when the Secretary-General may consider it necessary for the UN to step in. Another possible category of situations demanding direct action by the UN may involve vulnerable communities facing grievous danger at the hands of armed fanatics. In many situations the extent of the danger and the breadth of territory will be such that only the Security Council can effectively deal with it, but there may be more localized situations where quick and decisive action by a highly mobile and competent military force could be an option. I am thinking of the Chibok girls and the Yazidi women.

How much would it cost? Again, I am not sure of the answer except to say that it would be a tiny fraction of world military expenditure which, according to the Stockholm International Peace Research Institute rose to $1822 billion in 2018.[39] A quarter of one percent would come to around $5 billion. The combined arms-sales of the top 100 largest arms-producing companies and military services companies (excluding China) totaled $420 billion in 2018.[40] A one percent tax on all arms transfers would be sufficient to fund the S-G's Division.

The question that would be asked today is how could this possibly be made to work in a Westphalian world? What about the sovereignty of the countries in which these actions take place? Once again, the precedent may lie in three words used in the Charter. Returning to Article 43, the drafters foresaw that the armed forces would need to be able to operate effectively and so they added to the issues to be covered in the special agreements "rights of passage." A set of rights would need to be established to allow the Secretary-General's armed forces to operate. This could be achieved by a resolution of the General Assembly requesting the Security Council to take action under Chapter VII, and a subsequent binding resolution by the Council. The legal platform can be constructed if the will exists.

Diplomats and government ministers reading this will be startled by its audacity. The governments of Member States like to see the UN Secretariat and its Secretary-General as meek servants kowtowing to their demands. After all, they hold the financial reins, and they hold the military reins. To them, the UN is simply a convenient place for meetings between governments, a place to play the word games they have busied themselves with for decades. It is not seen as a place that initiates decisive action.

But cut those reins and it all changes. Governments would remain important players. The Security Council would continue to be the predominant chamber dealing with peace and security and, at least, a place for the concert of powers to occur. Troop contributing countries would remain central to the viability of peacekeeping missions. But an important new actor would join them—the Secretary-General. The Secretary-General would be the positive disruptor of the current cozy game. His authority would draw from beyond governments to civil society and corporations. His access to funds would be assured. And he would have limited but effective military clout.

## NOTES

1. Covenant of the League of Nations, preamble, https://avalon.law.yale.edu/20th_century/leagcov.asp
2. Charter of the United Nations, preamble, https://www.un.org/en/charter-united-nations/
3. Article 16

4. Kenneth N. Waltz, "Toward nuclear peace," in Kenneth N. Waltz, (Ed.). *Realism and international politics* (New York: Routledge, 2008) 260–275

5. United Nations. n.d. "Growth in United Nations membership, 1945-present." https://www.un.org/en/about-us/growth-in-un-membership

6. Sebastian von Einsiedel, David Malone, Bruno Stagno Ugarte (eds.) *The UN Security Council in the 21st Century*, Boulder: Lynne Rienner Publishers, 2016.

7. Edward C. Luck, "The Security Council at Seventy: Ever Changing or Never Changing," in von Einsiedel et al, ibid., 195–214

8. Kishore Mahbubani, "Council Reform and the Emerging Powers," von Einsiedel op. cit., 157–173

9. Permanent Mission of France to the UN, "The UN Reform," https://onu.delegfrance.org/France-and-the-UN-Reform-8615

10. ACT Explanatory Note, 1 September 2015, https://centerforunreform.org/wp-content/uploads/2015/09/Final-2015-09-01-SC-Code-of-Conduct-Atrocity.pdf

11. Delia Paul, "Elders Present Four Proposals for UN Reform" IISD, SDG Knowledge Hub, 11 Feb. 2015, http://sdg.iisd.org/news/elders-present-four-proposals-for-un-reform/

12. Christian Wenaweser, "Working Methods: The Ugly Duckling of Security Council Reform," von Einsiedel et al, op. cit., 175–194

13. Edward C. Luck, "The UN Security Council: Practice and Promise," (Oxford: Routledge 2006), 14.

14. See Christopher Layne, "This Time It's Real: The End of Unipolarity and the 'Pax Americana'," *International Studies Quarterly*, Vol. 56, No. 1 (March 2012), 203–213

15. Kenneth Anderson, "United Nations Collective Security and the United States Security Guarantee in an Age of Rising Multipolarity: The Security Council as the Talking Shop of the Nations," *Chicago Journal of International Law*, Vol. 10, No. 1, 2009, 55–90, 71–72

16. Roland Rich, "Crafting Security Council Mandates," in *The UN Role in Promoting Democracy—Between Ideals and Reality* eds. Edward Newman and Roland Rich (Tokyo: United Nations University Press, 2004)

17. Steven Erlanger, "Macron Says NATO Is Experiencing 'Brain Death' Because of Trump," *New York Times*, 7 November 2019

18. Krishnadev Calamur, "Trudeau Reaches His Breaking Point with Trump," *The Atlantic*, June 2, 2018

19. Scott Wilson, "Obama dismisses Russia as 'regional power' acting out of weakness," *Washington Post*, March 25, 2014

20. Mark Cartwright, "The Seven Voyages of Zheng He," *Ancient History Encyclopedia*, 07 February 2019, https://www.ancient.eu/article/1334/the-seven-voyages-of-zheng-he/

21. Ibid.

22. Chris Buckley, "China Takes Aim at Western Ideas, " *New York Times*, August 19, 2013

23. David Bosco, "Assessing the UN Security Council: A Concert Perspective," *Global Governance*, Oct.–Dec. 2014, Vol. 20, No. 4, 545–561

24. R.J. Delahunty, "Towards a Concert of Asia? A Proposed International Security Régime," 11 U. Penn. Asian Law Rev. 1 (2017)

25. See Roland Rich, "Recognition of States: the Collapse of Yugoslavia and the Soviet Union," *European Journal of International Law* 4 No. 1, March 1993, 36–65, http://ejil.oxfordjournals.org/content/4/1/36.full.pdf+html

26. Portrayed in the 2019 Keira Knightley film *Official Secrets* about Katherine Gun who blew the whistle on the spying operations.

27. Sue Eckert, "The Role of Sanctions," in von Einsiedel et.al., op.cit., 413–439 at 422

28. Ibid.

29. United Nations Security Council Resolution 2139 of 22 February 2014.

30. United Nations, "Meetings Coverage and Press Releases," https://www.un.org/press/en/2019/sc14066.doc.htm

31. Boutros Boutros-Ghali *Unvanquished: A US-UN Saga* (New York: Random House, 1999)

32. Kofi Annan and Nader Mousavizadeh, *Interventions: A Life in War and Peace* New York: Penguin Press, 2012) 357

33. James Traub, *The Best Intentions: Kofi Annan and the UN in the Era of American Power*, (New York: Farrar, Straus and Giroux, 2006) 264

34. Susan Williams, *Who Killed Hammarskjold?* (Oxford University Press, 2014)

35. I am borrowing the title of this section from my friend Simon Chesterman (ed.) *Secretary or General? The UN Secretary-General in World Politics* (Cambridge University Press, 2010)

36. Elaborated from the original table in Roland Rich, "Crafting Security Council Mandates" in *The UN Role in Promoting Democracy: Between Ideals and Reality*, eds. Edward Newman and Roland Rich, (Tokyo: United Nations University Press, 2004) 65. Updated with the assistance of Kate Ann Brace.

37. United Nations, "United Nations Truce Supervision Organisation." https://untso.unmissions.org/background

38. Moisés Naím, *The End of Power* (New York: Basic Books, 2013) in particular chapter 6 "Pentagons versus Pirates: The Decaying Power of Large Armies."

39. SIPRI press release of 29 April 2019, "World military expenditure grows to $1.8 trillion in 2018," https://www.sipri.org/media/press-release/2019/world-military-expenditure-grows-18-trillion-2018

40. SIPRI publication, *The SIPRI Top 100 arms-producing and military services companies, 2018,* December 2019, https://www.sipri.org/publications/2019/sipri-fact-sheets/sipri-top-100-arms-producing-and-military-services-companies-2018

# *Chapter 6*

# Democracy and Human Rights

The United Nations Leviathan will not succeed unless it can have a significant impact on human rights and democracy. The protection and promotion of human rights have been among the UN's great achievements. This chapter will elaborate the various steps in favor of human rights in which the UN has been a central player. The chapter will also track the more limited role of the UN in promoting democracy around the world. Yet, for all the progress that has been made, the situation on both issues is unsatisfactory. Much more needs to be done, and the chapter will propose some major steps the UN Leviathan must take.

## THE UNITED NATIONS AND HUMAN RIGHTS

Human rights, along with peace and development, has been a fundamental purpose of the United Nations since its inception. While its roots in moral codes may be ancient, the articulation of what has come to be known as the human rights canon is modern. It springs from President Roosevelt's Four Freedoms speech in 1941. He declared that the four fundamental freedoms that people everywhere in the world have the right to enjoy were:

- freedom of speech and expression
- freedom of worship
- freedom from want
- freedom from fear[1]

Three of the four freedoms would become the principal purposes of the UN. Freedom of speech would articulate into the human rights canon. Freedom from want would morph into the UN's development agenda. And freedom from fear was the underlying basis for the peace and security preoccupation. The necessarily secular UN Charter makes no mention of any god but includes religion as one of the ascriptive human qualities that cannot be the basis of discrimination, as in Article 1(3) calling for respect for human rights "without distinction as to race, sex, language, or religion."

Flowing from the Four Freedoms speech, the newly minted United Nations embarked on one of its great quests, to draft a Universal Declaration of Human Rights (UDHR). The story of the document has been told many times highlighting the leadership by Eleanor Roosevelt, the admonition of China's Peng Chung-chang that the document must transcend Western ideas, and the careful drafting by John Humphrey of Canada (from the Secretariat), René Cassin of France and Charles Malik of Lebanon.[2] The Australian representative on the eight-person drafting committee[3] was Col. William Hodgson who is little remembered. His contribution was to insist, hedgehog-like, for the establishment of an international court to enforce the protection of human rights, the subject of which will be further explored in this chapter.

It is remarkable how prescient was the UDHR. It understood the interlinkages between the various rights. It drew on concepts enunciated in the American Declaration of Independence about the inherent nature of rights. And it anticipated the yearning for dignity, that would be the rallying cry of the Arab Spring sixty years hence, in its opening preambular sentence: "Whereas recognition of the inherent dignity and of the equal and inalienable rights of all members of the human family is the foundation of freedom, justice and peace in the world." In its mere 1,773 words (in English) it laid down the blueprint for a new way to look at the worth of each individual.

The Universal Declaration of Human Rights, for all its power and prestige, is, however, simply a non-binding resolution passed by the UN General Assembly. The next step was to have its provisions adopted in binding treaty form. The UN, by this time locked in the Cold War struggle, was pulled in opposite directions by the United States and the Soviet Union. In retrospect, the UN took the erroneous decision to divide the Universal Declaration of Human Rights into two covenants: the International Covenant on Civil and Political Rights and the International Covenant on Economic, Social and Cultural Rights. The Soviet Union was disdainful of the former, while the United States had little interest in the latter, which, to this day, it has not ratified. The situation became analogous to an old story about a rabbi who is upset that his students are spending so much time playing soccer. The students invite the rabbi to watch a game and ask him his opinion. The rabbi duly spectates and then announces the solution; give each team its own ball and they will not have to spend so much time fighting for it anymore. This was the solution the international community found in relation to human rights over the Cold War period. Needless to say, speaking past each other and deploying the tools of propaganda did not enhance respect for human rights around the world.

## THE UNITED NATIONS AND DEMOCRACY

I have elaborated on this topic in previous writings and so I will attempt the most cursory summary.[4] The word "democracy" does not appear in the Charter for the simple reason that the Soviet Union refused to countenance its presence. It is not a pillar of the UN as is human rights. It took the end of the Cold War to rehabilitate the word within the UN and much of the credit should go to three succeeding Secretaries-General.

Boutros Boutros-Ghali had the courage to introduce the issue at the UN in An Agenda for Democratization, which he boldly saw as leading to fewer authoritarian societies.[5] Kofi Annan's contribution, In Larger Freedom: Towards Development, Security and Human Rights for All,[6] describes democracy as a "universal right." And Ban Ki-moon made a significant contribution in his 2009 Guidance Note on Democracy.[7] The Guidance Note makes clear that "democracy, based on the rule of law, is ultimately a means to achieve international peace and security, economic and social progress and development, and respect for human rights—the three pillars of the United Nations mission as set forth in the Charter of the UN." Aside from its universal value, democracy is seen by the UN as an instrument through which to achieve the organization's purposes.

It was on the basis of this instrumental value that the UN accepted the relevance of democracy to its ongoing work and embarked on its promotion. Perhaps the greatest expression of this support was at the 2005 World Summit Outcome document which welcomed the establishment of the UN Democracy Fund, which I had the honor to head, in the following paragraph:

> 136. We renew our commitment to support democracy by strengthening countries' capacity to implement the principles and practices of democracy and resolve to strengthen the capacity of the United Nations to assist Member States upon their request. We welcome the establishment of a Democracy Fund at the United Nations. We note that the advisory board to be established should reflect diverse geographical representation. We invite the Secretary-General to help to ensure that practical arrangements for the Democracy Fund take proper account of existing United Nations activity in this field.[8]

Other parts of the UN were deeply involved in aspects of democracy promotion. The UN Development Program then had a Democratic Governance division; the Department of Political Affairs still has an Electoral Assistance Division; and the Security Council included democratization aims in the mandates of several peacekeeping missions.[9] Democracy enjoyed a dozen halcyon years at the UN.

## "MUTUALLY REINFORCING"

The end of the Cold War provided the opportunity for democracy to be accepted as relevant to the work of the UN. It also provided the opportunity to redress the bifurcated situation in which human rights found itself, and to restore it to its rightful place as the world's universal moral code. There was also a need to articulate the relationship between democracy and human rights from the UN's perspective. The event that would take up these challenges was the 1993 World Conference on Human Rights in Vienna which formulated the proposition that the two concepts were mutually reinforcing:

> 8. Democracy, development and respect for human rights and fundamental freedoms are interdependent and mutually reinforcing. Democracy is based on the freely expressed will of the people to determine their own political, economic, social and cultural systems and their full participation in all aspects of their lives. In the context of the above, the promotion and protection of human rights and fundamental freedoms at the national and international levels should be universal and conducted without conditions attached. The international community should support the strengthening and promoting of democracy, development and respect for human rights and fundamental freedoms in the entire world.[10]

Furthermore, paragraph 8 linked the concepts of democracy and human rights to that of development, the overriding consideration of the countries of the global South. What was required was a reinterpretation of the human rights canon incorporating all the rights and putting them in an inclusive historical context. Karel Vasak, then Legal Adviser at UNESCO, provided that perspective, describing the emergence of human rights in generational terms. The first generation flowed from ideas arising during the English Glorious Revolution and the key pronouncements of the subsequent American and French revolutions. These led to the formulation of civil and political rights. The second generation rights flowed from the October Revolution in Russia and the creation of welfare states in Europe. These led to the formulation of economic, social and cultural rights. There is also a third generation of human rights. These are referred to as solidarity rights, and sometimes called the rights of peoples. The first born of that generation is the universally acknowledged right of self-determination. The most contested solidarity right is the right to development.[11]

The three generations of rights have something of a counterpart in the three waves of democratization. Clearly, the first generation and the first wave share common parenthood. Because the "waves" formulation comes from Samuel Huntington,[12] a doyen of American political science, it tends to be accepted without qualification. But I have always found his periodicity confusing and his underlying causation unconvincing. I have tried my hand at improving the argument by relating the three waves in turn to the defeat of absolutism, fascism, and communism.[13] This would have the Third Wave begin around the time of the collapse of the Soviet Union, not, as Huntington argues, fifteen years earlier with the collapse of the Iberian fascist dictatorships (which, along with the fall of military dictatorships in Latin America that followed, was the final part of the second wave, in my view). The waves have a Eurocentric flavor until one comes to the global application of the third wave. The generations also have Eurocentric origins until one comes to the third generation which owes much to the decolonization movement and the subsequent influence of newly independent states from the global South. It was, for example, a jurist from Senegal, Kéba M'Baye, who launched the debate on the right to development.[14]

Other links between democracy and human rights are readily identifiable. By definition, authoritarian regimes do not respect human rights, whereas democratic regimes tend to do so, though even the actions of elected governments require constant monitoring. And democracy cannot operate without human rights. The freedoms of speech, assembly and association are essential for the conduct of political campaigning and fair elections as well as the need for monitoring the executive between elections. Article 21(3) of UDHR goes further, in effect making voting a right, when it notes: "The will of the people shall be the basis of the authority of government; this will shall be expressed in periodic and genuine elections which shall be by universal and equal suffrage and shall be held by secret vote or by equivalent free voting procedures." The right to vote was put in binding form in Article 25 of the International Covenant on Civil and Political Rights (ICCPR) and interpreted by the Human Rights Committee, a body of experts under the ICCPR, in General Comment 25 of 1996 which elaborated meticulously on the right to vote including the right to vote for a candidate other than the incumbent.[15]

The next key linkages between democracy and human rights were established by Ban Ki-moon's Guidance Note on Democracy.[16] In part IV (4), the Note states:

> Political pluralism requires that more than one political party participate in elections and play a role in governance. Political parties play an essential role in democracy by aggregating interests and integrating citizens into the political process. Decisions are more likely to be accepted, even by those who oppose them, if citizens feel that their views have been represented.

This explicit reference to the need for multi-party democracy had not been articulated by the Human Rights Committee, though it had asked governments to explain how different political views in the community are represented in elected bodies. And, in part IV (2), the Guidance Note makes explicit another important link, that between democracy and the right of self-determination when it states:

> Popular participation, collective deliberation and political equality are essential to democracy, and should be realized through a framework and structure of accessible, representative, transparent and accountable institutions subject to periodic change or renewal. Democracy is a reflection of self-determination, and must be based on the freely expressed will of the people, both women and men, facilitated through free access to information, opinion, expression, association and assembly. Based on respect for all human rights, in a democracy, the rights, interests and "voice" of minorities, indigenous peoples, children, disempowered majorities, and vulnerable, disadvantaged and unpopular groups or individuals must be safeguarded.

The mutually reinforcing nature of democracy and human rights is evident. Indeed, without human rights, electoral democracy can easily become an exercise in majoritarianism. But the Vienna declaration includes a third concept as being mutually reinforcing, namely development. Here, the links are less immediately evident. One reason why the relationship between development, democracy and human rights does not quickly spring to mind, is that we have been taught a skewed and narrow interpretation of the meaning of development by economists. They insisted on measuring development through national accounts and explaining its causation through capital formation. In the following chapter, I unpack this issue tracing its rationale from the early and quickly discredited but not abandoned concept of the "financing gap" to its current implementation in Xi Jinping's Belt and Road Initiative. The unarticulated and unrealistic assumption underpinning the theory of development as capital formation is that the capital investment is occurring in a well governed polity with a highly educated and engaged public and a critical investigative press.

The alternative vision of development is about people. In the 1960s, the intelligent oxymoron "human capital" was popularized,[17] leading to a recognition of the importance education, training and health played in economic development. By the 1990s, the UN Development Program had introduced a new measure, the Human Development Index pioneered by Mahbub ul Haq and Amartya Sen, which placed people at the center of the development process.[18] The change in perspective from machines to people was completed with Amartya Sen's magisterial book *Development as Freedom*, placing the engine of development in the hands of people and arguing that protecting their human rights in a democratic context will allow them to develop their full capacities and thus lead to economic development.[19] Hence, the inclusion of development, in the Amartya Sen interpretation, in the troika of mutually reinforcing forces.

## ACHIEVEMENTS—HUMAN RIGHTS

The most remarkable achievement of the human rights canon is that in the space of a couple of generations since the drafting of the UDHR, it has been accepted by nearly all people as their inherent right. Even dictators and cultural relativists must at least pay lip service to the existence of these inherent rights. The vast spread of literacy, the drumbeat of the global village and the strong reputation the UN enjoys in most places, have all contributed to this result.

Another significant achievement is the translation of the human rights canon to legal form. The six major human rights treaties[20] are generally accepted as articulating international law. They list the rights, distinguish between the aspirational and the immediately applicable, and spell out the limited exceptions. For example, the International Covenant on Economic, Social and Cultural Rights contains aspirational language. But that does not lessen the obligation under international law to strive for its fulfillment. And alongside the aspirational language is black letter law requiring primary schooling to be compulsory and listing the areas where discrimination is disallowed. The six major treaties have been widely ratified and many of their provisions are now *jus cogens*, peremptory norms of international law.

The next achievement sounds like a back-handed compliment given continuing egregious abuses, but it is nevertheless a great credit to the international community that, despite the obstacle of sovereignty, innovative enforcement mechanisms have been developed and put in place, brick by brick. There is the national reporting obligation which has now been streamlined and rationalized into the Universal Periodic Review (UPR) process. I once had the honor to serve as Assistant Secretary for International Organizations in the Australian Department of Foreign Affairs and Trade. One of my tasks was to chair meetings of civil society and academic activists to review draft reports prepared by the government for submission to the various human rights treaty committees. These were ugly and difficult meetings where the activists would harangue the officials about the shortcomings of the human rights situation in Australia and demand amendments to the draft reports. Some amendments were accepted, some criticisms were conceded, some governmental *mea culpas* were expressed until an acceptable stalemate was reached. The value to the government was that these discussions took place in Canberra, not in Geneva in front of the entire international community. As noted, the UPR has streamlined the process. And it has made another major stride. Whereas in the past, consultations with civil society were at the discretion of committee members, they are now a formal part of the UPR process. A significant achievement.

The reporting obligation is a useful but blunt tool. Sharper tools have been devised. One particularly useful tool is the system of special rapporteurs or independent experts:

> The special procedures of the Human Rights Council are independent human rights experts with mandates to report and advise on human rights from a thematic or country-specific perspective. The system of Special Procedures is a central element of the United Nations human rights machinery and covers all human rights: civil, cultural, economic, political, and social. As of 1 August 2017, there are 44 thematic and 12 country mandates (Belarus, Cambodia, Central African Republic, Democratic People's Republic of Korea, Eritrea, Islamic Republic of Iran, Mali, Myanmar, Palestine, Somalia, Sudan, Syria).[21]

The rapporteurs provide independent and expert reports on the country situations allowing the international community to draw authoritative conclusions on which to base any action. The thematic topics may at times have some political coloration depending on the group of countries sponsoring the topic, but they are nevertheless based on key aspects of the human rights canon. They not only provide expert commentary on state actions in the human rights field, but they often also provide recommendations to rectify or alleviate problems. When Philip Alston submitted his report[22] concerning the use of drones by the United States for execution of "unlawful combatants," he argued that the operational process should be removed from the CIA, over which there is limited public oversight, and given to the military, which is subject to more checks and balances and has a better understanding of international humanitarian law.

Reports and rapporteurs are a useful addition to the enforcement panoply, but an even sharper tool is the capacity of individuals who are claiming that their human rights have been violated by a government, to complain to a legal body outside the borders of that country. All the major human rights treaties have established such complaints mechanisms.[23] Of course, this remedy remains inchoate until a country has formally signaled its acceptance of the complaint procedures. For example, the optional protocol allowing citizens to complain to the Human Rights Committee under the International Covenant on Civil and Political Rights, has been ratified by 116 states.[24] The decisions of the various committees hearing the complaints are not binding on states, but they are nevertheless powerful tools. In fact, there are times when the state in question welcomes the decision. In Australia, a federal country, criminal law is under the jurisdiction of the various states. One state, Tasmania, refused to follow the other states and decriminalize sodomy. A resident of that state, Nick Toonen, complained to the Human Rights Committee, which found that his right to privacy had been violated.[25] The federal government then asserted that, given the intervention by an international body, the matter was no longer a criminal issue, under which the states have jurisdiction, but an international relations issue, under which the federal government has jurisdiction, and threatened to overrule the state law. Faced with this situation, Tasmania complied and amended its criminal law.

Europe has gone one step further and turned its human rights complaint procedures into juridical appeals, the decisions of which are binding on states. Under the auspices of the Council of Europe, the European Court of Human Rights based on the European Convention on Human Rights was established in 1959 and has delivered 10,000 judgements.[26] Continuing with similar issues as those dealt with in the Toonen case, in 2016, a chamber of the European Court of Human Rights ruled that legislation in Russia banning the promotion of homosexuality, especially to minors, violated three gay activists' rights to the freedom of expression and the prohibition of discrimination, enshrined in articles 10 and 14, respectively, of the European Convention on Human Rights. Tellingly, in 2018, 37% of the violations determined by the court from the cases it heard were by the Russian government, and 17% by the Turkish government.[27]

There have also been important advances at the international level. In the field of criminal law, the International Criminal Court (ICC) was established in 2002 upon the entry into force of the Rome Statute, to which, as of February 2022, there are 123 parties.

> The Court may exercise jurisdiction in a situation where genocide, crimes against humanity or war crimes were
>
> - committed on or after 1 July 2002 and:
> - the crimes were committed by a State Party national, or in the territory of a State Party, or in a State that has accepted the jurisdiction of the Court; or
> - the crimes were referred to the ICC Prosecutor by the United Nations Security Council (UNSC) pursuant to a resolution adopted under chapter VII of the UN charter.[28]

While the jurisdiction is limited, membership is not universal, and the United States has taken a particularly hostile attitude to the court, the ICC example provides a precedent for criminal prosecution at the international level.

And it has something of a counterpart at the international political level in the responsibility to protect doctrine:

> The responsibility to protect embodies a political commitment to end the worst forms of violence and persecution. It seeks to narrow the gap between Member

> States' pre-existing obligations under international humanitarian and human rights law and the reality faced by populations at risk of genocide, war crimes, ethnic cleansing and crimes against humanity.[29]

The doctrine had a surprisingly short gestation period which began with the publication in 2001 of the report of the International Commission on Intervention and State Sovereignty (ICISS) established by Canada, and then unanimously adopted in 2005 at the UN World Outcome Summit,[30] and operationalized in the 2011 humanitarian operation in Libya under Security Council resolution 1706. One of the two co-chairs of the ICISS, Gareth Evans, describes the need for the responsibility to protect as taking away the state's "license to kill."[31]

While there is much more to be said on each of these issues, the purpose here is simply to note the existence of these advances in human rights enforcement machinery upon which a United Nations of the future would continue to build.

## ACHIEVEMENTS—DEMOCRACY

The mechanisms in defense of democracy are not as elaborate, but there are, nevertheless, some notable achievements in this area as well. We cannot assert that democracy has achieved the near universal adoption that human rights have achieved. But in rhetoric at least, we can say, following the argument by Amartya Sen, that in the twentieth century, democracy achieved the status of a universal value, in that everybody saw something of value in it.[32] In our Westphalian world, democracy lives in the nation state. Because it is so tied to the nation, it is difficult to elevate the issue to the international realm. There were attempts in the late 1990s to proclaim democracy as a human right,[33] but these did not achieve the requisite support and consistent articulation. Accordingly, one would not anticipate the existence of international mechanisms in support of national democracy. Yet, several such mechanisms exist.

One such mechanism is to make democracy a requisite for membership of certain international bodies. The most overt is the Organisation for Security and Cooperation in Europe (OSCE) which describes democracy as "the only system of government for our nations."[34] Further, "democracy is one of the fundamental principles of the European Union."[35] A similar situation pertains to the Americas where Article 9 of the Charter of the Organisation of American States (OAS) makes democracy a condition of membership. The Commonwealth of Nations in its 1995 Millbrook Action Programme, empowers the Commonwealth to suspend membership where the unconstitutional overthrow of a democratically elected government occurs.[36] Among the governments that have thus been suspended are Fiji, Nigeria, Pakistan, and

Zimbabwe. Under Article 25 of the African Union's Charter of Democracy, Elections and Governance, a member state where an unconstitutional change of government has taken place, may be suspended.[37] Among the governments that have thus been suspended are the Central African Republic, Egypt, and Sudan.

Another mechanism, primarily employed by the European Union, is to make democracy a condition for concessional benefits. In the multilateral arrangements under the Cotonou Agreement between the EU and 78 African, Caribbean and Pacific states governing trade and aid relations, the European Union is empowered to terminate or suspend benefits where there are serious and persistent human rights violations or interruptions in the democratic process.[38] In 2016, the EU cut its financial support for the government of Burundi but continued its support for Burundi civil society.[39]

International election observation has become a common practice. It has its own codes of conduct[40] and its own handbooks.[41] An extent of foreign assistance for national elections can be gauged from the work of the UN Electoral Assistance Division which has assisted more than 100 countries conduct more than 300 elections.[42] And one of the pioneers of the election observation process, the Carter Center, has observed 110 elections in 39 countries.[43] The leading actor in the field, the National Democratic Institute for International Affairs, has almost 300 election observation reports on its website.[44] Writing in 1992, Thomas Franck saw election observation as the path to an emerging right to democratic governance.[45] This has turned out to be overly optimistic, but election observation has become another important tool of the international community in enhancing the quality of elections around the world. A country refusing international observers is basically calling into question the probity of its election process. As this tool has developed, the accent has been placed far more on competent local election observers with the international team playing a supportive role.

The most advanced mechanism for the international protection of democracy, comes from the UN Security Council. Chapter VII of the Charter provides the international community with its sharpest tool in the use of legitimate force to maintain or reclaim peace. There was little recourse to Chapter VII in the Cold War years, other than the major intervention in Korea while the Soviet Union was boycotting meetings of the Council. In the post-Cold War period, however, the Council became active in numerous situations, launching many peacekeeping operations. The Council was on a steep learning curve as demonstrated by the growing sophistication of its mandates. It was readily understood that simply interposing peacekeepers between warring parties did not provide a solution to conflicts and that the peacekeeping mandates had to be proactive. Among the actions authorized by these mandates[46] are several that deal directly with democratization:

**Table 6.1. Key UN Security Council Action for Elections and Democracy.**

| *Situation* | *Peacekeeping Operation* | *Resolution* | *Mandate* |
|---|---|---|---|
| Namibia | UN Transition Assistance Group (UNTAG) | 435 of 29/9/1978 | "to ensure the early independence of Namibia through free elections under the supervision and control of the UN" |
| Haiti | UN Mission in Haiti (UNMIH) | 940 of 31/7/1994 | "the restoration of democracy," "the organization of free and fair elections" |
| Eastern Slavonia (Croatia) | UN Transitional Administration for Eastern Slavonia (UNTAES) | 1037 of 15/1/1996 | "To organize elections, to assist in their conduct, and to certify the results" |
| Sierra Leone | ECOWAS later joined by UN Mission in Sierra Leone (UNAMSIL) | 1132 of 8/10/1997 | "Demands that the military junta take immediate steps to relinquish power" "make way for the restoration of the democratically elected Government" |
| Kosovo | "international civil and security presence, under UN auspices" | 1244 of 10/6/1999 | "establishing and overseeing the development of provisional democratic self-governing institutions" |
| Timor Leste | United Nations Mission in East Timor (UNAMET) | 1246 of 11/6/1999 | "to organize and conduct a popular consultation on the basis of a direct, secret and universal ballot" |
| Liberia | United Nations Mission in Liberia (UNAMSIL) | 1497 Of 1/8/2003 | "transitional government until such a time when free and fair elections can be held" |
| Haiti | United Nations Stabilization Mission in Haiti (MINUSTAH) | 1542 of 30/4/2004 | "assist the Transitional Government to organize, monitor, and carry out free and fair municipal, parliamentary and presidential elections" |
| Burundi | United Nations Operation in Burundi (UNOB) | 1545 of 21/5/2004 | "contribute to the successful completion of the electoral process" |
| Côte d'Ivoire | UN Mission in Côte d'Ivoire (UNOCI) | 1933 of 30/6/2010 | "reaffirms its full support to the Special Representative of the Secretary-General in his (election) certification role" |
| South Sudan | UN Mission in South Sudan (UNMISS) | 1996 of 8/7/2011 | "holding of elections in accordance with the constitution" |
| Mali | Coordination with the African Union, Economic Community of West African States (ECOWAS) | 2100 of 25/4/2013 | "Urges the transitional authorities of Mali to hold free, fair, transparent and inclusive presidential and legislative elections" |
| Central African Republic | International Contact Group including the UN | 2149 of 10/4/2014 | "hold free, fair, transparent and inclusive presidential and legislative elections |

As can be seen from the table, the Council demonstrated its understanding that the key to enduring peace and stability is for the government to enjoy legitimacy. And the best way to ensure that legitimacy is through free and fair elections. Accordingly, in the cases listed above, the Security Council was working to restore or strengthen democracy under Chapter VII.

## ENTER THE LEVIATHAN

In relation to both democracy and human rights, the principal structural vulnerability can be summarized in one word—sovereignty. Sovereignty is the Great Wall of China that keeps barbarians out. But sovereignty is also the Berlin Wall that keeps citizens locked in. Sovereignty is the safety net of the welfare state. But sovereignty is also the horrors of the gulag archipelago. Sovereignty allows for national institutions of rule of law. But sovereignty also permits state capture by strongmen and oligarchs. We cling to the certainty and comfort of sovereignty in many instances. We despise and belittle it in other circumstances. The aim of the Leviathan is not to banish sovereignty but to tame it.

It is the excesses of sovereignty that need taming. The Leviathan must ensure that sovereignty can no longer be a "license to kill," or torture, or unjustly imprison, or discriminate against. Sovereignty must no longer shield human rights abusers. Nor should sovereignty be allowed to protect those who win national executive office by cheating or intimidation. If democracy, human rights, and development are mutually reinforcing, then those wanting the benefits of development need to defend democracy and protect human rights. If democracy is the instrument that will bring about peace and development, then those cherishing peace and development need to defend democracy. If the human rights canon is the key to human development, then those aspiring to human development need to protect human rights. In all these circumstances, the UN Leviathan must be their ally.

Some have argued that globalization is already taming sovereignty,[47] but as set forth in the chapter on globalization below, that process must be governed and not become a cloak for international economic anarchy. Globalization as the economic expression of might is right, will not advance human wellbeing. Globalization as a form of ruthless bilateralism unencumbered by any notion of rules or arbitration, will only benefit the strong. So, undermining sovereignty and leaving anarchy in its place is a recipe for heightening the Hobbesian *bellum omnium contra omnes*. Globalization itself needs taming by the same UN Leviathan.

The twenty-first century Leviathan does not aspire to a Weberian monopoly on the legitimate use of force. That goal is unwarranted and unachievable.

But the twenty-first century Leviathan does aspire to be the world's key normative influencer, to be the global leader in determining right from wrong, and to be the most accepted arbiter of governmental conduct. To achieve this status, the Leviathan must pierce the veil of sovereignty behind which governments attempt to defend their conduct. Because of their mutually reinforcing impact on each other and on development, the fields of democracy and human rights are critical. What can be done?

As with other subjects covered in this monograph, there is no need to reinvent the wheel. The basic ideas are already out there and have been employed, at times in developed form and at other times embryonically. The challenge is to scale up the use of these ideas and to have them accepted by "we the peoples." Governments will object. As previously noted, it is not the burden of this book to find the ways of countering government objections. Those ways will be found once the ideas find broad acceptance. In that sense, envisioning the structures is an end in itself.

In the field of human rights, certain structures already exist: the responsibility to protect, the International Criminal Court and supranational complaints procedures. R2P is in the hands of the Security Council, which has demonstrated both a willingness to act (Libya) and a refusal to do so (Syria). The issues of peace and security are dealt with in the previous chapter. In that chapter, the argument put forward is that the key factor for positive disruption is the currently underutilized office of the Secretary-General. A Secretary-General not selected for meekness and not subject to the overpowering influence of governments, will become the moral voice of "we the peoples" and may make the pivotal difference in the decision on whether to discharge the responsibility to protect vulnerable communities from genocide.

The International Criminal Court (ICC) represents a remarkable achievement by the international community although, in the eyes of some, it was fifty years late. As noted, the Australian representative on the UDHR drafting committee in 1948 was Colonel William Roy Hodgson, a tough, no-nonsense survivor of the Gallipoli campaign who was the Australian Ambassador to the UN at the time. He insisted, in vain, throughout the process, that the only way to ensure respect for human rights was to have an international tribunal to enforce these rights.[48] The Rome Statute establishing the court was drafted in spite of dogged American opposition which was overcome because the coalition in favor of the court, the then designated "Like-minded Group," was a collection of 60 nations that transcended the usual geographic and ideological cleavages in the UN, including the United Kingdom, a permanent member of the Security Council.[49] The Clinton Administration, by then in lame duck mode, grudgingly signed the 1998 Rome Statute on the last day of 2000.[50] A signature of a treaty is not a ratification which is the step that establishes the obligation to respect the provisions of the treaty. But signature is a step not without some responsibility. According to Article 18 of the 1969 Vienna Convention on the Law of Treaties, signature imposes the obligation "to refrain from acts which would defeat the object and purpose of the treaty." But the Bush Administration policy was in fact to defeat the object and purpose of the treaty and, accordingly, it took the unusual step of unsigning it.[51]

The need to fight impunity for egregious breaches of human rights was demonstrated by the decisions of the Security Council to establish *ad hoc* Tribunals for Yugoslavia and Rwanda.[52] It made little sense to continue the practice of establishing *ad hoc* tribunals as the need arose. The ICC is a major milestone in the process of protecting human rights around the world, but it has not been smooth sailing. The main criticism has come from African countries who discern a bias towards prosecuting leaders from that continent. The court argues it simply follows the law, even when doing so may be unpopular with some. Regardless of the inevitable criticism in individual cases, we can conclude that the ICC has had a positive impact. It has ended the period of impunity for crimes against humanity, it has brought some comfort to the victims of these crimes, and it has arguably had a deterrent effect on other national leaders.[53]

The ICC has a jurisdiction limited to crimes against humanity and genocide, the concept that needs to be developed and institutionalized is the capacity to bring other human rights abuses to the attention of a supranational court. We have the precedent of the European Court of Human Rights. We need to scale up the UN machinery to that level to complement and complete the work of the ICC. Just as the reporting procedures were streamlined and made more efficient in the universal periodic review, the complaints machinery needs to be scaled up and made more effective. There needs to be established a UN Human Rights Court.

## A UN Human Rights Court

Binding judicial decisions are not new to the UN. At the apex of the system sits the International Court of Justice (ICJ). But it is not alone in handing down binding decisions. The Permanent Court of Arbitration predates the ICJ and remains active in providing judicial services in cases of inter-state disputes and disputes between states and investors. The International Criminal Court has already been examined. Specialized bodies have their own judicial or arbitral bodies. The World Trade Organization is endowed with arbitration power in its dispute settlement procedures. The International Tribunal for the Law of the Sea adjudicates disputes arising out of the interpretation and application of the UN Convention for the Law of the Sea. The World Intellectual Property Organization offers arbitration and mediation services to resolve disputes. The Administrative Tribunal of the International Labour Organization is currently open to more than 58,000 international civil servants who are serving or former officials of 57 international organisations. The point is that there is nothing particularly radical or new about a United Nations judicial capacity. What would be new is applying it to human rights complaints.

What needs to be done is unifying the existing complaints procedures by dovetailing them to one court, the United Nations Court of Human Rights. In theory, putting aside for the moment the issue of states' consent to be bound by the court's rulings, the concept presents no particular theoretical difficulty. We have the major human rights treaties, and they are written in legislative language that courts commonly interpret. We have the Comments by the various committees established under these treaties, and they represent helpful interpretative precedent, though they clearly lack the status of *stare decisis*. Like any court, there will be a difficult issue of determining the facts of the case. I would suggest that the UN Court of Human Rights not adopt the common law adversarial system wherein the parties would usually be the individual complainant and the government about which the complaint is being made which would be the respondent, but rather, opt for the civil law inquisitorial system where witnesses and experts are called by the bench. The adversarial system would be weighed in favor of governments because of the resources at their disposal. Which system lends itself better to complaints of human rights abuses would, however, be a good subject for discussion.

The main problems for the successful operation of such a court would be practical. The European Court of Human Rights is experiencing a severe seven to ten years backlog on cases, and even after judgments are handed down, execution of those judgments could take a further five years.[54] The adage that justice delayed is justice denied holds firmly for human rights cases. Solutions can be found. The existing human rights treaty committees could continue to act as preliminary decision makers with the possibility of appeal to the Human Rights Court. This would spread the workload. But a further limitation would also be required. This can be seen from the experience of other complaint receiving institutions:

> One of the universal problems of the Ombudsman is the chronic complainer; people who feel passionately about their own cause and are uncompromising in their reaction to a negative conclusion on the part of the Ombudsman. Such people can sometimes cause a great deal of disproportionate disruption to the work of the Ombudsman and his staff.[55]

To survive the expected massive workload, the court should be limited to hearing appeals on matters of particular importance to the human rights canon such as complaints about "massive" or "persistent" or "systemic" breaches of human rights. Following the practice of most apex courts, the Human

Rights court would determine if the case should proceed to a full hearing. An individual case would therefore be heard if it fell within those categories as determined by the Human Rights Court in a preliminary hearing, probably before a single judge or perhaps a panel of three.

How will the Human Rights Court's judgement be enforced? One could hardly expect the government in breach to comply readily with a distant court's ruling. Recalling Stalin's question about how many military divisions the Pope commanded, the abusive government would ask how many sheriffs the court commands. While this paper argues, in the previous chapter, the case for the Secretary-General of the UN to have his own effective military force, it is not envisaged that the task of this force is the enforcement of court judgements. Yet a penalty needs to be devised. That penalty could be that in the case of a judgement of the court directing a government to take or desist from taking certain actions, non-compliance within a reasonable period would make the head and other key officials of the executive branch of that government liable to prosecution by the International Criminal Court. This is hardly a fool-proof remedy. The ICC also does not have military divisions under its command. But it personalizes the penalty. It makes a particular individual liable. That individual must contemplate the repercussions of travel abroad or a change of leadership at home leading to a decision to offer him or her up for trial. The line of least resistance may well be compliance with the human rights court's decision. Integrating the ICC into the human rights judicial structure also makes sense in theory and in practice. It would establish a hierarchy of courts and integrate them into a single system. This would assist in maintaining the coherence of the jurisdiction.

## The UN as Election Certifying Authority

Can similar mechanisms be envisaged on the subject of national democracy? Once again, precedents exist. Democracy is a complex process entailing many features. Issues such as the competence of representatives, the quality of debate and the voting culture of the electorate defy institutional solutions. The Leviathan cannot impose high quality democracy on a polity. That task will remain with the people of that polity. But the Leviathan can be involved in the mechanics of democracy, elections and unconstitutional changes of executives. The precedents in this regard concern the observation and certification of elections, and the use of the criterion of constitutionality as a qualification for international membership and services.

It is already the case that a refusal to allow proper observation of elections, through a mix of international and local expert observers, will establish a presumption that the incumbent has something to hide. That presumption needs to be articulated in legal form, perhaps as an additional protocol to the

International Covenant on Civil and Political Rights. Observation of elections including oversight of the rules and practices concerning voter registration, candidate selection and access to media, need to be part of the standard oversight role of the international community. In a practical sense, we are already there. The next step is legal articulation.

The UN Leviathan also must be armed with a critical new role. Let us recall what happened in Côte d'Ivoire in 2010. President Gbagbo lost the election but tried to manipulate the results in what he no doubt expected to be standard incumbent operating procedure. He was surprised by the level of local opposition to his maneuvers and perhaps even more surprised that the Special Representative of the UN Secretary-General, Choi Young-jin, adopted the resolute position that the winner was the opposition candidate Alassane Ouattara. Gbagbo did not anticipate that both the Security Council and the African Union would turn against him and with some French military steel in its back, the international community would step in to ensure respect for the election result. The reason the international community could take action was because Security Council Resolution 1933 gave the top UN official the power to certify the election results. It was not the first time the UN had been endowed with this power. The UN Transitional Administration for Eastern Slavonia under UNSCR 1037 of 1996 also had the power to certify election results. Here are the precedents that requires elaboration and legal articulation. The Leviathan must become the certifying authority for all national elections! All means all: Côte d'Ivoire and Canada, Malaysia and Madagascar, United Republic of Tanzania and United States of America.

The UN currently has a rather sleepy outpost called the Electoral Assistance Division. It would be transformed into a political behemoth, the UN Election Certifying Authority (UNECA). It would authorize observation of all national elections with a mix of international and local observers. That mix would vary depending on the availability of local expertise and the strength of local civil society. UNECA would acknowledge problems and propose responses, making clear that certification could be denied if the recommendations were not addressed. UNECA would not impose any particular electoral system, which would remain a national decision, but would ensure the system is credible and then monitor how the system is implemented. It would have the benefit of comparative experience and consequent knowledge of best practices. In most cases, UNECA would ratify the decision of the national election management body as its form of certification. But in exceptional circumstances, UNECA would withhold certification and thus withdraw legitimacy from those claiming victory. Once again, the penalty for defying UNECA could involve referral of the uncertified claimant to office to the International Criminal Court.

These steps would give the UN Leviathan powers to improve the current situation for democracy and human rights. They may not provide a total solution. But they would lead to a situation in which national leaders would need to determine whether they will comply with the decisions of the Leviathan or, instead, become North Korea. For the UN to get to that position would require the drafting or amendment of treaties and the adoption of resolutions of the General Assembly and the Security Council. Technically, not difficult.

Let us return once again to "that old bugaboo of sovereignty"[56] because it is the Member States of the UN, for which read governments, that negotiate treaties and vote on resolutions. Will they vote for such a radical departure? It depends, as does so much, on "we the peoples." If there is enough concern about the increasingly anarchic global system and consequent support for the UN Leviathan, most governments, however reluctantly, will toe the line. Others will pretend to toe the line while thinking they can game the system. Others will stand on the principle of the inviolability of sovereignty and refuse to toe the line. But this is the way all advances in the international system have been achieved. Often against the opposition of a small group of countries. There will always be some North Koreas. Hopefully, China, Russia and the United States will not be among them. Powerful countries such as these are likely to be in the second group, pretending to accept the system in the belief that they are sufficiently powerful not to be indicted by it.

The United Nations as Leviathan is not a panacea for the world's problems. It is a constructive and workable step to bring key elements of global governance into being. Yes, the ideas will be seen as radical, but they are, as demonstrated, a continuation of the arc of history. Supranational judicial involvement in human rights, and international certification of elections, already exist. They need to be brought to scale. The impact of the Leviathan on democracy and human rights should not be underestimated. Instead of the trickle-down policies based on sovereignty that have repeatedly been attempted with limited success, protecting democracy and human rights will have an upward projecting multiplier effect with the UN responsive to "we the peoples." Not only will it strengthen democracy and human rights, it will also contribute sharply to better governance, less corruption and more rational policy making.

## NOTES

1. F. D. Roosevelt, "Four Freedoms Speech," https://www.fdrlibrary.org/four-freedoms
2. United Nations, "History of the Document," https://www.un.org/en/sections/universal-declaration/history-document/index.html

3. The other three were Hernán Santa Cruz (Chile), Alexander E. Bogomolov (USSR), and Charles Dukes (UK).

4. Roland Rich, "Bringing Democracy into International Law," *Journal of Democracy* 12, No. 3 (July, 2001), 20–34. Edward Newman and Roland Rich (eds.) *The UN Role in Promoting Democracy—Between Ideals and Reality*, United Nations University Press, Tokyo, 2004. Roland Rich, "Situating the UN Democracy Fund" *Global Governance* 16 (2010), 423–434.

5. Boutros Boutros-Ghali, *An Agenda for Democratization*, New York: UN Department of Public Information, 2006

6. Kofi Annan, *In Larger Freedom: Towards Development, Security and Human Rights for All*, UN Doc. A/59/2005 (21 March 2005).

7. "Special Document: United Nations," *Journal of Democracy* 21, no. 2 (2010): 182–186.

8. United Nations General Assembly Resolution A/RES/60/1, 2005.

9. Roland Rich, "Crafting Security Council Mandates," in *The UN Role in Promoting Democracy—Between Ideals and Reality*, eds. Edward Newman and Roland Rich (Tokyo: United Nations University Press, 2004) 62–85.

10. Vienna Declaration and Programme of Action. Adopted by the World Conference on Human Rights in Vienna on 25 June 1993. https://www.ohchr.org/Documents/ProfessionalInterest/vienna.pdf

11. See Roland Rich, "The Right to Development: A Right of Peoples?" in *The Rights of Peoples*, ed. James Crawford (Oxford: Clarendon Press, 1988) 39–54.

12. Samuel P. Huntington. *The Third Wave—Democratization in the Late Twentieth Century*, (Norman and London: Oklahoma University Press, 1991).

13. Roland Rich, *Pacific Asia in Quest of Democracy*, (Boulder: Lynne Rienner Publishers, 2007) 5–8.

14. See Eunice N. Sahle. "On Kéba M'Baye and the Right to Development at 30," in *Human Rights in Africa Contemporary Debates and Struggles*, ed. Eunice N. Sahle (New York: Palgrave Macmillan, 2019).

15. Human Rights Committee General Comment No. 25, U.N. Doc. CCPR/C/21/Rev.1/Add.7 (1996). Discussed in Roland Rich, "Bringing Democracy into International Law," *Journal of Democracy* 12, No. 3 (July, 2001), 23–24.

16. Op. cit.

17. Gary Becker, *Human Capital: A Theoretical and Empirical Analysis, with Special Reference to Education*, (Cambridge, MA: Harvard University Press, 1964).

18. United Nations Development Programme, "Human Development Reports." http://www.hdr.undp.org/

19. Amartya Sen, *Development as Freedom*, (New York: Anchor Books, 1999).

20. The Conventions on Civil and Political Rights; Economic, Social and Cultural Rights; Women's Rights; Children's Rights; Racial Discrimination; and Torture. The UN Office of the High Commissioner for Human Rights considers there to be 9 "core treaties" by including the Migrant Workers convention, the Enforced Disappearances Convention and Disabilities Convention. https://www.ohchr.org/EN/ProfessionalInterest/Pages/CoreInstruments.aspx

21. Office of the High Commissioner for Human Rights, "Special Procedures of the Human Rights Council," https://www.ohchr.org/en/hrbodies/sp/pages/welcomepage.aspx

22. Philip Alston, "Report of the Special Rapporteur on extrajudicial, summary or arbitrary executions," A/HRC/14/24/Add.6 of 28 May 2010.

23. Office of the High Commissioner for Human Rights, "Human Rights Treaty Bodies - Individual Communications," https://www.ohchr.org/en/hrbodies/tbpetitions/Pages/IndividualCommunications.aspx

24. UN Treaty Collection, https://treaties.un.org/Pages/ViewDetails.aspx?src=TREATY&mtdsg_no=IV-5&chapter=4&clang=_en

25. Toonen v. Australia, Communication No. 488/1992, U.N. Doc CCPR/C/50/D/488/1992 (1994).

26. The International Justice Resource Center, "The European Court of Human Rights," https://ijrcenter.org/european-court-of-human-rights/

27. European Court of Human Rights, "Violations by Article and by State 2018," https://www.echr.coe.int/Documents/Stats_violation_2018_ENG.pdf

28. International Criminal Court, "Jurisdiction," https://www.icc-cpi.int/about/how-the-court-works/Pages/default.aspx#legalProcess

29. The United Nations Office on Genocide Prevention and the Responsibility to Protect, "Responsibility to Protect," https://www.un.org/en/genocideprevention/about-responsibility-to-protect.shtml#

30. Ibid, paras 138–140.

31. Interview with Gareth Evans by SEF News (Stiftung Entwicklung und Frieden), 22 May 2008, https://www.gevans.org/opeds/oped91.html

32. Amartya Sen, "Democracy as a Universal Value." *Journal of Democracy* 10.3 (1999), 3–17.

33. See UN Commission on Human Rights resolution 1999/57 entitled Promotion of the Right to Democracy.

34. OSCE, Charter of Paris for a New Europe, 1990, https://www.osce.org/files/f/documents/0/6/39516.pdf

35. European Parliament, "Democracy," https://europarlamentti.info/en/values-and-objectives/democracy/

36. Millbrook Commonwealth Action Programme on the Harare Declaration, https://thecommonwealth.org/sites/default/files/history-items/documents/millbrook%20declaration.pdf

37. African Union Charter of Democracy, Elections and Governance, http://archive.ipu.org/idd-E/afr_charter.pdf

38. European Commission, "The Cotonou Agreement," https://www.consilium.europa.eu/en/policies/cotonou-agreement/

39. Council of the European Union, "Burundi: EU renews sanctions until 31 October 2019," https://www.consilium.europa.eu/en/press/press-releases/2018/10/25/burundi-l-ue-renouvelle-les-sanctions-jusqu-au-31-octobre-2019/

40. International Institute for Democracy and Electoral Assistance, "The Declaration of Principles for International Election Observation and the Code of Conduct for

International Election Observers," 2005, https://www.idea.int/publications/catalogue/declaration-principles-international-election-observation-and-code-conduct

41. E.g., Organization for Security and Co-operation in Europe, "Election Observation Handbook: Sixth Edition," 2010, https://www.osce.org/odihr/elections/68439

42. ACE Electoral Knowledge Network, "United Nations Electoral Assistance Division," http://aceproject.org/about-en/ace-partners/UNEAD

43. The Carter Center, "Waging Peace Through Elections," https://www.cartercenter.org/peace/democracy/observed.html#table

44. National Democratic Institute, "International Election Observation Reports," https://www.ndi.org/international-election-mission-chronological

45. Thomas M. Franck, "The Emerging Right to Democratic Governance," *The American Journal of International Law*, Vol. 86, No. 1. (January 1992) 46–91.

46. Roland Rich, "Crafting Security Council Mandates," in Edward Newman and Roland Rich (eds.) *The UN Role in Promoting Democracy—Between Ideals and Reality*, United Nations University Press, Tokyo, 2004, 62–85. Updated with the assistance of Kate Ann Brace.

47. An early voice was C. Raj Kumar, "Corruption and Transparency in Governance and Development: Reinventing Sovereignty for Promoting Good Governance," in *Reinventing Sovereignty: The End of Westphalia?* Eds. Trudy Jacobsen, Charles Sampford and Ramesh Thakur (Farnham, UK: Ashgate, 2008) 251–265.

48. Bill Rowlings, "Dead to rights: how an Aussie hero framed the world's conscience," Civil Liberties Australia, https://www.cla.asn.au/News/dead-to-rights-how-an/#gsc.tab=0

49. William A. Schabas, *An Introduction to the International Criminal Court*, (Cambridge University Press, 2001) 15.

50. Statement by US President Bill Clinton, authorizing the US signing of the Rome Statute of the International Criminal Court, 31 December 2000, https://1997-2001.state.gov/global/swci/001231_clinton_icc.html

51. Curtis A. Bradley, "U.S. Announces Intent Not to Ratify International Criminal Court Treaty," *The American Society of International Law Journal*, Vol. 7, Iss. 6, May 11, 2002.

52. Established by UNSC Resolution 827 of 25 May 1993, and UNSCR 955 of 8 November 1994 respectively.

53. Nick Grono, "The Deterrent Effect of the ICC on the Commission of International Crimes by Government Leaders," *International Crisis Group*, October 5, 2012, https://www.crisisgroup.org/global/deterrent-effect-icc-commission-international-crimes-government-leaders

54. The Law Society Gazette of Ireland, "Ten-year backlog of 10,000 cases dogs ECHR credibility," 18/7/2019, https://www.lawsociety.ie/gazette/top-stories/ten-year-backlog-of-10000-cases-dogs-european-court-of-human-rights/

55. Hon. Justice Michael Kirby, "Ombudsman—The Future." Speech delivered on 7 September 1985. *Canberra Bulletin of Public Administration*, vol XII no 4, 300.

56. Daniel K. Tarullo, "Logic, Myth, and the International Economic Order," *Harvard International Law Journal* 26(2) 1985, p. 533.

# *Chapter 7*

# Against the Sustainable Development Goals!

Though something of an afterthought at the time of drafting the Charter, the concept of development has become a pillar of the United Nations. Colonialism had left the newly independent countries of the global South in a state of poverty and the solution was summarized in a single word—development. The wealthy world created the concept of official development assistance (ODA) and the UN jumped on board. Decades of fashions in ODA, from infrastructure to basic human needs to structural adjustment to governance and now to the Delphic term partnership, finally led to the Millennium Development Goals which in 2016 ceded their place to the Sustainable Development Goals. It all sounds terribly uplifting until one pauses to consider a key fact: No country was ever lifted out of poverty by ODA.

## FROM MDGS TO SDGS

Who could possibly be against the United Nations' Sustainable Development Goals? Who could in all decency oppose goals "to end poverty and hunger everywhere; to combat inequalities within and among countries; to build peaceful, just and inclusive societies; to protect human rights and promote gender equality and the empowerment of women and girls; and to ensure the lasting protection of the planet and its natural resources . . . to create conditions for sustainable, inclusive and sustained economic growth, shared prosperity and decent work for all, taking into account different levels of national development and capacities."[1] Who would dare stand up to the delegations and Secretariats that have made the 2030 agenda a sacred UN document to be worshipped at every occasion?

The answer will become clear as this chapter develops. The first hint of doubt comes from the fact that this is an agenda for everything and everybody for the next fifteen years and yet it was agreed unanimously by 193 delegations. When does that sort of thing happen? Yes, it happens in the Democratic People's Republic of Korea. And it might happen among lemmings. But, remarkably, it happened in September 2015 among delegations representing every government of the world. These are governments of capitalist economies, supposedly socialist economies, donor states, recipient states, least developed countries, and most developed countries. Among these governments are climate change deniers, human rights abusers and narco traffickers. Some of these governments are from patriarchal theocracies, patriarchal traditionalists and patriarchal developmentalists. Yet, they all supported the resolution establishing the SDGs. Why?

There is no economic, political or strategic thread tying all these governments together. Indeed, the one and only commonality is that they are *governments*. That is the thread tying together the SDGs. It is a document of the governments, by the governments and for the governments. But wait a minute, didn't more than one million people have their say on what the SDGs should contain?[2] Didn't Amina Mohammed consult tirelessly for two years to gather every significant opinion on the subject? Yes, those things happened. But in the end, the resolution was decided in the same way every important decision is taken at the UN, by a couple of dozen significant delegations.

Which delegations? Any list at the UN begins with the five permanent members of the UN Security Council (P5) whether they have anything useful to contribute or not. After all, what could Russia contribute to such a debate given that it has been turned into a kleptocracy run by an autocrat where individual rights and opportunities are the least of the government's priorities. Irrelevant! It is one of the P5 and that is sufficient status at the UN. The delegation of the European Union was actively involved given that it manages a large slice of official development assistance. And so was Japan for similar reasons. Then there would be delegations representing large countries from the global South such as India, Brazil, and South Africa. And whenever these delegations are active, their geographic and strategic alter egos, Pakistan, Argentina, and Nigeria respectively, would also be active. And then there are the delegations that deal themselves in through their expertise and enthusiasm. The CANZ trio (Canada, Australia, and New Zealand) would be in this category, though until recently Australia had little to offer given its domestic policies on climate change. All the Group of 20 (G20) are in, as are governments of possible spoiler countries as diverse as Algeria, Cuba, Egypt, and Venezuela. Once that critical mass of key delegations agrees, the rest jump on board.

I was not negative about the Millennium Development Goals (MDGs) which ran from 2000–2015. They were more modest and more achievable. They did not try to eradicate poverty but focused on extreme poverty. They worked on infectious diseases and primary education. Most importantly, they worked well as a donor coordination device. The supposed success of the MDGs required the international community to become far more ambitious. So, instead of a donor coordination program in favor of the weakest countries, the new set of goals had to cover the whole world and just about every problem in it. Has anybody ever heard a politician from a wealthy country campaigning in her electorate on the basis of meeting SDGs? Just as occurred with the MDGs, the SDGs, though intended to apply to every nation, only become a parameter in the poor nations.[3] And instead of being a coordination device, the SDGs became a menu.

The substance of the SDGs is less important than the key actor identified to make them happen—governments. Civil society and most academic commentators were blinded by the goals themselves and did not go on to ask who they privileged as deliverers. But these goals have weakened civil society and strengthened governments on the international scene. They are already cosseted and protected by the doctrine of sovereignty, and governments have now been cast by the SDGs as the heroic actors that will deliver development to their people.

## THE PRIMACY OF GOVERNMENTS IN DEVELOPMENT

Governments hide behind the expression "Member States of the UN," giving the impression that the whole nation is supportive when, of course, only governments have a voice at the UN. This aspect of the SDGs has not drawn commentary because it has become the natural order of things. The international community has come to accept that this is a community of governments. And in no field of endeavor is this truer than in the murky field known as "development." Let us note at the outset, that the concept of development does not apply to Europe or America or the wealthy countries of the Gulf or East Asia. In those countries it is called economics. Development is a phenomenon that occurs only in the poor countries of the global South. It has its own history, its own discourse, and its own myths. To understand why the world was so inured to the perspective that development is a heroic responsibility of governments, we need to unpack that history.

I began a book review of William Easterly's *The Tyranny of Experts, Economists, Dictators and the Forgotten Rights of the Poor* with the following passage:

> When in New York City, do you prefer uptown or downtown? Uptown is where you will find Columbia University, the academic base of Jeffrey Sachs who argues that official development assistance (ODA) works well if properly

> designed and should be increased. Downtown is where you will find New York University, the academic home of William Easterly, ODA's most trenchant critic.[4]

As readers will have discerned, I am a downtown guy, and I will draw on the analysis of the curmudgeonly Easterly of how governments of poor countries were assigned their heroic central role in development. I use the adjective ironically, but Gunnar Myrdal did not when, speaking in Cairo, he described as "heroic," the policy of developing country governments taking charge of development.[5]

While kings, dukes and popes have forever been critical players in the economies of their domains, the concept of development is a new vintage. It has its genesis in the late colonial period, when, after centuries of ruthless exploitation, the metropolitan powers began to justify their occupations by claiming the role of developing their colonial possessions. The British Colonial Development Fund was established in 1929 with other colonizers later following suit.[6] In 1938, Lord Hailey published the *African Survey* announcing "a more scientific approach to the problems of health and material well-being" in Africa, and in subsequent interventions, he made clear that the role of managing this scientific approach lay with the colonial government using systematic planning, if necessary, supported by legal compulsion.[7] One need simply extrapolate such thinking to the governance of the United Kingdom to realize its unacceptability. But by adding a dollop of racism through the concept of white man's burden, compulsory scientific planning was seen as the correct formulation for the colonies. Lord Hailey sold his ideas to the United States by equating them with FDR's New Deal.[8] The seeds of authoritarian development had been sown.

It is, however, facile to condemn these actions using today's morality. The Universal Declaration of Human Rights was only adopted by the UN General Assembly in 1948 and it would take another couple of decades till the voices of the former colonial peoples were clearly heard in that chamber. The authoritarian impulse under guise of scientific progress is more understandable in the formative period of development economics. Friedrich Hayek's *The Road to Serfdom* was published in 1944,[9] but it could not match the forces calling for central control in favor of scientific manipulation of society. The crime is less in the inception of the concept than in its continuing stubborn defense.

In the first decade or so after the end of WWII, two phenomena seemed to lend credibility to the concept of government-led development. The first was the Marshall Plan, which at least in the public imagination, was the vehicle for the reconstruction of a Europe left in rubble by war. There may be debates about the extent of its actual impact, but its generosity cannot be doubted. At its peak in 1948 and 1949, aid from the Marshall Plan accounted for around

5 percent of West Germany's national income.[10] It is also the case that the aid was subject to extreme conditionality set by the United States which retained broad decision making about its utilization.[11] The second phenomenon was the apparent success of the Soviet State Planning Committee (Gosplan) in rebuilding the USSR after the long and brutal war against Germany. It was only in the late 1970s that Soviet economists began to question its efficacy.[12]

It is therefore no surprise that the 'development as planning' model was adopted by the United Nations in the form of a 1951 publication entitled *Primer for Development*.[13] African countries followed this model as each became independent. Political authoritarianism was supported by economic authoritarianism in the form of central planning of the development processes. The issue of human rights was quarantined for discussion in Geneva with little application on the ground. Advocacy for human rights in this period focused primarily on civil and political rights with minimal linkage to the issue of economic development. The Cold War saw the question sidelined as secondary to the more critical question of allegiances. And as the Cold War began to wind down in the 1980s, yet another persuasive argument emerged in favor of the central role of governments in development.

By this stage, it was clear to most that central planning was not working well in the Soviet Union, that it had mired India in bureaucratic red tape, and that it had not lifted any African country out of the poverty colonialism had left behind. But a form of it was working wonders in East Asia. The "developmental state" concept[14] had turned Japan into an economic powerhouse and that model was being replicated in half a dozen other East Asian tiger economies. The formula required an authoritarian government, military or civilian, a competent but pliant bureaucracy, and a managed market economy dominated by favored titan corporations prepared to share the spoils with the government and the bureaucracy. South Korea and Taiwan, both under military dictatorship, as well as Singapore, effectively under a dominant party system, were quick to follow Japan's lead with considerable success. Malaysia, Thailand, and Indonesia also drew from the concept with some success. When the Cold War ended and Southeast Asia wished to form a geographically coherent regional body, the issue was whether Vietnam would fit into the Association of Southeast Asian Nations (ASEAN). The problem was that the former remained communist while the members of the latter were unabashedly capitalist. But what tied them together, and allowed for the expansion of ASEAN, was their common adherence to government-led developmentalism.[15]

Government-centered developmentalism has had successes, but these successes have arisen in limited circumstances. The Marshall Plan, even if accepted as the catalyst for the reconstruction of Europe, did not build nations or societies. Those viable nations and societies already existed. The Marshall

Plan provided food aid and the hard currency that allowed those viable nations to rebuild their ruined infrastructure. The post-war Soviet Gosplan model of forced savings and government directed investment, provided the impetus to rebuild Soviet infrastructure, but that was a clear and common post-war national purpose. Once the complexities of an economy for a modern society became apparent, the Gosplan proved to be worse than useless. The East Asian tigers emerged, phoenix-like, as they enjoy saying, from the ashes of war to middle income and, some, to wealthy or OECD status. They did so in a single generation. But wealth does not necessarily mean health. The legacies of East Asian developmentalism include persistent and systemic corruption; either dominant party politics or deep difficulties in alternation of power; and immature civil society organizations.

There is one last argument in favor of government-led development—China. Because it is a current phenomenon, it will be discussed separately below.

## GOVERNMENT-LED DEVELOPMENTALISM'S FAILURES

The systematic planning supported by legal compulsion method has not helped Africa, its intended beneficiary. There is no developmental state dividend on that continent. It was a policy initially designed to justify and sustain colonial administration, but it seeped into development economics orthodoxy with hardly a word of dissent. It became the instrument of the leaders of national liberation movements who took over from the colonial administrations and, by and large, adopted the government-led development model.

A case study of the largest country in sub-Saharan Africa, the Democratic Republic of Congo, formerly Zaire, formerly a Belgian colony and prior to that the personal possession of King Leopold of Belgium, is emblematic of the situation in Africa. Adam Hochschild's gripping book, *King Leopold's Ghost: A Story of Greed, Terror, and Heroism in Colonial Africa*, will serve as our guide.[16] Prior to contact with Europe in 1500, the region was ruled by a king chosen by an assembly of clan leaders. But Portuguese traders exploited the existing institution of slavery and turned it into an industry to service the mines and plantations of its colony in Brazil. Society in the Congo basin was deeply disrupted, but the interior of the country was partially protected by its inaccessibility. Henry Morton Stanley penetrated the interior using riverine and cross forest routes thus "opening up" the area for commercial exploitation. King Leopold of Belgian craved his own colony and based on the promise to bring Christianity and civilization to the natives, was granted the Congo basin at the 1885 Berlin Conference. Thus began 23 years of brutal absolutist rule, not overseen by the Belgian government or parliament. At first, wealth was generated by the slaughter of elephants for their tusks, but an even more lucrative commodity materialized with the popularity of automobiles and their need for rubber tires. The rubber needed to be laboriously milked by hand from vines in the canopies of tall trees. The method employed was for the King's mercenaries to hold hostage whole villages to force the men to go to the forest and tap the rubber. It took a massive campaign throughout Europe, sensitized by books such as Joseph Conrad's *Heart of Darkness,* which was set in Leopold's Congo, to force the Belgian state to relieve the King of his personal possession in 1908 and govern the Belgian Congo as a colony until its independence in 1960.

In the 23 years that Leopold governed Congo, a territory he never visited, it is estimated that he personally benefitted by a dividend of more than one billion dollars in current value. (It is little consolation that the bulk of his estate went to a Parisian teenage prostitute, Caroline, who he married late in life.) But at what cost to the people of the Congo? Hochschild researches this question deeply and settles on the generally accepted conclusion that in the couple of decades of Leopold's rule, the territory under his administration lost half of its population, which decreased from around twenty million to ten million inhabitants. The next half century saw a more normal process of colonization—exploitative but less barbaric. This was followed by President Mobutu, a junior officer in the Belgian colonial forces who conspired with Belgium and the CIA to murder the putative post-independence leader Patrice Lumumba, and subsequently ruled for the next 32 years in much the same way as did King Leopold, amassing a $4 billion fortune.[17] And little changed when Joseph Kabila chased Mobutu from power and ruled until he was forced to step down in 2018.[18]

In a case such as that of the Congo, whose history, but for the nasty Leopoldian idiosyncrasy, is not dissimilar to that of many African countries. The "systematic planning supported by legal compulsion" method is simply a formula for continuing an autocratic kleptocracy. But do these misgivings travel beyond Africa? A key feature that characterizes African society is deep and enduring trauma. Sadly, Africa is not alone in this regard. The Congo lost half its people in the space of two decades. Central and South American civilizations were decimated by the arrival of the conquistadors from the 1500s onwards. Drawing on Peter Watson's *The Great Divide: Nature and Human Nature in the Old World and the New,*[19] an ambitious comparative study of the civilizations on both sides of the Atlantic, it is important to note that, just as is the case for the figures for the Congo, the population figures for the Americas are educated estimates. Henry Dobyn's 1966 study, controversially arrived at by extrapolating back from death rates, found that in 1500, the population of Central and South America was between 80–108 million. To put this in perspective, it would be greater than the then population of Europe. By 1650, the number of indigenous people had been reduced to four million. Disease was the primary cause. Smallpox arrived around 1525, brought to Mexico apparently by a single sick Spaniard, it swept south and eliminated more than half the population of the Incan empire. Then came typhus in 1546, influenza and smallpox together in 1558, smallpox again in 1589, diphtheria in 1614, and measles in 1618, with the effect of reducing the native population by more than 90%.

Jared Diamond's magnificent *Guns, Germs and Steel: The Fates of Human Societies*,[20] explains the massive advantages enjoyed by the enormous East-West Eurasian landmass, including the presence of so many domesticatable mammals. They provided the protein surplus to enlarge populations. But they also caused zoonotic diseases, against which, over the millennia, pastoral people built their herd immunity. The people of the new world had no such immunity.

If I may be so bold as to suggest a footnote to Diamond's geographic determinism in the form of a response to the question—why was the conquest by Europe, and not the other way around from the populous and powerful civilizations of the new world? I believe the answer lies in the uniqueness of first the Aegean Sea, and then the Mediterranean Sea. Both were readily navigable with the technology of the day given the various adjacent and even opposite coastlines within island-hopping reach, and which, over the millennia, has seen many competitive littoral civilizations employing maritime warfare. This dynamic established the aggressive seafaring culture of Mediterranean peoples which ultimately facilitated the age of exploration and conquest. It was not the defeat in 490 BCE of the Persians by the vastly outnumbered Athenians at Marathon, nor, ten years later, the heroic yet suicidal stand of King Leonidas and his 300 Spartan warriors against an overwhelming Persian foe at Thermopylae, that safeguarded the cradle of European civilization. It was the Athenian navy's defeat of the Persian navy in the battle of Salamis in 480 BCE that ultimately put an end to the Persian threat.[21] Mediterranean peoples have been fighting naval battles ever since. In comparison, the Incas had large rafts of balsa wood which they used for trade along the Pacific coast, but they did not develop seafaring vessels to challenge the vastness of the largest ocean.[22]

Alongside physical genocide came cultural genocide. The ascetic and monopolistic form of Spanish Catholicism brought not only the Inquisition, but also a single-minded determination to destroy all pre-Columbian artifacts and cultural materials. From literate civilizations of tens of millions of people, only sixteen indigenous written works remain.[23] The Spanish colonizers would behave similarly in the Philippines. The loss of 90% of the people of the Americas meant a loss of memory, depriving the anthropologists the wherewithal to reconstruct those civilizations. We are therefore left in the hands of the archaeologists. The implications of the genocide continue to play out to the present day. The nations of the Americas all have remnants of their indigenous people, often numbering in the millions. Bolivia has an indigenous majority, Guatemala's population is 40% indigenous, and Mexico has more than seven million indigenous people.[24] The policies of the governments of these countries cannot wish these people away.

Though the decimation of native American peoples stands alone in its severity, incidents of mass murder, dislocation and enslavement of locals accompanied all the colonial powers right up to the last century. The Genocide Museum in Rwanda has a history of genocide in the twentieth century which begins with the genocide of the Herero people of Namibia under German colonial rule in the first decade of that century. Societal trauma is an inescapable part of the colonial legacy. The governance these people require should be restorative, not authoritarian. Making governments the central actors in the economic development process inevitably leads those governments to stand in the shoes of their colonial predecessors. When the economists of the former colonial masters, like Lord Hailey, considered the means of development, they came upon the sort of authoritarian solutions colonial administrations would typically craft. When they turned these ideas into an economic discipline, it became difficult for others to resist applying them.

There is an alternative concept of development, but before we examine it, it is important to rid ourselves of one of the great and popular myths of planning, that infrastructure equals development.

## THE MYTH OF INFRASTRUCTURE AS DEVELOPMENT

In 2013, Chinese President Xi Jinping announced that he wanted to resurrect the legendary Silk Road; he proposed a titanic project to build hundreds of roads, bridges, and railroads to connect China and Europe. The Belt and Road Initiative (BRI) has grown beyond this historical resurrection to encompass any large foreign project sponsored by China, just about anywhere in the world. It is planned to take fifty years. But beyond any benefits this might have for trade, China is attempting to export its development model by relying on massive investment in infrastructure to be delivered by Chinese corporations and funded by Chinese bank loans, all under the direction and purview of the Chinese Communist Party.[25] That development model is well understood—a Leninist party, making top-down decisions and imposing its will on the population about economic development.

The current generation in power in China understands the transformative effect of infrastructure. It has seen the country transformed from a backward rural economy into an urban economic powerhouse. That transformation required a lot of infrastructure to be built. There are today more than one hundred cities in China with a population of at least one million people.[26] We learned something about infrastructure construction in China during the 2008 Sichuan earthquake:

> Many schools in the earthquake zone crumbled while buildings around them remained standing. According to some estimates, as many as 7,000 classrooms collapsed and up to 10,000 students may have died.[27]

Chinese officials eventually admitted that schools were built in fault zones, often with inferior materials.[28] This is the Chinese model of development, where private buildings are properly built but schools are corruptly built in the wrong places with the wrong materials. Indeed, anybody living in China understands full well the Chinese infrastructure model because they cannot breathe clean air and they cannot be sure they are eating clean food. This is the "cut the ribbon" style of leadership where infrastructure is first and foremost a testament to the leader. Xi Jinping owns the BRI. It is the crown on the head of the colossus.

Unfortunately, the infrastructure as development idea is not distinct to China. It is widely believed by people and leaders all over the world. It formed the original basis for official development assistance (ODA) and it was the center piece of ODA projects in its first couple of decades. William Easterly traced the intellectual underpinnings of ODA in a paper he wrote while still at the World Bank.[29] In 1946, Evsey Domar published an article which assumed that production capacity was proportional to the capital stock. In other words, capital investment would return a fixed amount of production. It does not take much consideration to understand that while this might be arguable in a perfect frictionless world, it is based on unrealistic assumptions in the real world. Domar soon disavowed the idea and said it could not be employed as a model for economic growth. Yet, that is exactly what happened to Domar's model, it became the foundational concept for ODA. The model required high capital accumulation to ensure economic development. But developing countries did not have the growth rates or the tax receipts to fund such rates of capital accumulation. Into the breach would step ODA to fill "the financing gap." "Since virtually all of the aid advocates used the Harrod-Domar/Financing Gap model, this was one of the largest policy experiments ever based on a single economic model."[30] Easterly concluded that "there is no theoretical or empirical justification for using such a 'financing gap' calculation to influence policy or the allocation of foreign aid. After forty years, the Ghost of Financing Gap can finally be laid to rest."[31] But it lives on among the infrastructure boosters and, sadly, in the public imagination. It is no longer a yard stick for the Bretton Woods institutions or the OECD donors, but it has been enthusiastically adopted by China.

The BRI will build infrastructure for the purpose of exporting Chinese expertise and labor. It will be used to implant Chinese corporations on foreign soil. It may at times come in at exorbitant costs, with the local government and the Chinese corporation splitting the corrupt dividend and the taxpayer (current and future, foreign and Chinese) picking up the tab. It will generate enormous debt, well beyond the capacity of the local economy to absorb. That debt will be repaid by granting commercial favors to Chinese companies and strategic favors to the Chinese government. And, needless to say, the Chinese government, unconstrained by civil society, will not tolerate any sort of Jubilee Campaign to forgive the debt. The BRI is an authoritarian program by an authoritarian government in support of an authoritarian mode of development.

It does not take long for any traveler to countries in the global South and beyond to understand the fallacy of the Domar infrastructure model in which savings or ODA are invested in capital, mainly in the form of infrastructure, supposedly leading inevitably to economic development. There are many weak links in the model, one of which concerns the tenuousness of constructed infrastructure. We have all seen the ghosts of capital investment. On Iloilo Island in the Philippines, I have stood on what the locals called a dam. The basin was simply scrubland. The surrounding mountains had been denuded of trees. The rains washed the mountain soil into the dam which now stood as a mark of folly in the belief of the inevitable productive capacity of infrastructure. In Sagaing, Burma (now Myanmar), I was shown silos built with Australian aid. They work well as wheat silos in Australia, but they cracked the rice they were meant to store in Burma thus greatly reducing its value. In Northern Samar, in the Philippines, the Australian built road was intended to foster local trade, but its main use turned out to be for military vehicles fighting the communist insurgency and harassing villagers along the way. The morose villagers I spoke to were caught in the middle. In defense of the managers of the Australian aid project, they switched some of the funds to livelihood support, mainly in the form of simple fish tanks to breed tilapia. That was the infrastructure the villagers valued.

One cannot be against infrastructure *per se*. Those one hundred cities in China need housing. Factories are needed for production and employment. Infrastructure is needed for energy generation and transport. But infrastructure must be demand driven. It must meet the needs of the people it is meant to service. Its construction must be debated and contested and finally accepted. If it is publicly built, it needs to meet the tests of transparency and then accountability. If it is privately built, it needs to comply with the regulations designed to protect the public and advance its interests, within a framework of informed contestation. In 1966, Jagdish Bhagwati caused a stir when he said policy makers in developing countries faced a "cruel dilemma"—they had to choose between democracy and development.[32] He argued that it was the indiscipline, the clientalism and the absence of scientific planning in democracies that forced this choice. This was an argument, whether intended or not, for the school of forced savings to fill the financing gap, and, ultimately, for the authoritarian school of development. Three decades later, Bhagwati apologized for his earlier view. He argued that it was difficult to be certain about the relationship between democracy and development, but he did draw one critical conclusion: quality development requires quality democracy![33]

## THE HUMAN DIMENSION OF DEVELOPMENT

Earlier in this chapter, the concept of restorative governance was mentioned. It remains a broad and amorphous term, but a sense of its meaning may be found from a definition of the concept of restorative practices:

> (The concept of) restorative practices is the science of restoring and developing social capital, social discipline, emotional well-being and civic participation through participatory learning and decision-making.[34]

These are the practices governments should utilize in development. They are a long way from scientific planning supported by legal compulsion. They put the emphasis on civic participation and decision-making. They are bottom-up practices. Although state-centric development became economic orthodoxy for the developing world, there were voices expressing doubt and proposing countervailing ideas.

An early contrarian was Kéba Mbaye, a Senegalese jurist, who in a 1972 lecture at the International Institute of Human Rights in Strasbourg and a subsequent journal article, asked whether development should be seen as a human right.[35] The right to development has thereafter been the subject of half a century of debate and contestation, lionized by the global South, grudgingly accepted by some others, and rejected by the United States. The first decade of that debate was conducted in French, often within the august halls of UNESCO. I was at the time a diplomat posted to Paris, and I plugged into the debate. I was one of the first to publish a scholarly article on the subject in English, a case of language arbitrage with a few original ideas thrown in.[36] My enthusiasm for the new concept was based on the hope that the right to development would leverage support in the global South for the other human rights. Karel Vasak, UNESCO's legal advisor who we met in the preceding chapter, wrote an article in 1977 in which he described three generations of human rights.[37] The first generation has come to be associated with civil and political rights, the second generation with economic, social and cultural rights, and the third, which Vasak called Solidarity Rights, were rights of peoples and included the right to development. In a subsequent contribution, I added the right of self-determination to the putative list of rights of peoples.[38] In 1986, UN General Assembly resolution 41/128 adopted the Declaration on the Right to Development by 146 in favor, 1 against (USA), and 8 abstentions (Denmark, Germany, Finland, Iceland, Israel, Japan, Sweden, UK). The story since that adoption has been about the attempt to give meaning to this new right of peoples.[39] The closest this came to fruition was the work accomplished by the special rapporteur, Arjun Sengupta, in the late 1990s.[40] Sengupta recommended that the right be translated into practical compacts for food, health and education. In a reversal of normal voting patterns, the OECD donor community was enthusiastic, but the G77 rejected the idea because this group preferred to retain the right to development as a political cudgel with which to bash the wealthy countries of the global North. Various attempts to resuscitate the right to development have foundered on the same division of views. It is now in the ironic and unenviable situation of being seen as sacrosanct by one group and substantively meaningless by the other.

The right to development debate may have led to a dead end, but the concept of linking development and human rights emerged from this debate, leading to far more fruitful results. It found a home in the ODA community, no doubt because its practitioners had witnessed decades of futility financing infrastructure projects and then programs to strengthen government capacity. An early source of ideas was the Human Rights Council of Australia which published a paper in 1995 on the Rights Way to Development.[41] Its thesis was deceptively simple—use the human rights canon as a means of designing, delivering, and evaluating development assistance programs. The concept ran counter to ODA orthodoxy which valued economic planning and, in theory, followed the economic priorities of the receiving government. In a later publication, one of the authors of the HRCA paper, Andre Frankovits, wrote "From an ethical, moral, and efficiency perspective it is only the human rights approach to development that can prove at once effective and sustainable."[42]

The "Rights Way" ideas have been accepted in the ODA community under the term the Human Rights–Based Approach to Development (HRBA) which is described by UNDP as:

> based on the recognition that real success in tackling poverty and vulnerability requires giving the poor and vulnerable both a stake, a voice and real protection in the societies where they live. A human rights-based approach is not only about expanding people's choices and capabilities but above all about

> the empowerment of people to decide what this process of expansion should look like.[43]

By the early 2000s, many international development nongovernmental organizations enthusiastically adopted the human rights-based approach, including ActionAid, Save the Children, Oxfam, and Care International, as well as a number of official governmental and intergovernmental development agencies, including the UK Department for International Development (DFID), Swedish International Development Agency (SIDA), United Nations Children's Fund (UNICEF), and the United Nations Development Program (UNDP).[44] Scholars have underlined how this approach affects the discourse of ODA as well as the mandates of the donors and the goals they set.[45]

If there is a criticism to be made of this set of ideas, it would be that they emerged from jurists, lawyers, and human rights defenders, rather than from economists. But any such criticism was made moot in 1999 when Nobel Prize winning economist, Amartya Sen, published *Development as Freedom*.[46] Sen had been working on the causes of famine, with a particular emphasis on famines in the sub-continent in colonial times, and he came to the remarkable conclusion that it was not lack of food that had caused those famines but a lack of democracy and a free press. He brought this unorthodox thinking to the question of development. He concluded that development was a function of freedom, not of infrastructure. Freedom is both the primary end, and the principal means of development. And it was not freedom in some vague abstract sense, but freedom in the sense of the application of the full human rights canon; civil, political, economic, social, and cultural. If not infrastructure, what drove development? Sen's answer is human capabilities. Individuals must have the freedom to develop their capabilities to the fullest extent. The role of governments is to facilitate capability development. And, Sen concludes, that democracies provide the best political systems for the fulfillment of human capabilities.

The economist had come to the Rights Way of development by a different path from the human rights defenders. That both paths led to the same destination bolstered the conclusion. And it also bolstered Fukuyama's conclusion that democracy and market systems provided the best setting for individuals, the fulfillment of their capabilities and the economic development of the nation. It may not be the end of history, as Xi Jinping does not accept any aspect of the Sen perspective, but it provided people and institutions working in the field of development, a new true North.

The United Nations has played a considerable role in moving towards a people-centered concept of development, and as noted above, both UNDP and UNICEF have adopted HRBA. UNDP also made a telling contribution in designing the Human Development Index, the origins of which are discussed in a previous chapter. In a world where metrics matter, UNDP provided a single figure that combines sets of data on standards of living, health and wellbeing, and access to education, to gauge the state of an entire nation. As noted, Sen's first reaction to the idea was that it was "crude and inelegant," but it provided a useful snapshot, and as the years have passed since the first index was published in 1990, it provides a highly useful longitudinal perspective on each country's path.

The Human Development Index is accompanied by a report focusing on a particular issue or a specific region. The 2004 report focused on the Arab world. The causes of the Arab Spring uprisings have come to replace the causes of WWI in education and discussion circles. The demographers will point to a large bubble of unemployed youth. The economists will focus on the lack of opportunities. The agronomists will look at poor wheat harvests and high bread prices. Historians who believe in agency theory will zero in on the self-immolation of Mohamed Bouazizi in a small Tunisian town. They all have a point. But, in the view of the author, the 2004 Arab Human Development Report, subtitled "Towards Freedom in the Arab World,"[47] played a key role by fomenting anger and distress among Arab intellectuals. It was written by Arabs for Arabs, and it did not pull any punches portraying misogynistic societies with corrupt governments and poorly educated citizens. It prepared the intellectual ground for the Arab Spring.

## OFFICIAL DEVELOPMENT ASSISTANCE

The field of development where the debate about state-centered versus people-centered development has become acute is official development assistance. This is a relatively new, and in some ways, artificial process. While, as noted, it could be seen as having its origins in the late colonial period, it found a place in the Charter, where the preamble speaks of the determination "to promote social progress and better standards of life in larger freedom," and its formal launch was in 1949 when Harry S. Truman announced the establishment of a foreign aid program. It is artificial insofar as there is no historical precedent for the government of one nation assisting another nation to grow its economy. The usual historical prospect is for one nation to conquer another and bleed it of its wealth. The political justification behind the existence of ODA is that it is a form of enlightened self-interest because aiding poor nations to become successful will provide markets and investment opportunities and are more likely to become democratic and thus peace-loving. The justification is strong, it is the execution, as we have seen, that is problematic.

I have been involved in ODA on and off for many years. It is excruciatingly difficult to get things done and even harder to have a positive impact. Consider this example. I arrived as Ambassador in Vientiane and began the usual round of courtesy calls on Lao government ministers. To understand this story, it is important to know something about national naming cultures. In Myanmar, people are named based on the day of the week they are born. There is a small stock of names, and it is impossible, simply from the names, to know who is related to whom. In China and Korea, it is theoretically easier, but in practice family relationship detection is almost impossible for the newcomer. There is a small stock of single syllable family names in China like Mao or Deng or Xi or Lee, the world's most common surname, but they are so common that detecting family relationships is guess work. It is even harder in Korea where twenty percent of people share the family name Kim. But in Thailand and Laos, family names are often drawn from Sanskrit. They are multi-syllabic and distinctive. If two people share the same family name, one can be quite certain they are related, especially in a country like Laos with a small population. So, I studied the names of the various ministers and senior officials I was meeting. One of the first bits of paper to hit my in-tray was that year's list of winners of scholarships to study in Australian universities. I thought I had the wrong piece of paper because the names looked so familiar. I called in the aid team, and they confirmed that the list was compiled by the Lao side and that most of the names on the list were related to Lao political leaders.

To use an Australianism, I spat the dummy! We're not spending Australian taxpayer money to educate the children of the communist *nomenklatura*, I raged. We believe in meritocracy, I thundered. The damage had been done for that year's list, but I instructed the team to negotiate with the Lao side so that, henceforth, we would advertise scholarships and an impartial committee would select the most deserving applicants. The Lao side did not take this well. But Australia was a major donor and so, inevitably, a diplomatic compromise was reached whereby half the list would be nominated by the Lao side and the other half would be chosen by an impartial committee on merit. When the next list was presented to me . . . yes, the dummy was again spat. It was the same *nomenklatura* names as the previous year. The Embassy aid team explained that just about all those on the list, nominated and on merit, came from the one elite high school where the *nomenklatura* sent their children. You can always count on communist egalitarianism!

I was almost ready to concede defeat, but I had one last gasp of an idea. Let's offer the top boy and the top girl from the intermediate exam in each of Laos's fourteen provinces, scholarships to spend the last two years of secondary education in the elite high school. To my surprise, the Lao side accepted the idea. Even more surprising, the Australian side found additional money to fund this venture. During the balance of my posting, we focused on the logistical and welfare issues, and by the time I said my farewells, the system was up and running. As is often the case in diplomatic life, one moves on to the next assignment without knowing how things one may previously have initiated will work out. But some years later, I bumped into the desk officer in the Australian aid agency dealing with Laos and asked about results. He proudly said that for the first time, a provincial student had just won a scholarship to Australia. Maybe, I mused, she will be the first of many. And even without a scholarship for tertiary study, the 28 annual provincial high school graduates will have far better opportunities than had they stayed home. But what a herculean effort for a relatively modest outcome.

The Vatican of ODA is the Development Assistance Committee of the OECD. It believes in transparency, and practices it to a certain extent. It also, unusually, believes in honesty and empirically based conclusions. Its greatest attribute is its capacity for self-criticism. It is difficult to imagine another organization describing its own product as "incoherent." But that was the jarring term used in the discussion leading to the adoption of the 2005 Paris Principles on Aid Effectiveness.[48] The principles can be summarized as:

- Ownership: Developing countries set their own strategies for poverty reduction, improve their institutions and tackle corruption
- Alignment: Donor countries align behind these objectives and use local systems
- Harmonization: Donor countries coordinate, simplify procedures and share information to avoid duplication
- Results: Developing countries and donors shift focus to development results and results get measured
- Mutual accountability: Donors and partners are accountable for development results.

Of these five principles, the bottom four are basically policy bromides, often asserted and rarely delivered. The first principle was also not original but by listing it first, the donor community was expressing a determination to implement its purpose. It uses the term "developing countries," but as we have seen, this means the government of the country. Clearly, there was a problem in setting priorities for African countries in the corridors of power of Washington, London, Tokyo, or Paris. Decades of programs and projects flowing from donor priorities had failed because of lack of enthusiasm, resources, or commitment from the receiving side. The idea of "ownership" was to ensure that the projects and programs would be integrated into local policy and priorities. The problem was that receiving governments had priorities associated with enhancing the reputation of the leader-for-life, benefiting the ruling tribe, and building ribbon-cutting infrastructure.

The next iteration of the aid effectiveness process took place in Accra in 2008 and produced its own set of dot points.[49]

- Ownership: Countries have more say over their development processes through wider participation in development policy formulation, stronger leadership on aid co-ordination and more use of country systems for aid delivery
- Inclusive partnerships: All partners—including donors in the OECD Development Assistance Committee and developing countries, as well as other donors, foundations, and civil society—participate fully
- Delivering results: Aid is focused on real and measurable impact on development
- Capacity development—to build the ability of countries to manage their own future.

Of the next set of policy dot points, the critical innovation is expressed in two words: civil society. Here was an attempt to mitigate the opinions of the local leader-for-life by adding the views of local civil society organizations to the recipe. We can call this the ownership to partnership path. It was an attempt to correct the moral hazard of passing ownership of the aid program to unelected and unresponsive receiving governments. But it was flawed. Civil society can only have influence in an open society and a functioning democracy. In an authoritarian setting, the donors would need to become the defenders of civil society interlocutors and seek out their views. Otherwise, receiving governments would simply conjure up government organized groups to parrot its views, and apply coercive measures to silence any genuine civil society groups.

In describing the ODA phenomenon, the term "artificial" was employed above. Having a group of basically Western-educated local individuals with a direct line to the donors' embassies under the hostile gaze of receiving governments, added to that artificiality. And this artificiality was highlighted in a counter argument proposed by receiving governments. They rejected the very idea of donor programs, projects, and experts. The logic of ownership, they said, was to give us what we want—cash! ODA thus started moving towards general budget support under certain conditions of use and accountability. One estimate has it that, for several African governments, general budget support contributes up to 40% of the government budget.[50]

Ironically, this is what most taxpayers thought was happening all along, as in the Randy Newman song "Political Science":

We give them money but are they grateful?
No, they're spiteful and they're hateful
They don't respect us so let's surprise them
We'll drop the big one and pulverize them.

In a previous book, I advocated for a completely different system.[51] A review of that book argued that the proposal "should provoke further scholarly discussions."[52] In the hope of achieving this outcome, I will burden readers with it.

Twenty-first century aid needs to break free from its current Westphalian and *dirigiste* paradigms. Twenty-first century aid needs to move away from the government-to-government bottlenecks. Twenty-first century aid needs to help build societies from the bottom up instead of from the top down. Twenty-first century aid needs to be democratized to allow a flow of ODA to the private sector and to civil society in addition to a modest proportion for governments. It needs to invest in people—in the form of entrepreneurs, innovators, designers, risk-takers, civil society activists, consumer activists, environmental activists, public intellectuals, students, and others—who will bring about organic and sustainable economic and social development.

It is part of the current ODA planning and coordination philosophy that there be a host of experts at the giving and receiving ends of the process. If ODA were a success and countries were clearly benefiting from the process, the jobs of those experts would be justified. But ODA is not a success, it continues to be an incoherent mess. Those jobs are not justified and the bottlenecks at the giving and receiving ends should be swept away. This may sound like a radical approach, but the tools for achieving this result have already been invented and are already in use; it is simply a matter of scaling them up. The existing tools are civil society activism, corporate social responsibility and, critically, tax deductibility. So, allow civil society organizations, businesses, and individuals from the wealthy countries to give directly to civil society organizations, businesses, and individuals in the poor countries, and allow them to claim it as a tax deduction. This creates a type of ODA market. The money never passes through government hands at either end.

There would still be a place for government-to-government ODA, but it would be much diminished and would probably take the form of budget support. The job of the government of the wealthy country in the new scheme is to devise and police tax rules defining which contributions are tax deductible. That is what governments do well. Turning Dahomey into Denmark is beyond them. What is the job of the governments in the poor countries? It is to campaign and get elected, provide services including the rule of law, collect taxes fairly, and have infrastructure constructed as required by the people. The people would have the central role in legitimizing governments through elections and funding governments through taxation. This role is currently being played by ODA to poor reviews.

How would ODA be measured in the future? By adding whatever transfers in the form of budget support to the *tax foregone*, due to the deductions allowed for private and corporate transfers to aid eligible countries. It is the tax foregone by governments, by allowing these deductions, that makes it *official* development assistance.

Would this new method of delivering aid directly from people to people lead to a reduction in ODA? If governments were simply to commit to maintaining ODA at current levels but counting part of it as tax foregone, the amount of actual transfers will be considerably greater than at present. The following simplified example based on US ODA demonstrates the effect of this method. Assuming an effective tax rate of one third of income, it would take three times the amount of financial flows claimed as tax deductions to generate the amount of tax foregone claimed as ODA. Assuming US ODA is $10 billion, and assuming, generously, that half of it will be channeled by USAID in government-to-government flows. The remaining $5 billion in ODA as tax foregone will need to be generated by $15 billion in tax deductible aid flows. The ODA remains at $10 billion, but the aid flows from the US will then be $20 billion, a doubling of current flows and far better directed at the bottom of the pyramid.

I will not torture the evidence to portray the current system of development and development assistance as Hobbesian. It is not a war of all against all. It is not anarchy. But it is almost as bad because the best term to describe the situation remains "incoherent." From the perspective of the bottom of the pyramid, the difference between anarchy and incoherence is academic—the people at the bottom experience the same capriciousness, unpredictability, and unfairness. With government-led development, they do not obtain the benefits of the supposed planning, but they feel the lash of the enforcement. From the perspective of donor governments, they are the guinea pigs in wave after wave of experiment and fashion. From the actions of the receiving governments, they are the victims of corruption and oppression. Whether the current plight flows from anarchy or incoherence, the world needs a UN Leviathan to step in.

## WHAT IS THE ROLE OF THE UNITED NATIONS LEVIATHAN?

What does the UN do well, and what does it do not so well? The answer to the second part is easy: the UN is not good at project delivery. It is slow, cumbersome, bureaucratic and risk averse. UN people prefer talking to doing.

UN people are afraid of the governments at both ends of the ODA spectrum making them timid deliverers. The UN should get out of the project delivery game. In relation to projects, the UN is good at convening, brand sharing and, occasionally, flak catching on behalf of the risk takers on the ground. The UN should concentrate on these roles.

In answer to the first part of the question, one would have to say that the UN has been good at proclaiming, ratifying, and propagating normative ideas like the UN Declaration on Human Rights or the Human Development Index. That is what the UN's principal role should be; to declare and make known universal moral principles. A UN with moral authority, borne from independence and competence, speaking for "we the peoples" and not for governments, and based on agreement between the three chambers of the UN, would be perfect for that role.

That moral authority would underwrite the shift from government-centric development to people-centric development. Xi Jinping (no doubt remaining in power a decade or two from now) may still wish to parachute doubtful infrastructure projects along with his authoritarian model on poor countries, but it would not have the support of the UN. And this may cause people in those countries to question the process further and perhaps even cause their governments to pause before jumping on board with Xi. The UN should have opinions on the best development models. It has already taken a huge step in this regard by championing the concept of human development and the Human Rights–Based Approach to development. Today's UN would not dare pronounce on the Xi model because it fears China and lacks the independence and moral authority to take a stand. This must change.

The weapon at the disposal of a moral authority is that of naming and shaming. The effectiveness of this tactic is proportionate to the moral authority of the wielder. The UN already wields this weapon. The Human Development Index is a form of naming poorly performing governments. The World Bank has dozens of indexes of governance performance. The UN Intergovernmental Panel on Climate Change lists carbon emissions by country. The naming already takes place in certain limited settings, but the shaming is only implied because the UN lacks the courage and moral authority to draw the necessary conclusions. The UN Leviathan would not be so obsequious.

The UN Leviathan should also be prominent in calling for the direction of aid to be directed where it will do the most good. It will come as little surprise that the strongest indicator of the direction of bilateral ODA is whether there was a preexisting colonial relationship.[53] Understandable though this may be, given the linguistic, migration and business links, it is not a rational basis for the direction of ODA. This is where a Leviathan should step in and point to the needs of the least developed countries and the merits of directing ODA to countries with the best conditions for its effective use. The UN might currently provide a forum for such discussions, but it dares not take a position.

Finally, if the people-to-people method of disbursing ODA were to be accepted, there would be a need for bundlers of financial assistance. The new aid market needs information, and the bundlers would provide it. There would be bundlers at the donor end, probably being or replicating the existing civil society organizations focusing on development. And there would be a need for bundlers at the receiving end, probably again comprising local civil society groups and academics. There may even be bundlers who act to link individuals from both ends. Kivu International, through which individual investors in the global North can finance individual entrepreneurs in the global South, is an example.[54]

The UN would have a critical role as a forum for such ventures and as an evaluator of their effectiveness. Those roles could be delegated with care. The idea being that the UN brand would be used to build confidence in the system and the individuals and organizations playing important roles. The UN would not be a Leviathan by the sword, but a Leviathan by the judicious use of its brand.

## NOTES

1. UN General Assembly resolution of 25 September 2015, A/RES/70/1 - Transforming our world: the 2030 Agenda for Sustainable Development, para 3.

2. UN Development Group, *A Million Voices: The World We Want*, 11 September 2013, https://www.undp.org/publications/million-voices-world-we-want

3. Elham Seyedsayamdost, "MDG-based National Planning: An Assessment," 2015, https://oxfamblogs.org/fp2p/wp-content/uploads/2015/07/MDG-Assessment_ES.pdf

4. Roland Rich, book review of William Easterly, *The Tyranny of Experts: Economists, Dictators, and the Forgotten Rights of the Poor* (New York: Basic Books, 2013), *Population and Development Review*, 40(3): 559–572 (September 2014).

5. Gunnar Myrdal, "Development and Under-development: A Note on the Mechanism of National and International Economic Inequality," (Cairo: National Bank of Egypt, 1956), 63.

6. Paul Hopper, *Understanding Development*, (New York: Polity Press, 2012), 4.

7. William Easterly, *The Tyranny of Experts; Economists, Dictators and the Forgotten Rights of the Poor*, (New York: Basic Books, 2013), 88–89.

8. Ibid., 95.

9. It was unfairly brought back to life by Margaret Thatcher to justify market absolutism.

10. Basainey E. Jammeh, "The Post-War Economic Miracle in West Germany," (Berlin: Hochschule für Technik, 2009), 7.

11. P. Waller, "Aid and Conditionality," *D+C Development and Cooperation* 1(January–February 1994), 4–5.

12. An interesting source is a CIA document entitled "USSR: Role of the State Planning Committee" prepared at the request of Alan Greenspan in 1975, a version of which was released to the public in 1998, https://www.cia.gov/library/readingroom/docs/DOC_0000308042.pdf

13. Easterly, op. cit., 98–101.

14. The term was crafted in 1982 by Chalmers Johnson in *MITI and the Japanese Miracle: The Growth of Industrial Policy 1925–1975*, (Stanford University Press, 1982).

15. Nguyen Vu Tung, "Vietnam's Membership of ASEAN: A Constructivist Interpretation." *Contemporary Southeast Asia: A Journal of International and Strategic Affairs*, Volume 29, Number 3, December 2007, 483–505.

16. Adam Hochschild, *King Leopold's Ghost: A Story of Greed, Terror, and Heroism in Colonial Africa*, (New York: Mariner Books, 1999).

17. John-Thor Dahlburg, "Mobutu lost his power - but not his wealth," *Deseret News*, May 17, 1997, https://www.deseret.com/1997/5/17/19312407/mobutu-lost-his-power-but-not-his-wealth

18. Michael Kavanagh and Dan McCarey, "All the President's Wealth: The Kabila Family Business," *The Pulitzer Center*, July 20, 2017, https://pulitzercenter.org/reporting/all-presidents-wealth-kabila-family-business

19. Peter Watson, *The Great Divide: Nature and Human Nature in the Old World and the New*, (New York: Harper, 2013).

20. Jared Diamond, *Guns, Germs and Steel: The Fates of Human Societies*, (New York: Norton, 1999).

21. Chris Carey, "The Puzzles of Thermopylae," *History Today*, 10 October 2019.

22. Watson, op. cit., 490.

23. Ibid, 527.

24. Georgetown University, "Indigenous Peoples, Democracy and Political Participation," https://pdba.georgetown.edu/IndigenousPeoples/demographics.html

25. Julien Chaisse and Mitsuo Matsushita, "China's 'Belt and Road' Initiative: Mapping the World Trade Normative and Strategic Implications," *Journal of World Trade* 52, no. 1 (2018), 163–186.

26. Nick Routley, "Meet China's 113 Cities with More Than One Million People," *Visual Capitalist*, February 6, 2020, https://www.visualcapitalist.com/chinas-113-cities-one-million-people-population/

27. Edward Wong, "China Admits Building Flaws in Quake," *New York Times*, Sept. 4, 2008.

28. Ibid.

29. William Easterly, "The Ghost of Financing Gap: How the Harrod-Domar Growth Model Still Haunts Development Economics," *World Bank Policy Research Working Paper No. 1807*, (July 1997).

30. Ibid., 8.

31. Ibid., 25.

32. Jagdish Bhagwati, *The Economics of Underdeveloped Countries*, (London: Weidenfeld & Nicholson 1966).

33. Jagdish Bhagwati, "The New Thinking on Development," *Journal of Democracy* 6.4, (1995) 50–64.

34. Ted Wachtel, "Governance and the use of authority: encompassing diverse definitions of 'Restorative'," *European Forum for Restorative Justice*, September 2016 Newsletter Volume 17(3), 7–9, 8.

35. Kéba Mbaye, "Le Droit du Developpement comme un Droit de l'Homme," *Revue de Droit de l'Homme* 5, 503–534, 1972.

36. Roland Rich, "The Right to Development as an Emerging Human Right," *Virginia Journal of International Law* 23, No. 2 (Winter 1983): 287–328.

37. Karel Vasak, "A30-Year struggle The sustained efforts to give force of law to the Universal Declaration of Human Rights," *UNESCO Courier*, XXX 11, 28–32.

38. Roland Rich, 'The Right to Development: A Right of Peoples?' James Crawford (ed.), *The Rights of Peoples*, (Oxford University Press), 1988, pp. 39–54.

39. See Stephen Marks and Rajeev Malhotra, "The future of the right to development," Harvard University monograph, https://cdn1.sph.harvard.edu/wp-content/uploads/sites/134/2018/06/Marks-Malhotra-The-Future-of-the-Right-to-Development-2017.pdf

40. Arjun Sengupta, "On the Theory and Practice of the Right to Development," *Human Rights Quarterly* (2002) 24.4, 837–856, 876–889.

41. Human Rights Council of Australia, "The Rights Way to Development: A Human Rights Approach to Development Assistance," HRCA, Sydney, 1995.

42. Andre Frankovits, "Rules to Live by: The Human Rights Approach to Development," *PRAXIS The Fletcher Journal of Development Studies*, Volume XVII, 2002, 9–17, 16.

43. United Nations Development Programme, "A Human Rights-based Approach to Development: Programming in UNDP—Adding the Missing Link" Nov 11, 2015, 2.

44. Bård A. Andreassen and Gordon Crawford, *Human Rights, Power and Civic Action: Comparative analyses of struggles for rights in developing countries*, (Oxford: Routledge, 2013) 2.

45. Peter Uvin, "On High Moral Ground: The Incorporation of Human Rights by the Development Enterprise," *PRAXIS The Fletcher Journal of Development Studies* Volume XVII, 2002, 1–11.

46. Amartya Sen, *Development as Freedom*, (New York: Anchor Books, 1999).

47. United Nations Development Programme, "Arab Human Development Report 2004," http://hdr.undp.org/en/content/arab-human-development-report-2004

48. Organisation for Economic Cooperation and Development, Paris Declaration and Accra Agenda for Action, https://www.oecd.org/dac/effectiveness/parisdeclarationandaccraagendaforaction.htm

49. Ibid.

50. Andrew Lawson, David Booth, Meleki Msuya, Samuel Wangwe, and Tim Williamson, "Does General Budget Support Work? Evidence from Tanzania," in *Budget Support as More Effective Aid? Recent Experiences and Emerging Lessons*,

eds. Stefan Koeberle, Zoran Stavreski, and Jan Walliser, (Washington: World Bank publication, 2006) 121–138, 121.

51. Roland Rich, *Democracy in Crisis: Why, Where, How to Respond*, (Boulder: Lynne Rienner Publishers, 2017), 171–186.

52. Aurel Croissant (2019), book review of "Democracy in crisis. Why, where, how to respond," *Democratization*, 26:7, 1325–1327, 1327.

53. Peter Nunnenkamp, Gustavo Canavire-Bacarreza and Luis Triveño, "Targeting aid to the needy and deserving: nothing but promises?," *Kiel Institute for the World Economy Working Papers* No. 1229, 2004.

54. Kivu International, http://www.kivu-international.org/

# *Chapter 8*

# Governing Globalization

That we are living in the era of globalization has become axiomatic. But beyond this accepted observation, just about everything else concerning globalization is contested. Is it a new phenomenon or a continuation of previous forces? Is it spatial, social or both? Is it a single occurrence or the sum of many syndromes, synergies or scapes? Ultimately, there is the question over which nobody is permitted to be neutral—is it good or bad?

This chapter will grapple with some of these questions, not because this book is intended to definitively answer them, far from it, but because the questions are germane to one of the broader questions with which this book is engaged; how can globalization be governed? The underlying thesis of the chapter is that globalization needs governance. The basic conclusion of the chapter is that the world needs a Leviathan to provide and facilitate that governance. The aspiration is that the United Nations, as reconceived in this book, can mold itself into that provider of governance.

## WHAT IS GLOBALIZATION?

I am attracted to the clarity of the Anthony Giddens definition of globalization as "the intensification of worldwide social relations which link distant localities in such a way that local happenings are shaped by events occurring miles away and vice versa."[1] This was perhaps cast in even more parsimonious form by Marshall McLuhan when he coined the intelligent oxymoron "the global village."[2] The Giddens definition is both social and spatial, factors also implied in the McLuhan term. But these ideas come from the late twentieth century. By the dawn of the twenty-first century, it was clear that another dimension needed to be added: velocity! Hence, David Held defines globalization as "the widening, deepening and speeding up of worldwide interconnectedness in all aspects of contemporary social life, from the cultural to the criminal, the financial to the spiritual."[3]

It is a conceit of every age that it believes the phenomena it is witnessing are unprecedented. Some believe this is the case with globalization. But A. G. Hopkins has demonstrated quite convincingly that there have been previous globalization phases.[4] There have been various archaic forms of globalization associated with conquerors and explorers; Muslim globalization based on a lunar calendar that every devotee could easily interpret without the assistance of clergy; European plantation colonialism in the New World based on African slaves and appealing to European greed and taste buds; and gilded age globalization which only came to an end with WWI. The current age of globalization may be broader, deeper, and faster, but it picks up where its predecessors left off.

## UNITED NATIONS–BASED GLOBAL GOVERNANCE

It would be wrong to view today's globalization as taking place within global disorder. Globalization is primarily a win-win phenomenon and its participants have long realized that to maintain that quality, there is a need for some ground rules. Many of these ground rules have "become part of the furniture" and we look straight past them and take them for granted. When we shop, we do not see the elaborate rules governing the maritime transport of these goods. When we fly, we do not think of the many international rules to assure our safety. When we read a book, we may not realize the need for global rules necessary to protect the rights of the author. The United Nations is the premier institution to house these rules. The following allows for a glimpse at the range of UN rules in place:

- The *International Labor Organization* has adopted 189 Conventions dealing with fundamental rights concerning the right of labor to organize; the abolition of forced labor; minimum age requirements; proscriptions on the worst forms of child labor; and the right to equal remuneration.
- The *international human rights regime* which has nine major treaties dealing with civil and political rights; economic, social and cultural rights; racial discrimination; discrimination against women; rights of the child; prohibition on torture; rights of disabled people; protection against enforced disappearance; and the rights of migrant workers. It also has established an elaborate enforcement regime involving oversight committees, reporting obligations, special rapporteurs, and independent investigations.
- The *International Maritime Organization* has adopted numerous basic conventions concerning safety of life at sea, prevention of pollution from ships, prevention of collisions at sea, maritime search and rescue,

prevention of marine pollution by dumping of wastes, civil liability for oil pollution, the carriage of hazardous substances by sea, and the removal of wrecks.

- The *World Intellectual Property Organization* has dozens of conventions protecting all forms of intellectual property including trademarks and patents and the intellectual property of authors, performers, and artists.
- The *International Civil Aviation Organization* has some 25 conventions regulating all aspects of air transport and dozens of protocols to keep them up to date.
- The *UN Educational, Scientific and Cultural Organization* has adopted dozens of instruments globally and regionally protecting natural and cultural heritage; recognizing the international equivalence of educational qualifications; proscribing discrimination in education; as well as the International Convention against Doping in Sport.
- The standard-setting work of the *World Health Organization* coordinates responses to pandemics and its significant achievements include reducing the spread of communicable diseases, improving maternal and child health, and strengthening national health systems in the global South.
- The *World Meteorological Organization* focuses on weather and climate, and manages the Framework Convention on Climate Change with support from the *UN Environment Program*.
- The *World Trade Organization* is the forum for developing the rules of open trade and settling disputes about those rules, assisted by the research of the *UN Conference on Trade and Development* and the good offices of the *UN Centre for International Trade Law*.
- The *International Atomic Energy Agency* promotes the safe, secure, and peaceful use of nuclear technologies through treaties such as the Convention on Nuclear Safety and the Convention on the Physical Protection of Nuclear Material.
- The *Food and Agricultural Organization*, the *UN Office on Drugs and Crime* and other agencies perform indispensable tasks for the international community by setting norms and standards, and thereafter overseeing compliance.

There are other intergovernmental organizations that contribute to this work like the Organisation for Economic Cooperation and Development and the International Energy Agency, but the striking aspect of the existing set of global rules is the central role of the United Nations, to which the Bretton Woods institutions should be added. Most of these rules and norms are established in binding UN treaty form. Most of the treaties are routinely respected because it is in everybody's interests to do so. And, even though some of the human rights treaties may be far too often respected in the breach, it does not lessen the status of the rules as law. This is true of any body of law. International law is at times compared unfavorably with national legal systems because the latter has police enforcement. Yet if one were able to measure routine compliance rather than breach, international law would not compare unfavorably. Even police enforcement does not ensure that laws are respected. This is sadly true of the crime of rape, concerning which, fewer than one percent of perpetrators of sexual assaults are eventually convicted.[5] Weak enforcement does not lessen the status of rape as a crime. Nor do occasional lapses in enforcement reduce the status of international law as law.

Managing this vast array of rules and supporting mechanisms is one of the roles that sets the UN apart qualitatively from the League of Nations which had quite limited reach. It tells us that the UN has the vocation to manage and govern the globalization process, though perhaps not the ambition to go beyond the lowest common denominator benefits flowing to states. A UN Leviathan needs to be at the apex of the governance of globalization and to do so, it needs to further its capacities and ambitions.

Some trace the beginning of the current globalization era to the turn of the millennium,[6] but even at that point, the process had advanced to a significant degree. The International Telecommunication Union, founded in 1865, was the world's first international organization established by a multilateral treaty, followed by the Universal Postal Union in 1874. By the year 2000, there were 2,000 such organizations and 30,000 treaties in force.[7] They provide a good metric of the growth of globalization. Since the turn of the millennium, the numbers in both categories have continued to grow and the UN continues to play its role at the apex of many such systems, but another category has grown even more quickly—oversight regimes involving officials of national governments as well as non-governmental bodies such as civil society organizations and businesses.

## OTHER GOVERNANCE REGIMES

Following in part the taxonomy utilized in the groundbreaking Hale and Held *Handbook of Transnational Governance*,[8] this section will examine transgovernmental networks; multi-stakeholder initiatives; and voluntary codes by business and civil society. The UN may have greater or lesser involvement with some of these structures, but they are not, for the most part, formal parts of the UN architecture. The key point about these structures is that they respond to a need for governance which is not provided by the market-based processes of globalization. They represent interests and provide expertise which governments often prefer to engage with primarily within the domestic sphere. They may complement, contest, or even supplant the traditional role of governments on the international plane. As an organization of governments, the UN is often conflicted as to its relationship with transnational actors outside the bounds of its own architecture. Its inclination is to engage, but its subservience to governments can often override this willingness. The purpose of this section is to examine examples of these structures and analyze their effectiveness, to determine if some further step might be required.

While the Hale and Held taxonomy is useful, it is important to bear in mind the Venn diagram nature of these categories. They are certainly not watertight, and arguments can be made to move one institution or another into a different category. But our Aristotelian heritage requires categorization for better comprehension. Hence, even within the main categories, certain sub-categories may be of analytical interest.

## Trangovernmental Networks

Before turning to some examples of transgovernmental networks, a distinction is required between:

- Bodies practicing summitry or other forms of meetings at leadership levels between nations, such as the Group of 7 (G7) and the G20. This form of summitry has limited participation and tends to meet at regular intervals. Summitry meetings are managed by the participants, either through the host as in G7 meetings or through troika arrangements as in G20; and
- Standing bodies with defined terms of reference, which
  - may either be broad and general international organisations with physical headquarters and powerful Secretariats such as the Organisation for Economic Cooperation and Development (OECD) or the International Institute for Democracy and Electoral Assistance (IDEA); or
  - organisations, reviewed below, with a narrower and more technical focus and drawing authority from governments because they represent parts of governments such as the Financial Action Task Force (FATF) or because they have been delegated or contracted to act in ways governments accept, such as the International Accounting Standards Board (IASB) or, initially, the Internet Corporation for Assigned Names and Numbers (ICANN) respectively.

The following does not provide anything like a full explanation of the work of these bodies, nor is the list comprehensive. The underlying question concerns their effectiveness in governing aspects of globalization.

### *Financial Action Task Force*

The FATF was born in 1989 to combat money laundering flowing from illegal trafficking in narcotics and thus owes its existence to the 1988 UN Convention against Illicit Traffic in Narcotic Drugs and Psychotropic Substances, an international cooperation contribution to the ill-conceived "war against drugs." The FATF received a renewed relevance through its role in combatting terrorist financing and it has become the front-line organisation implementing the targeted financial sanctions regimes flowing from UN Security Council Resolutions relating to the prevention and suppression of terrorism and terrorist financing, such as UNSCR 1267 (1999) targeting the Taliban, and its successor resolutions, and UNSCR 1373 (2001) directed against Al-Qaeda. While FATF had attempted various enforcement processes in the past, such as peer reviews and "name and shame" publicity, its current powers flow from the authority of the UN Security Council under Chapter VII of the UN Charter. It also has "soft" normative powers through its widely respected 40+9 recommendations for best practice regimes in the fields of combatting money laundering and terrorist financing.

The FATF has 39 members including two regional groups, the Commission of the European Union and the Gulf Cooperation Council, as well as numerous observers including several UN bodies. Its membership criteria focus on size and significance of the economy and the quality of the applicant nation's financial regulation regime.[9]

The FATF is effective because of its powers of compliance, its recognized expertise, and its relative legitimacy due to its UN connection and its narrow but non-discriminatory (apart from size and wealth) membership criteria.

### *Basel Committee on Banking Supervision*

The BCBS is a committee comprising national banking supervisory bodies and aims to improve the quality of banking supervision worldwide. It is housed within the Bank for International Settlements in Basel. Beginning in 1974 with a narrower trilateral base, in 2009 it became an informal sub-group of the G20 with Hong Kong and Singapore also joining. By establishing basic banking regulatory standards for the twenty largest economies, it has in effect become the global standard setting body as other countries have little option but to follow suit. It operates with a small Secretariat and its meetings are closed though it also has a program of engagement and consultation with outside entities.[10]

Given its close links with the banking fraternity, the BCBS has been criticized as an example of "regulatory capture."[11] While the link with the G20 has allowed several developing countries to join its ranks, the BCBS also suffers from an impression that it is exclusive and closed, thus limiting its legitimacy, and denting its effectiveness. The UN Monterrey Consensus has called for it to extend its membership.[12]

### *Financial Stability Board*

The Financial Stability Forum (FSF) was established as a response to the Asian Financial Crisis of 1997/98. It began as a forum for key financial regulators to meet and discuss risk issues. The regulators came from the major economies as well as from international bodies such as the International Monetary Fund and other transnational regulatory bodies. As a forum, the body could discuss issues and even reach consensus views, but it had no regulatory function. The 2008/09 global financial crisis led to a reassessment, the forum was reconceived as a Board (FSB) and membership was realigned to parallel the G20. But the work of the FSB continued to be discursive and based on consensus. This becomes clear from its mandate which has verbs like assess, monitor, promote and collaborate.[13]

The FSB exists in a capitalist Westphalian context in which national authorities are primarily focused on national advancement and are thus "unlikely to rein in the speculative practices of private financial institutions where there are arbitrage opportunities to exploit within the unclear lines of national accountability."[14] Its effectiveness is compromised from the outset by its limited mandate, its exclusivity, and its tenuous legitimacy.

### *Global Forum on Transparency and Exchange of Information for Tax Purposes*

The GFTEITP, the world's least memorable acronym and therefore henceforth referred to as the Global Forum, was formed by the OECD in 2000 to tackle transnational tax evasion. It is primarily seen as a problem for OECD countries, but it is estimated that over six trillion dollars are held offshore by wealthy individuals from developing nations leading to a loss of tax revenue similar to the total amount received by those countries in official development assistance.[15]

While the Forum is a useful innovation for exchange of information among members of the OECD, one of its main challenges is to recruit support from outside that organization given the prevalence of developing countries among the world's tax havens. The G20's strong endorsement of the work of the Forum was a major step in enhancing its legitimacy beyond the OECD. In 2010, the OECD amended its Convention on Mutual Administrative Assistance in Tax Matters to make it open to all jurisdictions. The publication of the Panama Papers in 2016 added to the urgency for action according to the then OECD Secretary-General.[16] As of 2021, 137 jurisdictions participate in the Convention.

The Global Forum had its most significant achievement with the announcement in 2021 that those 137 jurisdictions had agreed to the 15% minimum corporate tax concept.[17] The Global Forum is an example of an institution that recognized both its strengths and its lack of legitimacy from the outset. Coming from the rich countries' club, the Global Forum had considerable muscle. But this limited provenance detracted from its attractiveness to the developing world. The G20 endorsement had a positive effect. And it should be noted that the issue of tax evasion was not on the UN agenda and nor did the UN Secretariat have the technical skills to manage such a process. The Panama Papers perhaps demonstrated more eloquently than any academic tome or political speech, the revenue cost to developing countries themselves, giving them an incentive to cooperate.

### *International Accounting Standards Board*

Accounting needs its own Esperanto without which it would be difficult to compare national and corporate accounts from country to country. The result is the International Financial Reporting Standards drafted and kept up to date by the International Accounting Standards Board.[18] The IASB is not an intergovernmental organization but a private company with headquarters in London and financial support from a charitable foundation registered in Delaware. That foundation has traditionally been funded by the Big Four accounting firms (Deloitte, E&Y, KPMG, PWC) though the funding base has since broadened. The International Financial Reporting Standards are used by 166 jurisdictions.[19]

This is an example of the delegation of state functions, the official setting of accounting standards, to the private sector. The fact that all the major global accounting firms participate enhances its expert status. The Anglo-American character of the Big Four has settled technical quarrels, for example between the use of the Anglo-American Fair Value method versus the Continental Historical Cost method of accounting, in favor of the former.[20] Its legitimacy comes from its undoubted expertise and the perception that the process is politically neutral. Contestation comes from within the industry and rarely from outside.[21]

### *International Organization for Standardization*

The International Organization for Standardization (usually referred to as ISO) is an intergovernmental organization, established at the same time as the creation of the UN and the Bretton Woods system, in which nearly all UN Member States are represented by their national standard setting bodies.

Many of the ISO standards are incorporated in national regulations.[22] Where national regulation is missing, the market pressures companies to meet the ISO standards. The standards have branched out to management and environmental issues. The main criticism of ISO is the subdued voice given to consumers and civil society.

### *Codex Alimentarius Commission*

The Codex Alimentarius Commission of state representatives was established in 1963 to implement the agreement between the Food and Agriculture Organization and the World Health Organization to set safety standards for trade in food. It was given additional weight as the basis for the binding phytosanitary rules by the World Trade Organization.[23] The main criticisms of Codex are that it is much more of an industry body than a consumer body, and that it is weighted heavily towards participation by countries of the global North than those of the global South.

### *International Competition Network*

The ICN is a community of interest comprising officials of national competition agencies and watchdogs. Accordingly, it is a like-minded club sharing problems and solutions but, given the growth in its membership, it has become more of a "self-disciplining transnational community."[24] Though only established in 2001 by a core group from thirteen countries, the ICN now comprises 132 members from 120 jurisdictions.[25] The ICN is not a regulatory body, but it has developed a "soft law" capacity by adopting best practices by broad consensus with holdouts being peer pressured and occasionally subject to "naming and shaming."[26]

The transition from club to soft law-making status has been facilitated by the ICN's qualities of openness, inclusivity, and informality. It is a virtual network with no headquarters, legal status or standing Secretariat. Its Steering Committee is self-perpetuating in that outgoing members appoint newcomers who are then approved by the general assembly. Yet, for all its positive qualities, the ICN continues to be dominated by the club of wealthy countries from which the original members came, a result created in part by the self-financing means of representation. The ICN has also come to accept that its soft law product will not necessarily translate into a global convergence of rules. Corporations may thus continue to engage in jurisdiction hopping. Two UN bodies, the World Trade Organisation and the UN Conference on Trade and Development, observe its proceedings.

### *International Conference on Harmonization of Technical Requirements for Pharmaceuticals for Human Use*

The ICH (we are thankful for acronymic mercies) is a transnational body that comprises regulators and industry associations from Europe, Japan and the United States. It provides guidance on how to evaluate new medicines. Since its inception, the ICH has been a success story because the three regulatory jurisdictions involved dominated world pharmaceutical innovation, development, and production. ICH guidelines enjoy authoritative status in the three regulatory jurisdictions and are often translated into national regulation. But, given the significance of these three jurisdictions in global pharmaceutical development and marketing, the ICH guidelines have broad influence in other countries.

The ICH's success has perhaps compromised its capacity to assimilate criticisms of its lack of accountability and transparency. As a body of regulators and industry insiders, it is set in its ways. For example, it was slow in responding to the criticisms coming from animal rights groups complaining about the massive use of animal subjects for testing, eventually leading to the implementation of the so-called 3Rs principles—replace, reduce, and refine—for the ethical use of animals in medicine testing.[27] It was also slow to respond to the needs of developing countries and it took a dramatic action by India to bring this matter to light. In 2014, India, working through the World Health Organization (the only UN observer to the ICH), blocked ICH harmonization efforts.[28] The underlying issue was the status of generic drugs, of which India is a major producer. The matter was ultimately resolved with both India and China now cooperating with the ICH.

### *Internet Corporation for Assigned Names and Numbers*

ICANN is an institutional descendent of the pioneers who first established the rules under which the Internet would operate. It is a not-for-profit corporation responsible for managing the Internet's Domain Name System. Unusually, ICANN initially held these responsibilities through a contract with the US Department of Commerce. Apart from a notion of founders' legitimacy, ICANN has a practical means of enforcement—it controls the root servers of the Internet.[29] ICANN can boast several decades of success and for many years sheltered behind the "it ain't broke" aphorism in relation to its governance. It may not be "broke," but it sure can be capricious, and sometimes even serendipitous. The tiny Micronesian island nation of Tuvalu was unaware that a committee halfway around the world was designating its Internet country name. Tunisia had already been assigned .tu, so Tuvalu was assigned .tv! The government of Tuvalu sold the rights to use this designation for $50m (a sum greater than its annual GDP).[30] The Federated States of Micronesia, another Pacific archipelagic nation, got in on the windfall when it was given the designation .fm.[31]

The United States government's "ownership" of the Internet was clearly untenable. The UN was the forum for complaints about this relationship which emerged at the World Summit on the Information Society (WSIS), a global multi-stakeholder forum co-organized by ITU, UNESCO, UNDP and UNCTAD. Some developing countries wanted the UN to take over ICANN's functions. ICANN transitioned in 2016 into a not-for-profit corporation sustained as a multi-stakeholder partnership and thus took the sting out of the original complaints of US control.[32]

## Multi-stakeholder Initiatives

The transition of ICANN from contractual legitimacy, as an agent of the United States government, to legitimacy based on a multi-stakeholder approach, requires some unpacking to understand the extent and significance of this new and unusual form of transnational governance.

The multi-stakeholder approach has its origins in the quest of civil society organisations to participate in the work of the UN as foreshadowed in Article 71 of the Charter. The UN implemented this provision grudgingly in the early decades and continues to place gatekeepers to limit civil society involvement (an issue discussed in chapter 3), but with the major conferences on the environment and food security in Stockholm 1972 and Rome 1976 respectively, the door was opened wider for civil society participation culminating in 30,000 people attending events at the Beijing Women's Conference in 1995.[33] The next step would be more formal participation as designated observers in meetings and conferences and, eventually, as partners in policy and project formulation and delivery.

Parallel to civil society engagement, came the philanthropists. Charity is what poor people do; philanthropy is for the super wealthy. The transition from charity to philanthropy was due to the size of the bequests by the American robber-barons of the late nineteenth century, perhaps to expiate their guilt for all the people they stepped on in accumulating their wealth. The first generation of philanthropists have household names like Rockefeller, Ford and Carnegie, and their eponymous foundations occasionally worked with the UN, including, of course, the Rockefeller gift of the 18 acres in Turtle Bay on which the UN Secretariat and conference buildings now stand. But the breakthrough came with a later generation of philanthropists and in particular, the 1998 decision by Ted Turner to give the UN one billion dollars through a tax-deductible eligible foundation that Kofi Annan, perhaps imprudently, gave permission to call itself the UN Foundation. Turner's example of working with the UN has been followed by others including the Gates Foundation (on which more will be said in chapter 11), George Soros' Open Society Foundations, and the Bloomberg Foundation. The philanthropic foundations have more than money. Their participation brings skills, contacts, and ideas that the UN lacks.

The final piece in the multi-stakeholder puzzle is participation by the business community. This is a book length topic and indeed, Bishop and Green have written just such a book.[34] It combines various concepts; that the brand is key to success and brands therefore need be made beloved; that corporate social responsibility requires corporations to have charitable arms; and the more recent concept that corporations must behave in socially responsible ways. One beneficiary has been the United Nations, itself a beloved brand in most parts of the world. The UN Office for Partnerships was involved in many examples of multi-stakeholder partnerships, such as that for the benefit of Haiti's mango farmers.

The story begins at Davos in 2010 where Bill Clinton, among other titles, the UN Special Envoy for Haiti, buttonholed Muhtar Kent, then CEO of Coca-Cola, to seek help for Haiti. It turns out that Haitian mango farmers produce a large crop but cannot find a sufficiently large domestic market. Apart from UNOP as convener, the project also involved UNDP on the ground to run interference with the authorities, and civil society groups to organize the mango farmers. Within a matter of months, the Coca-Cola bottling plant in Haiti was producing Haiti Hope mango juice based on an initial investment of $7.5m. None of the individual actors could have achieved this result working alone.[35] Some of my UN colleagues scoffed that Coca-Cola was only doing it to make money, to which I replied that the profitability of the enterprise is the only guarantee of sustainability for the Haitian farmers.

The following are examples of multi-stakeholder governance processes.

### *Global Fund to Fight AIDS, Tuberculosis and Malaria*

The Global Fund is a partnership designed to accelerate the end of AIDS, tuberculosis, and malaria as epidemics. As an international organization, the Global Fund mobilizes and invests more than US$4 billion a year to support programs run by local experts in more than 100 countries. It is a partnership of governments, civil society, technical agencies, the private sector, and people affected by the diseases.[36] It is the world's largest and most influential multi-stakeholder partnership.

The Fund's strength is its process of delivery by meritocratic competition through decentralized administration based on guidelines provided by the Fund. Its main weaknesses are the inevitable bureaucracy accompanying such a large fund and, more tellingly, the lack of capacity in local health systems (discussed further in chapter 11). The Fund has thus also focused on those health systems, but this brings it into the tenuous field of project aid.[37] An interesting innovation is that the Fund has a dedicated civil society oversight mechanism provided by a Kenya-based NGO, Aidspan.[38]

### *Global Polio Eradication Initiative*

The GPEI is a multi-stakeholder initiative, another name for which is a public-private partnership, led by national governments and the World Health Organization, Rotary International, the US Centers for Disease Control and Prevention, the United Nations Children's Fund, the Bill & Melinda Gates Foundation, and Gavi, the vaccine alliance. Its goal is to eradicate polio worldwide.[39] Eradication is a difficult goal, but it was achieved in the case of the successful eradication of smallpox which has been described as a gift from the twentieth century to the twenty-first.[40] The private aspect of the partnership is more than window dressing. Of the $16b spent from 1985–2019, private donors have contributed one third with the Gates Foundation providing 22% and Rotary International, an original member of the consortium, 11%.[41]

Governance of the Initiative is undertaken by the major donors who are a sufficiently small group so as not to have to formalize their arrangements beyond meeting quarterly as an Oversight Board.

### *The Framework Convention Alliance*

The FCA is a coalition of more than 350 civil society organisations formed to support the WHO's 2005 Framework Convention on Tobacco Control which is an evidence-based, legally binding treaty that does not focus on suppression of supply, like other drug policies, but on demand reduction. The FCA was formed in 1999 to strengthen civil society's voice in the negotiation process as "the public health conscience."[42] In this sense the civil society representatives are playing the classic role of watchdog while also contributing to the policy deliberations. By forming the Alliance, civil society not only strengthened its voice, but also simplified conference arrangements.

### *International Coral Reef Initiative*

The structure of ICRI reflects both a deep determination to arrest the degradation of coral reefs around the world, and a profound pessimism about the effectiveness of formal international action in doing so. There are already major UN agreements like the Biodiversity Convention, the Climate Change Convention and the Convention on International Trade in Endangered Species that should protect the world's coral reefs. But they have failed to do so. The damage to the reefs is caused by factors so complex that they are beyond simple legislative solutions. Accordingly, the burden has fallen on local and national governments and their multi-stakeholder allies to work as best they can, reef by reef.

Although coral reefs exist in some 100 countries, more than half the world's reefs are in Australia, Fiji, Indonesia, the Maldives, Papua New Guinea, and the Philippines.[43] Established in 1994, ICRI is a partnership of governments, international organisations, development banks, scientific institutions, and civil society groups. Partner countries take turns hosting the small ICRI Secretariat every two years. ICRI takes decisions on reef management, makes recommendations on various issues, and provides a forum for sharing scientific research. It behaves more like an advocacy group than an international governance mechanism. Various UN bodies cooperate with ICRI.

## United Nations Multi-Stakeholder Partnerships

Given the emergence of multi-stakeholder mechanisms as viable transnational policy and delivery vehicles, and given the participation by UN bodies in many such mechanisms, it is not surprising that the UN, under the leadership of then Secretary-General Ban Ki-moon, would launch four such initiatives. One is successful, the jury is still out on another, and two have clearly failed:

- Every Woman Every Child (EWEC) is an UN-based mechanism to mobilize international and national action by governments, multilateral bodies, the private sector, and civil society to address the major health challenges facing women, children, and adolescents around the world. More than $40 billion was pledged at its 2010 launch primarily by traditional donors, but this was bolstered by hundreds of pledges from groups, small and large, public and private, around the world. EWEC thus functions as a focused resource and coordination hub. It is administered by the UN Population Fund (UNFPA). It is governed by a high-level steering committee comprising senior UN officials, Ministers for development assistance, and representatives of philanthropic and civil society groups.
- The Sustainable Energy for All initiative (SEforALL) was launched in 2011 and its goals have become to support action toward achievement of: Sustainable Development Goal 7 which calls for universal access to sustainable energy by 2030; and the Paris Agreement, which calls for reducing greenhouse gas emissions to limit climate warming to below 2° Celsius.[44] It has been through turbulent leadership and structural changes eventually emerging as a separate international organization based in Vienna. Judged simply on the size of commitments ($14m to the end of 2016[45]), SEforALL can hardly be judged a success.[46] But the fact that

key donors would agree to transition this multi-stakeholder initiative into a new international organisation, argues in favor of its utility. The jury remains out.

- The five-year Global Education First Initiative (GEFI) was launched in 2012 to accelerate progress towards the Education for All goals.[47] It had a distinguished board of directors comprising senior UN officials and leading civil society activists including Bishop Tutu and Her Highness Sheikha Moza bint Nasser of Qatar. All we need to know about this initiative is that it was not renewed after its initial five-year span. One reason, no doubt, flows from UNESCO's perilous financial situation following the withdrawal of the United States.[48]
- The Zero Hunger Challenge (ZHC) launched in 2012, reflects five elements from within the SDGs, which taken together, can end hunger, eliminate all forms of malnutrition, and build inclusive and sustainable food systems. There have been no ZHC events since 2016.[49] The initiative was based at the Food and Agriculture Organization (FAO) in Rome, and it seems that in 2016 the ZHC was simply folded into the FAO's existing work plans and structures.

This is not what one would consider a Leviathan-like performance. One of the problems is based on personality. The four initiatives were identified with Ban Ki-moon and at least three of them seem to have lost their luster after the conclusion of his second term. The personalization of political initiatives is not an unknown phenomenon. But it points to organizational weakness because a basic test of any initiative should be its survival after a change in political leadership. Another problem endemic to UN bodies, except for the World Intellectual Property Organization which collects significant fees for service, is tenuous finances. Any new UN initiative must attract additional donor funding because the regular UN budgets are static or shrinking and, as noted in chapter 3, committed to national baubles on the UN Christmas tree. EWEC hit a sweet spot in existing donor priorities. SEforALL may yet survive its transition away from the UN. But neither UNESCO nor FAO could carry the multi-stakeholder initiatives bestowed on them by the then Secretary-General, and nor could they attract enough additional funding. For the UN to be the Leviathan needed by the international community, these factors would need to be dramatically altered. Finally, there was always a suspicion that the UN initiatives were packaged for presentational purposes more than substantive results. Ban Ki-moon had started his second term and was finally free of the structural stasis imposed on Secretaries-General in their first terms. He needed "announceables" to demonstrate his commitment and dynamism and these multi-stakeholder initiatives had the right timbre to them. Having been an insider at the time, I can vouch for the fact that the detailed planning processes involving the host UN agencies was insufficient.

## Voluntary Actions by Business and Civil Society

The foregoing examples concern initiatives to govern globalization in which governments are the initiators, principal actors or indispensable participants. Though extensive, these bodies do not cover the field. There is another set of initiatives to govern globalization springing, not from governments, but from business, investors, consumers, and civil society. These initiatives try to fill gaps left by the perceived inadequacy or limitations of governmental initiatives. They are quite numerous and therefore, instead of listing them comprehensively, it might be more enlightening to attempt a taxonomy based on their operating concept. While this taxonomy may be analytically helpful, it falls well short of establishing solid boundaries because the various initiatives tend to borrow aspects from the different operating models. But for the purpose of analysis, it may be useful to divide the voluntary initiatives between those that primarily use *standardization*, those that primarily use *accountability* and those that primarily use *transparency* as their key operating tool.

### *Standardization Initiatives*

The *Equator Principles* set standards for private financing of large infrastructure and development projects. They were initially devised in 2003 by ten big banks and have evolved to meet World Bank standards. As of 2020, 105 financial institutions in 38 countries have adopted the Equator Principles[50] which consider matters beyond risk management, such as environmental and social impacts, and do so with high technical specificity. Though bank led, civil society has a place in the deliberative process. Opinions differ on the effectiveness of this type of self-regulating standardization because of perceptions of conflicts of interest in a process ultimately reliant on reputational risk as the method of enforcement.[51]

Other bodies that produce voluntary guidelines based on self-enforcement are the *Global Reporting Initiative,*[52] the *Global Corporate Governance Principles*[53] and two initiatives to curb corruption, Transparency International's *Business Principles for Countering Bribery*[54] and the World Economic Forum's *Partnering Against Corruption Initiative.*[55] The provenance of these voluntary guidelines ranges from civil society, civil society in partnership with corporate actors, and business associations in cooperation with intergovernmental organizations. They produce and keep updated through a consultative process, sets of guidelines on actions ranging from environmental reporting to management practices. As with the Equator Principles, participation by industry actors ensures a high level of technical proficiency. Once again, enforcement is largely by market forces based on reputational risks with the involvement of civil society acting to encourage accuracy and earnestness. Unlike the products of the International Organisation for Standardization or Codex, these types of guidelines are unlikely to find their way into government regulations and thus will not be supported by state enforcement processes.

Examples of voluntary codes for labor relations initiated by civil society with some industry support, were the various *Clean Clothes Campaigns*.[56] Initiated in Sweden and the Netherlands, these campaigns attempted to require supply chain contractors in the global South to meet certain labor standards in clothes manufactured for major department stores and brands. Ultimately, however, they demonstrated the limitations of voluntary processes. There never was wide uptake by the retail sector leading to frustration at free rider problems. But there were also divisions among the proponents. Trade union representatives were concerned that the bargaining for labor rights was being conducted by civil society groups from the global North and not by the actual workers from the global South. Though intending to reach agreed ends, the initiatives fell apart over the question of means.

### *Accountability Initiatives*

The *Extractive Industries Transparency Initiative* is a classic accountability initiative initiated by civil society in a bid to combat the resource curse afflicting countries overly dependent on oil, gas, and mining revenues. It now encompasses 53 nations and many corporations including major oil companies like BP, Shell, and ExxonMobil.[57] The main tool employed is publication of accounts by both the producing country and the purchaser corporation. Enforcement is through suspension for being non-compliant. Ultimately, the price to be paid would be locally, in electoral terms, and internationally, in credit worthiness.

Another path-breaking accountability scheme is the *Kimberley Process* to combat the trafficking of blood diamonds. The role of blood diamonds in fueling conflicts was recognized by the UN Security Council in the cases of Angola, Liberia and Sierra Leone and its Sanctions Committee blamed the industry for facilitating the practice.[58] In response, key producer companies and countries, meeting in Kimberley, South Africa, devised a certification process to ensure diamonds were not from conflict zones. The certification process has reduced the percentage of conflict diamonds in world trade from as high as 15% to around 1%. Eighty-two countries participate in the process and the key criticism is that, given its self-regulating system, the process is only as strong as the weakest national link. Accusations have been made against countries like Israel, the United Arab Emirates and Zimbabwe for gaming the system.[59]

The US counterpart to the Clean Clothes Campaign was the anti-sweatshops campaign of the 1990s. It led to a more robust piece of architecture than was achieved by its Northern European counterparts in the form of the *Fair Labor Association*. The US market is big, and the initiative attracted key brands as well as universities which, as the breeding grounds for professional sports, have considerable brand power. It avoided doctrinal problems by adopting international standards and undertaking a regulatory role backed by the power to exclude non-compliant companies in the various supply chains.[60]

### *Transparency Initiatives*

Transparency is the main tool of voluntary governance mechanisms. Transparency figures in the standardization and accountability systems. It allows the market to work better. It provides the basis for rule of law actions. It informs the motives of investors, consumers, and voters. It is little wonder then, that many groups utilize this tool.

If a consumer wishes to be assured that the carpet she is about to purchase was not made by the nimble little fingers of child workers, she looks for the *Rugmark*[61] label (now known as GoodWeave International). If an ethical investor wishes to know about the carbon footprint of a particular company, he turns to the *Carbon Disclosure Project*.[62] If a furniture manufacturer wishes to ensure that her business uses only sustainably grown timber, she will look for certification from the *Forest Stewardship Council*.[63] And the same goes for the restaurateur who wishes to ensure that the fish served in his premises will not lead to the collapse of fish stocks—he will seek out the eco-label of the *Marine Stewardship Council*.[64] Even a big chemical company will want its customers to know it is following ecologically sound production and management procedures, so it will plaster its advertisements with the *ISO 14001* seal of good housekeeping. There are many more "eco," "fair" and "sustainable" labels.

When contracts and sales transactions are published under the Extractive Industries Transparency Initiative, there are specialized academic, media and civil society representatives on the lookout for them and armed with the knowledge to interpret them. But simple labelling has an inherently more difficult job in being effective; it must stand out in an ocean of information readily available to billions of people. The astute buyer may understand that the rug from India is guaranteed to be made without child labor by the Rugmark label, while the rug from Pakistan is not. But how astute are consumers? It is far more likely that they know the Woolmark logo, which has been aggressively marketed for decades to denote fine merino wool, than the Rugmark logo. Information regimes are excellent for the discerning, but of limited relevance to the mass market.

Apologies for the inordinate length of this section on governance regimes. The point being made is that globalization needs governance. The UN provides a shiny veneer of it and participates in many other governance activities. Civil servants, corporations and civil society try to fill the governance gap as best they can. They use the techniques of cooperation, standardization, and transparency to take the place of regulation. They do a fair job. But the harsh reality is that globalization remains, to a large extent, ungoverned. It remains the domain of all states against all, and all corporations against all, a Hobbesian world of competition and corruption, where the ultimate price is paid by the global commons.

## UNGOVERNED AREAS

The first ungoverned areas that spring to mind are territories where government has collapsed, where there is no Leviathan and hardly even an angel fish, though lots of sharks continue to prowl. The world was shocked when Somalia became an ungoverned social wilderness in the 1990s.[65] It has sadly been joined by others. Yemen now falls into this category as do parts of Afghanistan, Pakistan, Syria, and Congo (Kinshasa). Venezuela, Zimbabwe, and parts of the Sahel, as well as gang-infested parts of Central America are not far behind. Ungoverned areas are incubators of disease, lawlessness, and piracy. They provide the soft underbelly for evading effective governance of globalization.

But it is not even necessary to go to these failed and fragile states to find the physical gaps. The reality is that even in many states of the global South that have viable government structures, their reach is limited. They have limited state capacity, narrow rule of law systems, and no-go areas controlled by gangs or insurgents. And poverty is a limitation that insinuates itself into every point of weakness. Even where state capacities are adequate, state priorities may not be. Some East Asian tigers had authoritarian reach, but nevertheless claimed to be powerless to stop their nationals from ripping off intellectual property, though these problems pale next to China's rapaciousness. China's rise may be portrayed as peaceful insofar as no world war has yet broken out, but it was certainly not peaceful to its own air, soil, rivers, and groundwater.

In a world where sovereignty is the entry fee for power, what is to become of those areas, quaintly termed "beyond national jurisdiction?" They are in the unenviable position of being protected only by tenuous transnational regimes. Those transnational regimes, for all their good intentions and clever designs, are not preventing global warming, collapsed fish stocks, rising oceans, and air unsafe for children to breathe. The global commons are in effect ungoverned and unprotected areas.

The ungoverned areas go beyond the physical to the sectoral. The main tool for the exploitation of gaps in global governance beyond the physical, is described by economists employing the delicate term "arbitrage," which is the practice of taking advantage of a price difference between two or more markets. Not only are price differences exploited but also rule differences and tax differences. Arbitrage is the vehicle for the race to the bottom. The countries of the OECD are deeply concerned about tax havens mainly in the global South, but they regularly engage in undercutting each other's tax regimes by offering sweetheart deals to the biggest corporations.[66] The biggest corporations wrap themselves in whichever is the nearest national flag and then engage in transfer pricing to avoid, or at times evade, taxes. Arbitrage at the global level also involves finding jurisdictions with lax enforcement, finding politicians with lax ethics, and finding populations lacking options.

A treaty remains a treaty, a law remains a law and a regulation remains a regulation even if their means of enforcement is weak. But the weaker the enforcement regime, the less effective the treaty, law, or regulation. UN Treaties are regularly respected because they encapsulate areas of win-win agreement by states. But as soon as a state considers that its immediate interests are furthered by ignoring the treaty, it will often do so. The more difficult the compromise and the more distant the common good, the more likely that a state will be in breach.

This chapter has described dozens of transnational governance regimes that are not enshrined in treaties, that do not have the force of law and that are not backed by regulations. They are well-intentioned and some are well designed. But, for the most part, they are creations of those with wealth and with the luxury of expertise. They are creations of the global North, and though some have the blessing of the G20, they do not primarily represent the interests of the global South. There are transnational governance institutions in which industry has achieved regulatory capture and consumers are an afterthought. There are multi stakeholder regimes with catchy names but hollow substance. The term stakeholder is promiscuous, it will attach itself to nearly all claimants, often weakening the power and resolve of the resulting bloated body. And nearly all the mechanisms rely on transparency. But transparency only works where there is a democratic structure to protect speech and to encompass the resulting debate.

The result is vast ungoverned areas of economic activity. Congratulations to the Kimberley process for reducing conflict diamonds to only 1% of global trade, but in a $82 billion world market,[67] that is still $800 million available to fuel insurgency. Applause for the Marine Stewardship Council for its work in protecting fish stocks, but its labelling covers only 7% of the world fish catch.[68] And a hearty well done to the Forest Stewardship Council, but the reality is that it's labelling overwhelmingly covers temperate timber rather than tropical timber.[69]

What is missing from all the governance mechanisms is the presence of a Leviathan. Not in the form of a world government, which is a bridge too far. But in the form of a morally powerful United Nations. The Leviathan would significantly increase the cost of disrespecting treaties and laws. The approval of the Leviathan would make transgovernmental regimes more effective. The Leviathan would make information widely known and trusted thus providing a more solid foundation for regimes built on transparency. The UN Leviathan is the missing ingredient in governing globalization.

## THE SIGNIFICANCE OF GOVERNING GLOBALIZATION

Having discussed the "how" question, we come to the "why" question. Why is governing globalization so important? Yes, it is intrinsically important to have the common good as the aim of governance regimes. Yes, the global commons will finally catch a break. And yes, exploitation of individuals must be challenged. But beyond these "normal" reasons for governance, globalization must be governed for society's sake because it is increasing inequality in most parts of the world to the point of insurrection. And because it is beginning to undermine and unsettle our domestic politics.

### Globalization *Sauvage* is Fueling Inequality

In his magnificently researched 2017 book,[70] looking through eons of world history, Walter Scheidel argues that there were four transformative events that led to greater economic equality:

- Mass mobilization war
- Transformative revolution
- State collapse
- Pandemics

Scheidel was examining inequality within societies and his list of "cures" looks worse than the disease. But if we examine inequality between nations, there is another force at work leading to greater economic equality—globalization. This is the definitive conclusion of Branko Milanovic and his famous elephant curve.[71] Milanovic describes the process as "the greatest reshuffle in individual incomes since the industrial revolution."[72] It is a startling conclusion, but the evidence in favor is primarily generated by the growth of the middle class in two countries, China and India. The conclusion that globalization is leading to less inequality between nations is counter intuitive. The simple explanation, however, is to look at where these two nations began their ascent up the wealth ladder. China was emerging from decades of ruinous Maoism. India was mired in inefficient and anti-business bureaucracy sometimes called the "Licence Raj." These are great civilizations with enormous domestic markets and hundreds of millions of ambitious and educated citizens. Their departure from Maoism and bureaucratic domination coincided with the take-off of globalization, and they were on board that rocket ship. The greater global equality discerned by Milanovic, is simply the phenomenon of two countries using their extensive comparative advantages to catch up. It was not globalization *per se* that encouraged their greater equality with the wealthy world, it was China and India's just-in-time embrace of capitalism. It is a phenomenon limited in time and in circumstances; it is not a general rule.

If we wish to discern the general rule, we need to turn to the work of Thomas Piketty.[73] First, it is important to accept that globalization is not a distinctive and novel system, it is super charged capitalism on a global scale. It may not behave in exactly the same way as might capitalism in one country or another, because of variations in governance rules and systems as noted above in the discussion of arbitrage. But globalization has the same properties as capitalism, and similar strengths and weaknesses. Capitalism is a wealth creating system, as is its off-shoot globalization. That is its greatest strength. But capitalism and globalization alike, are indifferent to the human conditions in which that wealth is created, the resultant damage to the environment and the distribution of that wealth. These are considered irrelevant externalities.

In the domestic setting, it is the job of governments to deal with these externalities. Many governments are trying to improve the conditions of workers. Some governments are tackling the environmental damage caused by industry. Very few governments are engaged in wealth redistribution. Piketty's conclusion is that it is wealth that begets greater wealth, far more than does income. There is no reason to believe that this phenomenon does not apply to all capitalist countries. Indeed, the various measurements are showing growing inequality in just about every country. Governments do not have many tools at their disposal, but the one tool available to deal with this situation is taxation.

We are still living in the anti-tax world created by the Reagan/Thatcher market-as-guru philosophy. In Australia, we had an early preview of this world in the 1970s in a specific race to the bottom. Australia is a federation of six states and two territories, and in the 1970s, the premier of Queensland,

Joh Bjelke-Petersen, abolished death taxes to entice wealthy retirees to move to his sunny state.[74] Before long, all the other states and territories had little choice but to follow this example and no such tax exists in Australia to this day, though 19 out of 34 OECD members still have some form of estate duty on direct descendants.[75] The power of taxation is the only way to redress the inequality inevitably flowing from the discrepancies of inherited wealth. Piketty wishes to go beyond death taxes to institute a wealth tax. But he accepts that, given the mobility of money, a wealth tax in one country will simply lead to tax avoidance through wealth transfers to other countries. His startling conclusion: the wealthy countries of the world must band together to institute a common wealth tax!

Some countries in northern Europe have found a mix of policies to arrest the growth in inequality. Taxation, social safety nets and community solidarity are part of the mix. But they are the exceptions. A recent OECD report found that in 2012, the bottom 40% owned only 3% of total household wealth in the 18 OECD countries with comparable data. By contrast, the top 10% controlled half of all total household wealth and the wealthiest 1% owned 18%. "We have reached a tipping point. Inequality in OECD countries is at its highest since records began," said the then OECD Secretary-General Angel Gurría.[76] This is grist to the Piketty mill. But instead of adopting Piketty's suggestions, what we are seeing in many capitalist countries and especially in the United States is a type of capitalism *sauvage*, a Hobbesian form of capitalism. I use the French term because its English translation, wild, has lost its pejorative power. And because the only actor that can keep a check on capitalism *sauvage* is government, it follows that the global form of capitalism we are experiencing, with no global government and limited global governance, will only exacerbate inequality.

What we need is a Leviathan. Piketty's synchronized wealth tax needs a Leviathan. Governing globalization needs a Leviathan. Without the Leviathan, the environment will degenerate to a point near inhabitability. Without a Leviathan, arbitrage capitalism will race the world to the bottom. Without a Leviathan, inequality will continue to grow. If nothing is done about inequality, we will be left with a choice between Scheidel's tragic "cures."

## Globalization as the New Cleavage

All societies have divisions. When these divisions are expressed in consistent political choices, they are called cleavages. In the 1960s, Seymour Martin Lipset and Stein Rokkan described four basic political cleavages: center versus periphery; state versus church; rural versus urban; and owners versus workers or class cleavage.[77] These are not universal cleavages, they spring from the particularities of European history, including feudalism, the centuries long war between Christian sects, the Westphalian concepts centralizing power, and the industrial revolution leading to class divisions and the drift to the cities. Societies that have experienced different histories will have different cleavages. James Scott argues that the deepest cleavage in mainland Southeast Asia may be altitude-based, whereby the highland people resist the hegemony of the lowland rulers.[78] In India, caste may be the single greatest cleavage in politics, though religion is catching up under the influence of the Bhartiya Janata Party's Hindutva philosophy. In South Sudan, the civil war is fueled by a centuries-old tribal cleavage between the Dinka and the Nuer. And in South Korea, where it is difficult to discern linguistic, class or religious differences, geographic regions become the major molder of cleavages.

At a panel discussion at Rutgers, I was asked to speak about the political phenomenon in France known as the *gilets jaunes* (yellow vests) who had by then been protesting for a year. I decided to test the facts against the Lipset and Rokkan cleavages.

- Centre versus periphery: Many of the *gilets jaunes* demonstrators come from small towns and in fact, the trigger for the demonstrations was a carbon tax increase in petrol prices at a time when public transport to these small towns had been "rationalized." But this Lipset/Rokkan cleavage concerns restless regions like Scotland, Catalonia, or the Basque country. France has been centrally governed for a couple of millennia and there is no similar regional dynamic. So, this cleavage does not assist in understanding the *gilets jaunes*.
- State versus church: This is a cleavage between voters who turn to religion for political guidance and secular voters. France, however, is a deeply secular country, probably the most anti-religious nation in Europe. The church retains only small pockets of influence. It is probably not an overstatement to conclude that the only country in Europe that is still riven by this cleavage is Poland. A decade ago, Ireland may also have been included, but recent votes have demonstrated how Irish attitudes have become far closer to mainland Europe.
- Rural versus Urban: This may look initially like a relevant cleavage. But, as noted, most of the *gilets jaunes* are from small towns, not from the rural sector. France's farmers were bought off decades ago by exorbitant and inefficient subsidies known in Europe as the Common Agriculture Policy. Farmer protests occur occasionally in France, but they have a different look—dumping manure or releasing livestock in cities.
- Owner versus worker: the Marxist class cleavage is the key instigator for the formation of parties of the left and responding parties of the right. But the *gilets jaunes* protests did not involve the trade unions, the main voice of the workers. And although their vague demands had an

economic basis, it was directed less at the class enemy and more at the cosmopolitan elite.

The Lipset/Rokkan cleavages have held considerable sway in European political science. And the concepts are also relevant to the European settler societies though they become less acute the longer these societies have been politically independent. As noted, they have far less application outside these contexts. But even in Europe, it is becoming clear that half a century of political and economic change has left its mark on many aspects of politics, including the cleavages. There has been a process of dealignment as the classic cleavages lose their salience.[79] Yet the concept of cleavages remains relevant. There is a need, however, to identify new cleavages that explain today's voter behavior.

To find this new cleavage, we need to turn to the phenomenon of globalization. Political science is beginning to recognize the impact of globalization as the next key cleavage.[80] In relation to the *gilets jaunes*, one explanation comes from the French demographer Christophe Guilluy.[81] A process he calls *métropolisation*, has cut French society in two. Sixteen dynamic urban areas (Paris, Lyon, Marseille, Aix-en-Provence, Toulouse, Lille, Bordeaux, Nice, Nantes, Strasbourg, Grenoble, Rennes, Rouen, Toulon, Douai-Lens, and Montpellier) are home to all the country's major educational and financial institutions, as well as almost all its corporations and all the well-paying jobs that go with them. In these places, the economy is functioning well because it is plugged into the rest of the world. Traditional workers have largely been exiled from these spaces. The *gilets jaunes* resent this process and their protest is about having surreptitiously become second class economic citizens. They blame the cosmopolitan elites from the dynamic urban areas. In other words, they cast globalization as their enemy.

In their 2014 paper, de Wilde et al. debate whether this phenomenon can yet be said to be discernable outside continental Europe. I would argue that both the 2016 Brexit and Trump votes can largely be explained as votes against the cosmopolitan elites and votes against this group's pet project, globalization. I believe we can describe the new cleavage as dividing those who perceive they benefit, directly or indirectly, from globalization, and those who perceive they do not. The only plausible response is to govern globalization so as to soften its negative impacts. Otherwise, it will become the key cleavage and roil the democratic politics of the global North for years to come.

## GLOBALIZATION NEEDS GOVERNANCE

The major conclusion of this chapter is summarized in its title, globalization needs governance. It remains largely ungoverned, yet the need for governance is eloquently expressed by the many dozens of ways partial governance regimes have been constructed, or perhaps cobbled together, at times by governments and at other times by voluntary actors. The next inevitable conclusion is that, for global governance to work, a Leviathan must step up.

As noted in this book, a twenty-first century global Leviathan does not resemble Hobbes's seventeenth century national version. It is not the Weberian monopoly on the use of force that endows the Leviathan with power. It is moral authority, popular acceptance, and effective performance. But if it is not to be the gun barrel that tames globalization, how can the Leviathan achieve that goal?

This book has already described the attributes of the new Leviathan. It is built from the existing United Nations, but it is radically different from the frightened and hesitant current model. It is financially independent through Tobin taxes. It has a powerful boss and Secretariat freed of the blackmail applied by its Member States. And it has the ambition to work towards solutions to the world's most pressing problems, rather than simply describe and discuss them. How will this Leviathan-like United Nations tackle the governance of globalization? Not by pretending to be a world government. That would take us back to the barrel of the gun. Instead, the Leviathan would use three techniques: subsidiarity, certification, and legitimacy.

The principle of *subsidiarity* is defined in Article 5 of the Treaty on the European Union. It aims to ensure that decisions are taken as closely as possible to the citizen and that constant checks are made to verify that action at EU level is justified in light of the possibilities available at national, provincial or local level.[82] We need to add global at the head of the list of layers of governance. Decisions that can be taken at the local level should continue to be taken there. It is not for the UN to decide the maximum height of buildings in any particular neighborhood. Decisions that can be taken at the provincial level should continue to be taken there. It is not for the UN to decide what the region's official languages should be. Decisions that can be taken at the national level should continue to be taken there. It is not for the UN to decide the date of national holidays. But decisions that affect the whole planet should be elevated to the global level. How can this be achieved without world government?

The United Nations would use the technique of *certification*. The term is defined by Sidney Tarrow as "the validation of actors, their performances, and their claims by authorities."[83] The United Nations would provide the necessary certification. It already does so in a partial and state-centric way in the adoption of resolutions by the General Assembly. Very few new ideas originate at the United Nations. They often come from what was described in chapter 2 as the third UN—academic, civil society and corporate thinkers whose ideas gather interest and support until they achieve the critical mass of social gravitas to be recognized and ratified by the UN. By organizing global coordination, certifying voluntary codes, and championing multi-stakeholder initiatives, the Leviathan would add the missing ingredient to make them far more effective.

The final quality added by the Leviathan is *legitimacy*. Based on its moral authority, popular acceptance and effective performance, the United Nations Leviathan would have the legitimacy to rule on the subsidiarity division of responsibility and to certify the actions of others as well as to reach consensus on how to tackle global problems. This is not to say that contention and contestation will end. Ideally, the twenty-first century Leviathan would incorporate deliberative processes in its decision-making. Even so, there will be resistance at the various levels. It is the Leviathan's legitimacy that will overcome that resistance.

Globalization *sauvage* is leading us to a Hobbesian future. We need Hobbes' Leviathan solution.

## NOTES

1. Anthony Giddens, *The Consequences of Modernity*, (Cambridge: Polity, 1990) 64.
2. Marshall McLuhan and Bruce R. Powers, *Global Village: Transformations in World, Life and Media in the 21st Century*, (Oxford University Press, 1992)—though McLuhan coined the term in the 1960s.
3. David Held, A. McGrew, D. Goldblatt and J. Perraton, *Global Transformations: Politics, Economics and Culture*, (Cambridge: Polity, 1999) 2.
4. A. G. Hopkins (ed.), *Globalization in World History*, (London: Pimlico, 2002).
5. Rape, Abuse & Incest National Network, "The Criminal Justice System: Statistics" https://www.rainn.org/statistics/criminal-justice-system. Based on surveys showing only 230 out of 1,000 sexual assaults are reported, 46 perpetrators are arrested, 9 are prosecuted and 5 are convicted.
6. Thomas Friedman, *The World is Flat: A Brief History of the Twenty-First Century*, (New York: Farrar, Straus and Giroux, 2005) 49.
7. Thomas Hale and David Held (eds.), *Handbook of Transnational Governance: Institutions and Innovations*, (Cambridge: Polity Press, 2011) 5.
8. Ibid.
9. See its website, http://www.fatf-gafi.org/home/
10. See its website https://www.bis.org/bcbs/

11. Kevin Young, "The Basel Committee on Banking Supervision," Hale and Held, op. cit, 39–45, 42.

12. Monterrey Consensus of the International Conference on Financing for Development, "The final text of agreements and commitments adopted at the International Conference on Financing for Development Monterrey, Mexico, 18–22 March 2002," para 63. https://www.un.org/en/events/pastevents/pdfs/MonterreyConsensus.pdf

13. See its website https://www.fsb.org/about/

14. Randall Germaine, "The Financial Stability Board," Hale and Held, op. cit, 50–55, 53.

15. Tony Porter and Verónica Rubio Vega, "Global Forum on Transparency and Exchange of Information for Tax Purposes," Hale and Held, op. cit, 61–66, 61. This phenomenon perhaps supports E. F. Schumacher's aphorism that official development assistance is taking money from poor people in rich countries to give it to rich people in poor countries.

16. Statement from OECD Secretary-General Angel Gurría, *OECD Insights*, 5 April 2016, http://oecdinsights.org/2016/04/05/oecd-reaction-to-the-panama-papers/

17. OECD, "OECD releases Pillar Two model rules for domestic implementation of 15% global minimum tax," Dec. 20, 2021, https://www.oecd.org/tax/beps/oecd-releases-pillar-two-model-rules-for-domestic-implementation-of-15-percent-global-minimum-tax.htm

18. See its website https://www.ifrs.org/about-us/

19. IASB, "Who uses IFRS Standards?" https://www.ifrs.org/use-around-the-world/use-of-ifrs-standards-by-jurisdiction/

20. Andreas Nölke, "The International Accounting Standards Board," Hale and Held, op. cit, 66–70, 69.

21. Ibid.

22. Jonathan Koppell, "The International Organization for Standardization," Hale and Held, op. cit, 289–295, 292

23. Tim Büthe and Nathaniel Harris, "Codex Alimentarius Commission," Hale and Held, op. cit, 219–228, 220

24. Marie-Laure Djelic, "International Competition Network," Hale and Held, op. cit, 80–88, 80

25. ICN, "Members," https://www.internationalcompetitionnetwork.org/members/

26. Djelic, op. cit, 84.

27. European Medicines Agency, "Ethical use of animals in medicine testing," https://www.ema.europa.eu/en/human-regulatory/research-development/ethical-use-animals-medicine-testing

28. ECA Academy, "India blocks further Expansion of the ICH Harmonisation," 23 September 2014, https://www.gmp-compliance.org/gmp-news/india-blocks-further-expansion-of-the-ich-harmonisation

29. Jonathan Koppell, "Internet Corporation for Assigned Names and Numbers," Hale and Held, op. cit, 176–182, 179.

30. Danielle Kehl, "Dot What?," *Slate*, 7 May 2015, https://slate.com/technology/2015/05/icann-transition-the-interesting-history-of-the-internet-domain-name-system.html

31. Ibid.
32. ICANN, "Governance Guidelines," https://www.icann.org/resources/pages/governance/guidelines-en
33. Kathrin Böhling, "Multistakeholder Involvement in UN Conferences," Hale and Held, op. cit, 195–202, 197–8.
34. Matthew Bishop and Michael Green, *Philanthrocapitalism: How Giving can Save the World*, (New York: Bloomsbury Press, 2008).
35. Amy C. Edmondson and Jean-Francois Harvey, *Haiti Hope: Innovating the Mango Value Chain*, (Harvard Business School, 2016).
36. See https://www.theglobalfund.org/en/overview/
37. Johanna Hanefield, "Global Fund to Fight AIDS, Tuberculosis and Malaria," Hale and Held, op. cit, 161–166, 163.
38. See https://www.aidspan.org/
39. See the website http://polioeradication.org/
40. Matthia Koenig-Archibugi, "Global Polio Eradication Initiative," Hale and Held, op. cit, 166–176, 167.
41. See http://polioeradication.org/financing/donors/historical-contributions/
42. Ross MacKenzie, "The Framework Convention Alliance," Hale and Held, op. cit, 157–161, 159.
43. Radoslav S. Dimitrov, "International Coral Reef Initiative," Hale and Held, op. cit, 182–198, 183.
44. See https://www.seforall.org/about-us
45. See https://www.seforall.org/sites/default/files/gather-content/MPTF-2016_0.pdf
46. For comparison, in the first five years of the UN Democracy Fund, contributions topped $100m. See UNDEF, "State of Contributions in US Dollars," https://www.un.org/democracyfund/sites/www.un.org.democracyfund/files/contributions_undef_2005-2019_1.pdf
47. See http://www.unesco.org/new/en/gefi/home/
48. Eli Rosenberg and Carol Morello, "U.S. withdraws from UNESCO, the U.N.'s cultural organization, citing anti-Israel bias," *Washington Post*, October 12, 2017.
49. No events have been listed on the FAO website since 2016.
50. See EP Association Members & Reporting, https://equator-principles.com/members-reporting/
51. Christopher Wright, "The Equator Principles," Hale and Held, op. cit, 229–236.
52. See https://www.globalreporting.org/Pages/default.aspx
53. See http://www.oecd.org/corporate/principles-corporate-governance/
54. See https://www.transparency.org/whatwedo/tools/business_principles_for_countering_bribery/1
55. See https://www.weforum.org/communities/partnering-against-corruption-initiative
56. Niklas Egels-Zandén, "Clean Clothes Campaign," Hale and Held, op. cit, 259–265.
57. See https://eiti.org/supporters/oil-gas-companies

58. Sue Eckert, “The Role of Sanctions,” Sebastian von Einsiedel, David Malone, Bruno Stagno Ugarte (eds.) *The UN Security Council in the 21st Century*, (Boulder: Lynne Rienner, 2016), chapter 20, 416–17.

59. Global Policy Forum, “Kimberley Process,” https://www.globalpolicy.org/the-dark-side-of-natural-resources-st/diamonds-in-conflict/kimberley-process.html

60. Kate MacDonald, “Fair Labor Association,” Hale and Held, op. cit, 243–251.

61. See http://www.anti-slaverysociety.addr.com/rugmark.htm

62. See https://www.cdp.net/en

63. See https://fsc.org/en

64. See https://www.msc.org/home

65. A bracing account is provided by Michael Maren, *The Road to Hell: The Ravaging Effects of Foreign Aid and International Charity*, (New York: The Free Press, 1997).

66. The Biden Administration has now pushed through a 15% minimum tax as part of the Organization for Economic Cooperation and Development (OECD)/G20 international tax negotiations. OECD, “OECD releases Pillar Two model rules for domestic implementation of 15% global minimum tax,” Dec. 20, 2021, https://www.oecd.org/tax/beps/oecd-releases-pillar-two-model-rules-for-domestic-implementation-of-15-percent-global-minimum-tax.htm

67. See https://www.statista.com/topics/1704/diamond-industry/

68. Thomas Hale, “Marine Stewardship Council,” Hale and Held, op. cit, 308–314, 312.

69. Philipp Pattberg, “Forest Stewardship Council,” Hale and Held, op. cit, 265–273, 270.

70. Walter Scheidel, *The great leveler: violence and the history of inequality from the Stone Age to the twenty-first century*, (Princeton and Oxford: Princeton University Press, 2017).

71. Branko Milanovic, *Global Inequality: A New Approach for the Age of Globalization*, (Cambridge: Belknap Press, 2016).

72. Branko Milanovic, *Global inequality: A new approach for the age of globalization, a book talk*, 2016, https://www.piie.com/system/files/documents/milanovic20160509ppt.pdf

73. Thomas Piketty, *Capital in the Twenty-First Century (Le Capital au XXIe siècle)*, (Harvard University Press, 2013).

74. Michael Janda, “Inheritance tax: Combining the two certainties of life,” ABC News, 25 November 2016, https://www.abc.net.au/news/2016-11-25/inheritance-tax-combining-the-two-certainties-of-life/8058578

75. Ibid.

76. OECD, “In It Together: Why Less Inequality Benefits All” (2015), https://www.oecd.org/social/in-it-together-why-less-inequality-benefits-all-9789264235120-en.htm

77. Seymour Martin Lipset and Stein Rokkan, “Cleavage Structures, Party Systems, and Voter Alignments: an Introduction” in S.M. Lipset and S. Rokkan (eds) *Party systems and voter alignments: cross-national perspectives*. (New York: Free Press, 1967) 1–64.

78. James C. Scott, " 'Stilled to silence at 500 metres'—making sense of historical change in Southeast Asia," *IIAS Newsletter*, No. 48, Autumn 2008, pp. 12–13.

79. Z. Enyedi, "The Social and Attitudinal Basis of Political Parties: Cleavage Politics Revisited," *European Review*, 16(3), 2008, 287–304.

80. A good summary is available from Pieter de Wilde, Ruud Koopmans and Michael Zürn, "Conflicts or Cleavage? Contesting Globalization in Western Europe and Beyond" in a Paper presented at the ECPR General Conference, Glasgow, 4–7 September 2014, https://ecpr.eu/Filestore/PaperProposal/ce7978ec-3492-4c4f-ba81-459b6ad76667.pdf

81. Christophe Guilluy, *Twilight of the Elites: Prosperity, the Periphery, and the Future of France*, (Yale University Press, 2019).

82. EUR_Lex Glossaries, https://eur-lex.europa.eu/summary/glossary/subsidiarity.html

83. Sidney Tarrow, *The New Transnational Activism*, (Cambridge University Press, 2006) 194.

## *Chapter 9*

# Tackling Climate Change

This will not be a long chapter. The facts are well known and do not need to be rehearsed beyond the most skeletal of summaries. The Hobbesian international response is also clear for all to see. The world is behaving as if the true adversary is the free rider, not the change in climate that threatens us. So, a few examples will suffice. The bulk of this chapter will deal with the response to climate change. Once again, the menu has been before us for a while. It is really a *plat du jour*, we need to select green energy because the carbon burning economy is not a rational option. And along with green energy, we need a green economy and green lifestyles. Many people fear a change in their lifestyles. The chapter will take a peek at this issue as well.

This is a book about a (hopefully not too distant) future United Nations Leviathan. So, the main purpose of this chapter is to ask what such a Leviathan should do when facing the existential threat to humanity. Recalling that it is beyond the realms of possibility, or even preference, for the UN Leviathan to have a monopoly on the use of force, there is no magic wand to force the world to behave appropriately in the face of this existential threat. Accordingly, the UN is only one among many key actors in this fight. But, drawing on previous successes, the UN has a critical and, hopefully, pivotal role to play. The chapter will suggest three major avenues of action. The first concerns employing a name and shame tool. The second uses the UN's normative power. And the third is the one with the least pedigree but the most potential. I call it the Davos gambit.

### IT CAN BE DONE: THE MONTREAL PROTOCOL

Whenever my classes discuss international environmental issues, I always begin with the Montreal Protocol of 1987. The Montreal Protocol on Substances that Deplete the Ozone Layer is an international agreement designed to stop the production and import of ozone depleting substances and reduce their concentration in the atmosphere to help protect the earth's ozone layer. In the 1980s, we understood the concept of pollution of the land, the atmosphere, and the oceans, we understood that species, even charismatic megafauna, were becoming extinct because of human action, but the threat to the ozone layer was our first inkling there might be existential environmental threats to humanity beyond the stray comet hitting the Earth. The ozone layer blocks the sun's ultraviolet light which, among other problems, can cause increased rates of skin cancer. It is almost quaint to read back on the "science" of the day and note how convincing it was to one and all:

> Depletion of the ozone layer is a relatively new problem. It is the result of chlorofluorocarbons invented by General Motors' scientists in 1929. They did not come into general use until a bit later than that. Chlorofluorocarbons, or CFCs for short, have the great advantage of being very effective refrigerants for use in refrigerators and air-conditioning equipment, also as propellants in aerosols, and for cleaning electrical equipment and computers. Halons, a related chemical, are very effective at putting out fires, particularly in tanks and aircraft.[1]

There was initially some corporate resistance to regulating CFCs and the first attempt to do so in Vienna in 1984, only resulted in a Framework Convention which did not set measurable obligations. But as the scientific evidence gathered, the resistance of chemical companies weakened, and the resolve of governments strengthened. The Montreal Protocol of 1987 set measurable limits as well as a review process armed with the power to tighten these obligations, if necessary, by a qualified vote of two-thirds including fifty percent of the global producers of these chemicals. By 1990, it was decided that all CFCs would be phased out by 2000 with compensatory provisions for developing countries including China and India.[2] The Montreal Protocol process attracted near-universal support from governments and, ultimately, enthusiastic support from industry. Alternative engineering was developed for refrigeration and propulsion. By the new century, though not fully eliminated as planned, CFC use had been reduced by 95% and was still falling.[3]

It is hard to realize that this was only two decades ago. From the initial scientific realization of the ozone problem to the delivery of effective internationally coordinated action was only a matter of a couple of decades. The science was not contested by non-experts, and if it was, they were ignored. Public opinion was galvanized by leadership, scholarship, and culture. In the last category, the 1991 Julian Lennon (John's son) song "Saltwater" had an impact. Here is its opening stanza:

> We are a rock revolving
> Around a golden sun
> We are a billion children rolled into one

So when I hear about the hole in the sky
Saltwater wells in my eyes

From an international relations perspective, the system worked. The UN played is convocation role and even though the initial framework convention did not decisively tackle the problem, it took some key steps including establishing a Secretariat that would be the link between the scientific community and the national delegates. The framework convention was given some dynamism to review developments and when the science became both unimpeachable and dramatic, governments acted. Free rider problems were resolved. Industry was regulated and responded progressively. The hole in the sky remains, but it has not grown bigger. The lesson from the Montreal Protocol is that humanity can deal with existential environmental threats.

## THE INTERGOVERNMENTAL PANEL ON CLIMATE CHANGE

As the ozone issue receded, the climate change issue came to the fore. This is oddly ahistorical as the study of the Earth's temperature has been in the scholarly inbox for two centuries. The American Institute of Physics has a wonderfully accessible history of climate change research.[4] It begins in the 1820s with a French theoretician, Joseph Fournier, asking himself why the Earth, constantly bombarded by the sun's rays, remains at a constant temperature. He intuitively understood that heat is reflected back into space through the atmosphere. The next two hundred years would witness the growth of this discipline in accordance with scientific traditions and methods. Intuitions would be challenged by calls for evidence. Hypotheses would be attacked by scholarly skeptics thus forcing the proponents to sharpen their theorization. A discourse, impenetrable to laymen, would develop within the scientific cohort, some of whom would attempt to explain and popularize the scholarship to a lay audience. Thus would arise analogies and simplifications, like the "greenhouse effect," which may be readily understandable but does not withstand criticism from those initiated into the complexities of the issue. As hypotheses were refined into well accepted theories supported by a growing body of evidence, broad in its geographic range and sufficiently deep in time to provide longitudinal direction, it was time for the modelers to step in. They were greatly assisted by the advances in computing and various base assumptions could now confidently be projected into models of future climate change. All the findings were alarming.

Buoyed by the success of dealing with the ozone issue, the UN acted on the same playbook, the first step was to gather the scientific evidence.

The Intergovernmental Panel on Climate Change (IPCC) was established by the United Nations Environment Programme (UNEP) and the World Meteorological Organization (WMO) in 1988 and endorsed by the UN General Assembly in resolution 43/53 of the same year. According to the resolution, the job of the IPCC "was to prepare a comprehensive review and recommendations with respect to the state of knowledge of the science of climate change; the social and economic impact of climate change, and potential response strategies and elements for inclusion in a possible future international convention on climate." The IPCC is not a research body, it is an intergovernmental panel that reviews scientific research and summarizes it in regular reports. IPCC assessments are written by hundreds of leading scientists who volunteer their time and expertise. They enlist hundreds of other experts to provide complementary expertise in specific areas. IPCC reports undergo multiple rounds of drafting and review to ensure they are comprehensive and objective and produced in an open and transparent way. Thousands of other experts contribute to the reports by acting as reviewers, ensuring the reports reflect the full range of learning in the scientific community. For example, the Fifth Assessment Report of 2014 was compiled by a total of 831 experts.[5] I think I need to articulate an obvious point at this stage. With nearly two hundred governments and almost one thousand experts involved in writing these reports, it is beyond the realms of feasibility that they are all engaged in a massive and secret conspiracy.

The IPCC prepares comprehensive Assessment Reports about knowledge on climate change, its causes, potential impacts, and response options. The IPCC also produces Special Reports, which are an assessment on a specific issue and Methodology Reports, which provide practical guidelines for the preparation of greenhouse gas inventories. To date, it has more than 40 reports on its website.[6] The very first report in 1990 put the matter succinctly:

> Emissions resulting from human activities are substantially increasing the atmospheric concentrations of the greenhouse gases: carbon dioxide, methane, chlorofluorocarbons and nitrous oxide. These increases will enhance the greenhouse effect, resulting on average in an additional warming of the Earth's surface.[7]

And in 2019, it released a special report on a 1.5% increase in global temperature, noting:

> Warming from anthropogenic emissions from the pre-industrial period to the present will persist for centuries to millennia and will continue to cause further long-term changes in the climate system, such as sea level rise, with associated impacts (*high confidence*) . . . Future climate-related risks depend on the rate, peak and duration of warming. In the aggregate, they are larger if global warming exceeds 1.5°C before returning to that level by 2100 than if global warming

> gradually stabilizes at 1.5°C, especially if the peak temperature is high (e.g., about 2°C) (*high confidence*). Some impacts may be long-lasting or irreversible, such as the loss of some ecosystems (*high confidence*).

The science has been consistent for the 30 years of the IPCC's reporting. There may be variations in the anticipated levels of severity, but all the levels are nevertheless high. So, why did the international community act so decisively on the ozone issue while behaving with such willful myopia with regard to climate change? While the issues appear to present themselves in a similar way, there are deep differences. The ozone issue was presented as a problem with a single scary symptom: if we're not careful, the sun will fry our asses to a crisp! People could easily understand and relate to this. The climate change issue is complex and so are its impacts: wild weather, rising sea levels, uninhabitable land, food emergencies, death of coral reefs etc. It triggered a response reminiscent of Jack Nicholson's famous line in the movie *A Few Good Men*, "you can't handle the truth." It was simply too much to handle, too ominous, too imminent, and as Al Gore told us, too inconvenient. And while the ozone issue presented a surmountable challenge to the chemical industry, the climate change issue is ringing the death knell of the carbon burning economy. One industry in particular, the world's third largest,[8] the oil and gas exploration and production industry, will need to be sacrificed and its commodity stranded. That industry is fighting back.

## TACKLING CLIMATE CHANGE

As noted in the opening paragraph of this chapter, this will not be a blueprint of how to tackle Climate Change. Instead, I aim to demonstrate the scale of the problem. I also aim to highlight the Hobbesian response to date.

I begin with an anecdote. I am using that rather belittling term because I simply cannot remember the name, date and title of the talk I attended at the Australian National University around 2000 given by a World Bank official, and nor have I found the information on the World Bank Climate Change Knowledge Portal. My recollection is that he examined the problem from an economic cost perspective. The problem was well understood by then, and the steps needed to ameliorate the situation by retooling to green energy were also known. He did not engage with the politics of taking the necessary steps but focused on the costs and I remember the numbers because they left a strong impression on me. He said (in 2000) that the world could fix the problem by spending 2% of global income. Well, world domestic product in 2000 was around $34 trillion[9] (12 zeroes), so two percent would amount to $680 billion which was more than twelve times the total amount of official development assistance in 2000.[10] That is an enormous amount but, in retrospect, what a wonderful investment it would have been. He went on to say that the cost of fixing the problem is compounding cumulatively and that in ten years' time, the cost would be 5% of world GDP. Well, by 2010, world GDP was $66 trillion and 5% amounts to $3.3 trillion. He went on to speculate about a time so distant in the future that it seemed like science fiction. He said by 2020, the cost would rise to over 10% of world income. The World Bank has a figure of $87.75 trillion as global domestic product in 2019, so a ten percent bill comes close to $9 trillion. The amount of $680 billion sounds like a bargain now, and the figure of $9 trillion will sound readily affordable in twenty years by which time the cost of taking action simply to mitigate and adapt will again have ballooned because the objective of fixing the problem will no longer be available.

In a review of Mark Lynas's new book, *Our Final Warning: Six Degrees of Climate Emergency,* the noted environmentalist Bill McKibben quotes a paragraph from the book:

> If we stay on the current business-as-usual trajectory, we could see two degrees as soon as the early 2030s, three degrees around mid-century, and four degrees by 2075 or so. If we're unlucky with positive feedbacks . . . from thawing permafrost in the Arctic or collapsing tropical rainforests, then we could be in for five or even six degrees by century's end.[11]

McKibben calls it an aggressive but not outlandish reading of the climate science, noting that the scientists have been conservative in their projections, some of which have come to pass decades before their "due date." It makes $680 billion sound like a trifle. We need to change our economy and our lifestyles, but we still need money to tackle the problem.

A key element in raising the sort of money needed to tackle climate change is a carbon tax. It is logical, efficient, and focused. But it is also deeply unpopular. So rather than have governments impose a tax, some governments have toyed with the idea of a "cap and trade" system whereby the market would set the price while governments set a cap on pollution. This is politically astute but has yet to be effectively designed and deployed.[12] So we fall back on a carbon tax. But political experience has been uniformly negative. In 2017, Mexicans took to the streets to express outrage at fuel tax increases. During the 2018 US midterm elections, residents of Washington state again rejected a ballot measure aimed at introducing a carbon fee. Several Canadian provinces have started legal proceedings against a federal carbon pricing framework. Germany and Ireland recently backed away from carbon tax expansions.[13] And Australia has yo-yoed back and forth, mainly back. But the cautionary tale comes from France where President Emmanuel

Macron followed Cartesian logic, while displaying poor political instincts, in introducing a singeing and regressive carbon tax in 2018 which launched the revolutionary *gilets jaunes* movement that persisted long after the tax was abandoned. The best hope for the future is to link the issue of a carbon tax with systemic reforms that also deal with the dramatic rise of income inequality and wealth disparities. This is the idea behind the Green New Deal launched by several American politicians.[14]

The political complexity is mirrored in the economic and technical complexities of tackling climate change. The big step method, like the Kyoto and Paris Agreements within the United Nations Framework Convention on Climate Change, is necessary as a coordination and goal setting exercise, but it is bound to fail for Hobbesian reasons without a Weberian Leviathan to enforce it, something that is almost impossible to conceive. As noted, governments are more serious about fighting free riders than fighting climate change. That is why Elinor Ostrom's polycentric approach commends itself.[15] Recognizing the world's Hobbesian inclinations, she argues:

> A polycentric approach has the main advantage of encouraging experimental efforts at multiple levels, leading to the development of methods for assessing the benefits and costs of particular strategies adopted in one type of ecosystem and compared to results obtained in other ecosystems. Building a strong commitment to find ways of reducing individual emissions is an important element for coping with this problem, and having others also take responsibility can be more effectively undertaken in small to medium-scale governance units that are linked together through information networks and monitoring at all levels.

So, has the world followed the script? Well, it did not fix the problem when it was still possible to do so. Instead, it engaged in pious rhetoric disguising myopic behavior. China talked a good game but continued to build a new coal-fired power plant every other week.[16] Europe was particularly pious, but we all saw the *gilets jaunes* reaction when France attempted to put piety into action. And the United States has behaved as if climate change is a second or third order issue, not worthy of its attention. Indeed, candidate Trump called it a hoax, and President Trump acted accordingly. This may not be a war of all against all as Hobbes imagined it in a national context, but it is the twenty-first century international equivalent. It is every country for itself. It is refusing to take action because others are not taking similar action. It is pretending that we do not live on spaceship Earth but rather in arbitrarily cobbled together pieces of property defined by lines on a map and walls on the ground. And some of this Hobbesianism is driven by pique. There is a view in China and India that the West became wealthy by treating the environment as an irrelevant externality and now it is their turn!

This is not a propitious situation for a Leviathan armed only with competence, independence, and moral authority to rectify. In many ways, the UN has behaved appropriately and done as much as its convocation and persuasive powers will allow. The UN followed the ozone playbook but has not achieved the sought-after results. As foreshadowed, I believe there are several significant additional steps a UN Leviathan must take.

## THE NAME AND SHAME TOOL

I was at a dinner party for some official event some years ago. At the table was an enthusiastic activist from the Robert F. Kennedy Human Rights Foundation. She said their main tool was to name and shame and it was employed in all settings; local, state, national and global. Her foundation was fearless in the way it directed this tool to all and sundry, from slum lords to recalcitrant governments. I was present in my capacity as head of the UN Office for Partnerships and, feeling a little provocative, I said that the UN also uses the "shame" tool but in a slightly different way—we shamelessly flatter big corporations and philanthropists. Also sitting at the table were people from New York law firms, insurance companies and big tech companies, and they immediately piped in with "yeah, that will work!" The name and shame tool needs to be wielded in a calculated manner. The more scatter gun the approach, the less effective it becomes. The more authoritative the approach, the more effective it becomes.

The UN's most effective use of the tool is not in the occasional resolution criticizing the human rights situation in a particular country but in an instrument that does not look like a name and shame tool—the Human Development Index. It purports to be an apolitical statistical analysis in comparative longitudinal form shorn of value judgements and criticism. But its effect is to demonstrate which governments are effective and which are not, which governments are meeting their people's basic needs, and which do not. If one needs evidence of a failed or fragile state, the HDI will provide it. It is an effective name and shame tool because of the rigor of its production and the credibility of its statistical basis and the authority of its provider.

The IPCC reports provide little boxes of examples and lists of countries taking certain actions, but it does not add up to the power of an annual index. The UN needs a climate change performance index to name and shame governments. Luckily, the UN need not invent it because an excellent index already exists. Germanwatch, the New Climate Institute and the Climate Action Network publish the Climate Change Performance Index annually and have been doing so since 2005.[17] It tracks countries' efforts to combat climate change and publishes a scorecard of some sixty countries and of the European

Union (EU), which are together responsible for more than 90% of global greenhouse gas (GHG) emissions. The methodology is explained as follows:

> Aiming to provide a comprehensive and balanced evaluation of the diverse countries evaluated, a total of 14 indicators are taken into account. Around 80% of the assessment of countries' performance is based on quantitative data taken from the International Energy Agency (IEA), PRIMAP, the Food and Agriculture Organization (FAO) and the national GHG inventories submitted to the UNFCCC. The categories "GHG Emissions," "Renewable Energy" and "Energy Use" are each defined by four indicators: (1) Current Level; (2) Past Trend; (3) Well-Below-2°C Compatibility of the Current Level; and (4) Well-Below-2°C Compatibility of the Countries' 2030 Target. The remaining 20% of the assessment is based on the globally unique climate policy section of the CCPI. The index category "Climate Policy" considers the fact that climate protection measures taken by governments often take several years to have an effect on the GHG-Emissions.[18]

The 2020 Report lists the top five countries as Sweden, Denmark, Morocco, UK, and Lithuania while the bottom five are Iran, South Korea, Taiwan, Saudi Arabia, with the United States stone cold last. Australia and Canada were just above the bottom five.[19] That is shameful conduct, and it needs to be called out. I am not suggesting a UN takeover of this Index, but a partnership with it. Perhaps expanding the list and adding the UN brand and dissemination capacity to the annual report. The UN needs to do more and to become more effective and this is a relatively accessible step to do so. Of course, governments would block the UN from doing so in the current circumstances, but a UN Leviathan could certainly jump in.

## CLIMATE CHANGE DENIAL AS A CRIME AGAINST HUMANITY

Is climate change denial simply free speech? Well, when your irrelevant idiot cousin is the denier, then it is free speech. But what if the denier holds a prominent public or corporate position and benefits from the denial? That starts to resemble something akin to fraud. Fraud is a crime, and it thus requires either the intention to commit it or reckless indifference in its commission. Generally, in American criminal law, the following are the five elements of fraudulent concealment:

1. the defendant concealed or suppressed a material fact
2. the defendant was under a duty to disclose the fact to the plaintiff

3. the defendant intentionally concealed or suppressed the fact with the intent to defraud the plaintiff; that is, the defendant concealed or suppressed the fact for the purpose of inducing the plaintiff to act differently than she would have if she had known the fact
4. the plaintiff was unaware of the fact and would have acted differently if she had known of the concealed or suppressed fact
5. and, as a result of the concealment or suppression of the fact, the plaintiff sustained damages.[20]

The oil and gas industry knows full well that its product causes global warming yet lies to its customers who purchase the noxious product. The first three elements are established. The final element, the planet is becoming increasingly unlivable, is also established. The problem is the fourth element—did the customer already know about the noxious nature of the product? For this element to be established, it is necessary to go beyond the oil and gas company to its accomplices (or perhaps we should think of them as agents, given the political funding), the politicians who aid and abet in the denial. It is the politicians' reassurances that lull the customer into believing the product is not harmful.

The next step is to apply this legal structure to recent history and for this purpose, we have an excellent publication, James Hoggan's *Climate Cover-Up*.[21] It will come as no surprise that the oil and gas industry simply continued the scam undertaken by the tobacco industry which had established a foundation called The Advancement of Sound Science Coalition (TASSC) as an ostensibly credible source of information for the media and the general public. One of the tobacco industry's objectives was to broaden the debate to include other products under attack. The oil and gas industry was an obvious avenue and the funders soon included Amoco, Chevron, Exxon, Occidental Petroleum as well as General Motors and Dow Chemical.[22] The standard operating procedure of TASSC was to put out its propaganda under the name of a scientist. One example is Frederick Seitz, once President of the National Academy of Science, whose name was used prominently though some described him at the time as "quite elderly and not sufficiently rational to offer advice."[23] TASSC described success as being achieved when the media and average citizens recognized uncertainties about climate science as conventional wisdom; when the media adopt the practice of providing a "balanced" account of climate science; when those promoting the Kyoto treaty are seen as out of touch with reality.[24] Yet industry knew the truth. Exxon had a clear understanding of climate change and oil's role in it in 1977.[25] This is one of many examples of the industry's perfidy. The first three elements of fraudulent misrepresentation are clearly established.

The final two elements can also be readily demonstrated in the ways the oil and gas industry use politicians to comfort the public. Public documents demonstrate that the oil and gas industry spent almost $130 million in 2008 on lobbying in what was described as a "climate change lobby explosion" with 770 companies employing 2,340 lobbyists.[26] This money buys politicians, like Mitch McConnell, beginning all his statements about climate change with the phrase "I'm no scientist, but . . . " To allow oneself to be placated by the McConnells in Congress was simply the path of most convenience. The electorate is no doubt guilty of contributory negligence in buying this line, but the actions of politicians are nevertheless sufficient to establish the final two elements of the crime. Of course, fraudulent concealment is a crime under national law. What about international law? That is where the UN Leviathan must step in.

In his poignant book *East West Street*,[27] Philippe Sands tells the story of two men born around the same time not far from each in (what was then) Poland, of Jewish heritage, who both studied law at the same Polish university, and who both had a profound impact on international law. Hersch Lauterpacht became a leader of the academic establishment in the UK and was a key member of the British prosecution team at Nuremberg. He relentlessly pursued the idea that there must be crimes against humanity that were punishable in international law. These were crimes against individuals in wartime. His view formed the main basis for the prosecution and conviction of war criminals at the Nuremberg trials which began in 1945. Born several years after Lauterpacht, Rafael Lemkin, lived his life, in the United States after the war, more on the edges of academia. He obsessively pursued the idea that the intent to murder an ascriptively identifiable group of people must be a crime under international law, a crime he called genocide. Genocide was briefly noted at the Nuremberg trials, but the main focus was on crimes against humanity. It seemed that Lauterpacht's influence had prevailed. But the concept of the crime of genocide captured a corner of the public imagination. Spurred by Lemkin's lobbying, the Convention on the Prevention and Punishment of the Crime of Genocide was unanimously adopted by the United Nations General Assembly on 9 December 1948, the day before UNGA adopted the Universal Declaration of Human Rights. It seemed that Lemkin got the last laugh. But Lauterpacht's idea would catch up half a century later. The concept of crimes against humanity was central to the International Tribunals for Yugoslavia and Rwanda, and was then defined in the Rome Statute of the International Criminal Court of 1998 to include the list of acts as follows:

> (a) Murder; (b) Extermination; (c) Enslavement; (d) Deportation or forcible transfer of population; (e) Imprisonment or other severe deprivation of physical liberty in violation of fundamental rules of international law; (f) Torture; (g)

> Rape, sexual slavery, enforced prostitution, forced pregnancy, enforced sterilization, or any other form of sexual violence of comparable gravity; (h) Persecution against any identifiable group or collectivity on political, racial, national, ethnic, cultural, religious, gender as defined in paragraph 3, or other grounds that are universally recognized as impermissible under international law, in connection with any act referred to in this paragraph or any crime within the jurisdiction of the Court; (i) Enforced disappearance of persons; (j) The crime of apartheid; (k) Other inhumane acts of a similar character intentionally causing great suffering, or serious injury to body or to mental or physical health.[28]

I think we can call the competition between Lauterpacht and Lemkin a tie because the jurisdiction of the International Criminal Court was listed as dealing with the following crimes: (a) The crime of genocide; (b) Crimes against humanity; (c) War crimes; (d) The crime of aggression.[29] The first three are well defined. The concept of aggression, though it appears in the Charter, has yet to be definitively defined.[30] The point of this little digression is to note the open-ended nature of the last-mentioned crime against humanity—acts intentionally causing great suffering.

The next chapter will deal with climate change refugees. There could be one billion of them by the end of this century. The instability, conflict and suffering that will ensue will be intense. The next chapter will again make the argument in favor of the need for a UN Leviathan to at least provide a system to manage this flow of refugees, though no Leviathan could solve the problem. One step that needs to be taken in this regard is to stop the disinformation and obfuscation coming from corporate and political leaders denying the reality of rapid anthropogenic climate change. As noted above, this is not a case of free speech but one of fraud.

The UN General Assemblies should designate climate change denial as a crime against humanity. While it does not fit comfortably into the existing structure because it is not an act "of a similar character" to the other listed crimes, it has the profound advantage of being literally true. Denying climate change and sabotaging efforts to deal with its consequences will lead to "great suffering" for the whole of humanity. A UN Leviathan would have the courage to call it what it is. Yes, enforcement will not be simple. But the designation of climate change denial as a crime against humanity would establish some doubt in the minds of those planning to perpetrate this crime. They should ask themselves some searching questions. What if I travel abroad and find myself in the Pinochet position, prosecuted in a foreign court? What if the regime in my country changes and delivers me for prosecution? What if world opinion turns so resolutely against the deniers that no government would have the courage to refuse to act on an indictment by the International Criminal Court?

Colleagues who have read this chapter say the preceding argument makes them uncomfortable. That it is a reach. That it will antagonize too many people. They may be right. On examining my own motives, I realized that I had another set of readers in mind, those from future generations. They will inherit a broken planet with a diminished quality of life, and they will know that their children will have it even harder. They will look back on this period, the turn of the millennium, with disgust. We could have fixed the problem with a mere 2% of global income! And even the greater sums in the following years will seem to them a bargain. They will see the decision makers of this era as having committed a crime against all humanity. My selfish motivation is to let them know that some of today's people agree with them.

## THE DAVOS GAMBIT

Governments think short-term, most big corporations think longer-term. Government's must fight fires. Their agenda is invariably hijacked by outside forces. Lobbyists have immediate demands. Elections are always just around the corner. To think about the future is a luxury, to act on it is politically foolhardy. Dictators may have longer-term horizons, but all their energy is spent on burnishing their personal legacies and establishing their dynasties. From a strategic perspective, putting one's faith in governments to deal with anthropogenic climate issues is bound to lead to disappointment. Yet, though we should have anticipated the results, that is exactly what the world has done—asked governments to think long-term, ignore forthcoming electoral prospects, and act for future generations rather than today's electorate. Then we act surprised when we get piety instead of action.

Corporations also think short-term given their quarterly reports, yearly dividends, and annual general meetings. But they are also expected to think longer-term. They have to grow their businesses, increase market share, and become a global brand. Yes, CEO bonuses are tied to annual performance, but the board and the shareholders expect those CEOs to have a future vision and a strategy to get there. Corporate leaders need to think ten or twenty years into the future, and some must grapple with generational processes. A strategy based on corporate activism to deal with anthropogenic climate issues is more likely to succeed. But, of course, we are not there yet.

I saw this first-hand at the United Nations. Delegates make well-crafted speeches on behalf of their governments calling for action and urging change. They repeatedly vow their fidelity to the big new stone tablets of the day, the Rio or Kyoto or Paris or Edinburgh document. As the Climate Change Performance Index demonstrates, very few were serious about taking action. Governments are among the first to recognize the political and economic inconvenience of tackling climate change in any effective manner. The UN Office for Partnerships co-hosted at the UN every two years the Investor Summit on Climate Change. This was a summit of major players in the corporate world organized by Ceres, a sustainability nonprofit organization working with the most influential investors and companies to build leadership and drive solutions throughout the economy. Having listened so often to the delegates of governments, it was encouraging to hear representatives of the corporate world. They had a different discourse. Far less piety and far more practicality. They spoke about investment strategies and divestment strategies. They spoke about deadlines and time frames as if they meant it. They knew that public pronouncements lead to market consequences, so they took care in the projections they made.

Earlier in this chapter I described the oil and gas exploration and production industry as the third largest in the world. Well, the two largest industries were well represented at the Investor Summit. They are global life and insurance carriers and global pension funds.[31] The insurance industry is sharply alive to the reality of the phenomenon of increasing wild weather events because of their liability to those insured against just such events. The sudden increase in the number of extreme weather events drew the interest of scientists and became a distinct subject of scholarship since the early 2000s. A think tank has mapped all the peer-reviewed papers in this new field,[32] providing a bracing summary:

- 69% of the 355 extreme weather events and trends included in the map were found to be made more likely or more severe by human-caused climate change
- 9% of events or trends were made less likely or less severe by climate change, meaning 78% of all events experienced some human impact. The remaining 22% of events and trends showed no discernible human influence or were inconclusive
- Heatwaves account for 47% of such events, while droughts, heavy rainfall, and floods each make up 15%
- Of the 125 attribution studies that have looked at extreme heat around the world, 93% found that climate change made the event or trend more likely or more severe: "For the 68 studies looking at rainfall or flooding, 54% found human activity had made the event more likely or more severe. For the 61 drought events studied, it is 61%."

The insurance industry understands that at a certain inflection point, the cost to the insured will be so high that a rational choice is to accept the climate risk. This is not, therefore, an industry that can simply continue to grow as the risks increase. At a certain point, the insurance formula will become untenable. The industry has a clear interest in mitigating climate risk. The pension industry is necessarily a long-term thinker. It accepts contributions knowing that a pension will need to be paid thirty or forty years hence. It also has a clear interest in mitigating climate risk.

The Davos gambit is to stop putting all our faith in governments and turn to the corporate world for climate change action. In relation to governments, we are constituents and voters, and therefore have some influence on their policies and we should continue to keep the blowtorch to the belly. But that has clearly not been sufficient. In relation to the corporate world, we are employees, consumers, investors, shareholders and, that promiscuous term again, stakeholders. We need to continue to vote climate change, but we need to start to be far more active in our other roles in public economic life. Sometimes flattery will work, sometimes the name and shame tool may be required, but the most influential nudges come from the economic power we hold. Reward companies that take climate change mitigation action, boycott those that do not. Invest in companies that do the right thing, divest from those that do not. With the fine profitability margins that competition forces on the corporate world, it will only take action by ten or twenty percent of consumers and investors to trigger a decisive impact.

I call it a gambit because it is not a strategy without risk of failure. The corporate world is quite unpopular around the world, understandably so given a history of tax evasion, oligopolistic behavior, planned obsolescence, production of noxious chemicals, race to the bottom tactics, and generally poor citizenship, local and global. Many people would prefer to retain their faith in governments than to place it in the corporate world. I sympathize to some extent. There are a few good governments. But the ugly truth is that putting our faith in governments has been a failed strategy, and that is unlikely to change. The gambit is that, given the awesome responsibility to be placed in corporate hands, their leaders will meet the challenge. After all, whereas previous orthodoxy was to maximize shareholder value, the new thinking is to make the brand beloved, causing all good things to flow. What could be more popular than to save the planet?

The UN Leviathan blends in well in this regard. Recall that there is a UN General Assembly of Business. The corporate world will be involved in global governance. It will not be able to hide behind governments as is its current wont. It will be front and center in the fight against anthropogenic climate change. The Davos gambit offers the world hope that is currently sadly missing.

## NOTES

1. Geoffrey Palmer, "An International Regime for Environmental Protection," 42 *Journal of Urban and Contemporary Law* 5, 1992, 5–19, 14.

2. Ibid.

3. Michael G. Faure, and Jurgen Lefevere, "Compliance with Global Environmental Policy," in *The Global Environment Institutions: Law and Policy*, eds. R.S. Axelrod, J.D.L Down, N.J. Vig, (California: CQ Press, 2004), 172–191, 181.

4. American Institute of Physics, "The Discovery of Global Warming," https://history.aip.org/climate/summary.htm. It is based on the book by Spencer Weart, *The Discovery of Global Warming*, (Harvard University Press, 2008).

5. IPCC, "IPCC Factsheet: How does the IPCC select its authors?," https://www.ipcc.ch/site/assets/uploads/2018/02/FS_select_authors.pdf

6. See https://www.ipcc.ch/reports/

7. IPCC First Assessment Report Overview and Policymaker Summaries, 1990.

8. IBIS World, "The 10 Global Biggest Industries by Revenue," https://www.ibisworld.com/global/industry-trends/biggest-industries-by-revenue/

9. World Bank data, https://data.worldbank.org/indicator/NY.GDP.MKTP.CD

10. OECD, "ODA Steady in 2000; Other Flows Decline," https://www.oecd.org/dac/stats/odasteadyin2000otherflowsdecline.htm

11. Bill McKibben, "130 Degrees," *New York Review of Books*, August 20, 2020.

12. Reuven S. Avi-Yonah and David M.Uhlmann, "Combating Global Climate Change: Why a Carbon Tax is a Better Response to Global Warming than Cap and Trade" (January 29, 2009). *Stanford Environmental Law Journal*, Vol. 28, No. 3, 2009, 3–50.

13. Michael Mehling, "Emmanuel Macron's carbon tax sparked *gilets jaunes* protests, but popular climate policy is possible," *The Conversation*, December 10, 2018.

14. Lisa Friedman, "What Is the Green New Deal? A Climate Proposal, Explained," *New York Times*, Feb. 21, 2019.

15. Elinor Ostrom, "A Polycentric Approach for Coping with Climate Change," World Bank Policy Research Working Paper 5095.

16. Daniel Oberhaus, "China Is Still Building an Insane Number of New Coal Plants," *Wired*, November 27, 2019.

17. See https://www.climate-change-performance-index.org/about

18. CCPI, "Methodology," https://www.climate-change-performance-index.org/methodology

19. Jan Burck, Ursula Hagen, Niklas Höhne, Leonardo Nascimento, Christoph Bals, "Results 2020," CCPI, https://www.climate-change-performance-index.org/sites/default/files/documents/ccpi-2020-results-the_climate_change_performance_index.pdf

20. Clear Counsel Law Group, "Fraudulent Concealment," https://www.clearcounsel.com/fraudulent-concealment/

21. James Hoggan with Richard Littlemore, *Climate Cover-Up: the Crusade to Deny Global Warming*, (Vancouver: Greystone Books, 2009).

22. Ibid., 41.

23. Ibid.
24. Ibid., 43.
25. Shannon Hall, "Exxon Knew about Climate Change almost 40 years ago: A new investigation shows the oil company understood the science before it became a public issue and spent millions to promote misinformation," *Scientific American*, October 26, 2015.
26. Hoggan, op. cit, 188.
27. Philippe Sands, *East West Street*, (New York: Vintage Books, 2017).
28. Article 7(1).
29. Article 5.
30. UNGA Res. 3314 of 1974 proposes a definition of aggression.
31. IBIS World, "The 10 Global Biggest Industries by Revenue," https://www.ibisworld.com/global/industry-trends/biggest-industries-by-revenue/
32. Carbon Brief, "Mapped: How climate change affects extreme weather around the world," April 15, 2020, https://www.carbonbrief.org/mapped-how-climate-change-affects-extreme-weather-around-the-world

# *Chapter 10*

# One Billion Refugees

In no area of United Nations activity is there such an unbridgeably wide gap between the Hobbesian problem and the Leviathan solution than the management of the world's refugees. Millions of terrified people stream across international borders often meeting a hostile reception, and their champion is a relatively small apolitical agency, the office of the UN High Commissioner for Refugees (UNHCR), that must then go cap in hand seeking funds for their upkeep. As noted on the UN homepage:

> The world is witnessing the highest levels of displacement on record. An unprecedented 70.8 million people around the world have been forced from home by conflict and persecution at the end of 2018. Among them are nearly 30 million refugees, over half of whom are under the age of 18.[1]

If we can barely meet the needs of seventy million displaced people, the question posed by this chapter is, how will we cope when up to one billion people are forced from their homes?

## WHO IS A REFUGEE?

There is an answer to this question in international law, but before we consult the relevant texts, it might be worth drawing on other disciplines like etymology and history. Etymology provides the first clue. According to Merriam-Webster:

> Refugee came directly from the French word *réfugié* with a very specific meaning: it referred to Protestants who fled France following the revocation in 1685 of the Edict of Nantes, the law that granted religious liberty and civil rights to the Protestant Huguenots for nearly a century.[2]

So, the earliest meaning did not describe a person seeking refuge, the logical construct, but a far narrower definition—a person seeking refuge to escape religious persecution. Succeeding centuries would continue to see religious persecution in Europe leading to population displacement as well as escape to settler communities in the new world.

The term "refugee" solidified its association with persecution during the First World War, during which time the term was put to wide use. The war engulfed the whole of Europe and generated an unprecedented flow of civilian "victims of war." One estimate puts the number of displaced people, either internally or having crossed an international border, at ten million.[3] The displaced included Belgians and French from the Western Front, Jewish refugees fleeing Galicia and Bukovina, then part of the Austro-Hungarian Empire, Italian refugees escaping the front in the war against the Habsburg Empire, Serbs fleeing in great numbers when the Central powers defeated the Serbian army, vast civilian displacement following the defeat of the Tsarist army, and Armenians escaping genocide at the hands of Ottoman forces.[4] All these victims of war sheltered under the name "refugee." There was no need to enquire why they fled. Fleeing war, genocide or oppressive foreign occupation is a natural human instinct. There was no need for a definition of refugee.

Whether formally defined or not, the vast numbers of refugees had to be dealt with. National governments set policies and, at times, took action, but the main burden was left to local authorities and civil society groups. There were issues, however, the resolution of which required international cooperation and the newly formed League of Nations stepped in. The noted polar explorer, Fridtjof Nansen, headed the Norwegian delegation to the League, and in 1921 he was appointed High Commissioner for Refugees and successfully dealt with the League's first large-scale humanitarian task—the repatriation of 450,000 prisoners of war.[5] He introduced the so-called "Nansen passport," which was the first legal instrument used for the international protection of refugees. A sense of the work of the League on the issue of refugee resettlement can be drawn from the following list of legal instruments setting out some of its responsibilities:

- Arrangements with regard to the issue of certificates of identity to Russian refugees of 5 July1922
- Arrangements relating to the issue of identity certificates to Russian and Armenian refugees, supplementing and amending the previous arrangements
- Arrangements relating to the legal status of Russian and Armenian refugees of 30 June 1928
- Convention Relating to the International Status of Refugees of 28 June 1933

- Provisional arrangement concerning the status of refugees coming from Germany of 4 July1936
- Convention Concerning the Status of Refugees Coming from Germany of 10 February 1938.[6]

The unprecedented refugee outflows of the First World War would be dwarfed by the Second. One estimate has it that 60 million people were involuntarily moved from their homes during the war or in the period immediately thereafter.[7] The figure breaks down to 20 million in Europe and 40 million in China, these people were prisoners of war, civilians who fled combat zones, individuals evicted to make room for colonists, laborers imported and forced to work, and persons relocated by the Axis powers in conquered territory.[8] According to former New York Governor and Director-General of the United Nations Relief and Rehabilitation Administration (UNRAA), Herbert Lehman: "Never before in the history of the world has so massive a problem involving so many millions of people been presented to the nations for solution."[9] One need only consult Timothy Snyder's epoch-defining *Bloodlands: Europe between Hitler and Stalin*[10] to understand the chaos and cruelty of this period. The term refugee was used interchangeably with the term displaced person to cover the survivors, even though international borders were in flux and movements were at times involuntary due to the policies of both Hitler and Stalin to move large numbers of people, many bound for slaughter or starvation. In 1945, the UNRAA, succeeded in 1948 by the International Refugee Organization, took responsibility for the administration of displaced persons in Europe and successfully repatriated most and resettled the balance.[11] This was a major achievement of international cooperation.

The Agreement for the establishment of the United Nations Relief and Rehabilitation Administration, concluded in 1943, does not attempt to define its beneficiary cohort beyond the general objective to work "for the relief of victims of war."[12] On 12 February 1946, the UN General Assembly adopted Resolution 8 (I)[13] dealing with the Question of Refugees, interchangeably using the terms refugees and displaced persons while adding the qualifier "genuine" to distinguish them from "war criminals, quislings and traitors." But there is a hint of things to come when the resolution, in paragraph c(ii) precludes sending people to their country of origin if they have a "valid objection" to doing so. The Constitution of the International Refugee Organization, of 15 December 1946, does not contain a definition of refugees but simply refers to the General Assembly resolution of 12 February 1946.

The Statute of the Office of the United Nations High Commissioner for Refugees was adopted by the General Assembly on 14 December 1950 as Annex to Resolution 428 (V).[14] It is the next iteration of the international community's pronouncements on its responsibilities towards refugees.

Whereas previous situations had not considered it necessary to devise a general definition of a refugee, considering the answer to be self-evident, the Statute adopts a definition, or perhaps it is better to say, definitions. Article 2 of the Statute states: "The work of the High Commissioner shall be of an entirely nonpolitical character; it shall be humanitarian and social and shall relate, as a rule, to groups and categories of refugees."

The reference to groups and categories is a link to the previous work generated by two world wars. It takes us back to categories previously mentioned: civilians who fled combat zones, individuals evicted to make room for colonists, laborers imported and forced to work, and persons involuntarily relocated. But these are categories of people requiring protection during periods of war or occupation. By the 1950s, the requirement was to tailor the definition to the realities of Cold War peace. Accordingly, Article 6A (ii) defines a refugee as:

> Any person who, as a result of events occurring before 1 January 1951 and owing to well-founded fear of being persecuted for reasons of race, religion, nationality or political opinion, is outside the country of his nationality and is unable or, owing to such fear or for reasons other than personal convenience, is unwilling to avail himself of the protection of that country.

The notion of a group is missing, the definition applies to individuals. Those individuals need to have crossed an international border because they have a "well-founded" fear of "persecution." That persecution needs to be based either on one or more of three ascriptive characteristics (race, religion, nationality) or on an acquired characteristic, political opinion.

The 1951 Convention Relating to the Status of Refugees which entered into force in 1954 (and was broadened to cover the world beyond Europe by its 1967 Protocol) attempts a combination of the two definitions in the Statute. Article 1A (2) retains the three ascriptive characteristics and the acquired characteristic of the definition in the statute and adds an additional ground of persecution: "membership of a particular social group." The addition of the new category of recognized persecution because of membership of a social group added an element of dynamism to the definition. The list of ascriptive and other characteristics against which discrimination is disallowed in Article 2 of the 1948 Universal Declaration of Human Rights is longer than that defining a refugee in the 1951 Convention and includes the term "sex." The meaning of that term at the time was closer to the term "gender" in use today. But by using the word "sex" the article opened the later possibility of proscribing discrimination for reason of sexual preference. "Sex" is missing from the 1951 Convention but the inclusion of "social group" may achieve a similar result.

The basic right enjoyed by refugees is the right of *non-refoulement*, the right not to be sent back to the country being fled. It is the basic protection offered to refugees under the 1951 Convention. Some regional instruments describe the right as a principle of *jus cogens*, a peremptory rule of international law that applies to all nations even without a basis in the acceptance of a particular treaty.[15]

According to the innovative 2017 book by Alexander Betts and Paul Collier, the "fear of persecution" formulation was insisted on by the United States delegation so as to apply to the "iron curtain" countries and thus preclude the forced return of escaped dissidents.[16] It was initially seen as a temporary measure, but it was thereafter extended in time and geographic scope until it became the lasting formal definition of a refugee, the only category of person who enjoys the right of *non-refoulement*. By contradistinction, people who are not persecuted do not enjoy this right. The definition also necessarily changed existing practices by requiring individualized determinations of refugee status. This might have been useful at the time to highlight individual cases, thus demonstrating the perfidies of a Cold War enemy, but it added a cumbersome step subject to legalistic delay to the entire process. Let us pose this counter factual question: could the return or resettlement of twenty million post-WWII European refugees, within a decade of the end of the war, have been accomplished if each had required a personalized legal and appealable determination of status?

By adding the element of persecution to the definition and the requirement that it be determined on an individual basis, the international community did more than simply complicate the process, it sacrificed what had previously been the self-evident understanding of the problem. It is understandable that governments should wish to limit their *non-refoulement* obligations. This is a powerful right that obliges a government to expend resources on a problem not of its own making which, on the face of it, provides little or no benefit to its own citizens. The tighter the definition, the smaller the problem.

It can plausibly be argued that the case of being forced to leave one's country because of persecution is *sui generis* and therefore should attract special protection. In such a case the refugee's own state has "not just failed to meet their needs but has actively turned against them."[17] But it should not be forgotten that the obligation to assist these people ultimately flows from humanitarianism because they were forced to leave their homes and escape their country. The receiving country therefore is morally bound to assist people who had no choice but to cross the border. The same humanitarian instinct need not necessarily extend to migrants seeking a better future because it cannot reasonably be said that they were forced to leave. Migrants choose to leave in search of a better life. That may be an understandable human reaction, but it does not trigger an obligation on other countries to open their doors.

## CLIMATE REFUGEES

In both Canberra and Wellington, there are detailed plans for the relocation and resettlement of Pacific islanders who lose their homes to rising seas. Countries like Kiribati, Nauru and Tuvalu have already seen low lying land areas underwater at high tide, the inevitability of the loss of their land lacks only a definite timeline. The islanders are not being persecuted by their governments. They do not qualify as refugees. But when the time comes to get on that last ship or aircraft headed to Australia and New Zealand, there will sadly be no place to which they can be returned. The populations of these island countries number in the tens of thousands and they are headed to countries of refuge where vibrant Pacific islander communities already exist. They will not pose a particular hardship for the receiving nations. But it is not the level of hardship that is the salient issue here, it is the principle. They are not climate migrants, who may prefer a less arduous and more certain future elsewhere, they are climate refugees because they have been forced to leave. And there are, no doubt, similar resettlement plans in Washington for the people of the Marshall Islands and the Federated States of Micronesia.

Oil was the key commodity of the twentieth century. Water will be the key issue of the twenty-first. It will be both about the lack of fresh water and the increase in sea water. The United Nations University publication *Water and Migration: A Global Overview*,[18] paints an ominous picture of the balance of the century. The tragedy of the disappearing Aral Sea between Kazakhstan and Uzbekistan will be repeated on other continents beginning with Lake Chad; sea level rise and salination will cause havoc in the heavily populated Nile Delta; the thin strip of land between Mexico and Panama will be buffeted by extreme water events; and small island states in the Pacific and beyond, including the Maldives and in the Caribbean, will see a high percentage of the population migrate, or ultimately, forced to abandon their uninhabitable countries.

The UNU study refers to projections that by 2050, there could be 250 million additional people fleeing climatic disasters.[19] That amounts to almost ten times the current number of the world's refugees. And the terrifying projection for the balance of this century is that "after 2050, this can reach as high as one billion environmental migrants."[20] A separate study estimated that thirty million migrants, many being climate refugees, would head to the US border in the next thirty years and that by the year 2050, 150 million people will be displaced by rising sea levels.[21] In fact, "survival migration will be a defining feature of the twenty-first century and beyond."[22]

There is a lively academic debate as to what the appropriate terminology should be for these people on the move.[23] The burden of this debate is to avoid the use of the term "refugee" for climate migrants and to seek euphemisms in its stead. The candidates include environmentally induced displacement, climate change-induced displacement, environmentally forced migrants, and involuntary environmental migrants. The reasons for the reluctance to employ the term refugee are, to maintain the status of a refugee as a person who escapes persecution and to limit the *non-refoulement* obligation of neighboring states. This is understandable from the perspective of the UN High Commissioner for Refugees who already cannot manage the current 30 million refugees and does not wish to increase that number. And it makes some sense for the government of a country like India, warily watching neighboring Bangladesh where tens of millions of people live precariously at sea level. But it does not make any practical sense. Climate refugees are people who are forced to leave their homes. They are fleeing against their will towards a dangerous and uncertain future. The current system may wish them away by designating them as beyond the entitlement to protection, but they will still be present. They still have to be dealt with.

## INCIPIENT HOBBESIANISM IN RESPONSE TO REFUGEE CRISES

The plight of the world's refugees is tragic. They often leave their homes with only what they can carry on their backs. They then mainly end up in inhumane camps where they are denied the right to work. The usual period of refugee status is now twenty years.[24] This is the life of more than half of the world's nearly thirty million refugees. But there is a positive side as well. There is at least a UN body dedicated to assist them. UNHCR is a major institution with an annual budget of $5 billion and offices in nearly every country.[25] It manages camps, negotiates with governments, and seeks return and resettlement options. It is the champion of the world's refugees and whenever there is a new crisis, it goes cap in hand to the usual donors to seek the necessary funding.

The UNHCR performed successfully in some situations such as the post-war Indochinese refugee crisis, and poorly in other situations such as the eternal Palestinian refugee crisis. Some countries, like Japan, only give money, while other donors also offer refugee resettlement places. If there is a major criticism to be made of the system it is that it treats a long-term problem as a temporary situation, hence the common twenty-year sentence in a camp. But one would not necessarily have described the situation as Hobbesian. The Syrian refugee crisis changed all that.

Memories are short. We now classify the event as the Syrian refugee crisis, but it actually began as the Libyan refugee crisis. The responsibility to protect (R2P) intervention by the UN in Libya was not followed by the discharge of the responsibility to nation-build. Libya was left to its own devices with anarchy, warlordism, and noxious foreign interference the inevitable result. Many wished to escape this anarchy. To the North, Europe had, by and large, transformed itself into Schengenland within which the internal borders had simply faded away. Let us do the math. Anybody arriving in Europe seeking asylum must have her status determined individually. While the determination of status process is ongoing, the right to *non-refoulement* attaches. Once in Europe, therefore, a prospective refugee has the run of the continent to make their fortune. The Italian island of Lampedusa is "only" one hundred and sixty nautical miles from Tripoli. Clearly, the situation was ripe for the people smuggling business and once that business got underway, it attracted customers from well beyond Libya. Young people, mainly young men, from countries South of the Sahara, were prepared to risk crossing the Sahara and then the Mediterranean to get to the promised Schengenland. Above all, Europe wished to have an orderly process and the Dublin agreement required that an asylum seeker would be registered in the country where she first entered Schengenland and restricted to remain within its notional national borders. Thereafter the determination of status process would begin, leading either to the return of the individual deemed not to be a refugee, or the protection and possible resettlement of those determined to have a well-founded fear of persecution. If resettlement was the outcome, there was an expectation of burden sharing among the countries of Europe.

One hundred and sixty nautical miles does not seem like a major journey. It is the equivalent of three hundred kilometers which can be traveled on an autobahn in around two hours. But the sea is not an autobahn and even the normally placid Mediterranean can be rough going, especially on a rickety craft often worth less than the sum of the fares being extracted from the desperate passengers. Boats sank, people died in their thousands, outrage ensued. The Italian government responded by ordering its navy to rescue people foundering at sea in an operation named *Mare Nostrum*. One can laud the humanitarian impulse behind this initiative, but its practical effect was to strengthen the business case of the people smugglers. They could charge more because the risks diminished, and their goal was now simply to get passengers out to sea because the Italian navy would get them to Lampedusa once their unseaworthy boat was spotted. In 2014, the navy rescued 100,000 people and by November of that year the reality dawned on the authorities that the rescue operation was working as a pull factor, and it was suspended.[26] The navy's place was eventually taken by civil society actors and Europe would conduct a bitter debate about ethics and law.

Meanwhile, the Arab Spring had spread beyond North Africa and into the Arab heartland where it would ravage Syria and Yemen. Of course, we cannot blame Syrian people for rising up against the Assad family dictatorship. *New York Times* correspondent Thomas Friedman coined the term "Hama Rules" to describe a method of governance based on an episode in 1982 when the local Muslim Brotherhood chapter killed dozens of officials and took control of the Syrian city of Hama. The Assad regime's response was basically to level the city by artillery, killing tens of thousands and displacing 100,000 more. A generation later, the Syrian people would again revolt, and the Assad regime would again respond using the Hama Rules, no doubt emboldened having recently witnessed the grisly fate of Colonel Gaddafi. Civil war ensued and some four million Syrians fled to seek refuge in neighboring countries, Jordan, Lebanon, and Turkey. This provided an enormous challenge to UNHCR and the international community which it ultimately failed to meet. Turkey hosted the largest number of Syrians, about two million, and as a relatively wealthy country with a population of 80 million, it was able to accommodate this large movement of people without much support from UNHCR. Lebanon only has a population of four million and adding one million refugees is a considerable burden, but Lebanon was reluctant to take the UNHCR path of establishing refugee camps because of memories of the Palestinian camps which had become de facto sovereign entities and had triggered a war with Israel. So, the Syrians largely melted into the local Lebanese population. Jordan, however, called on UNHCR's help, and the normal camp formula was established. As far as Europe and the rest of the world was concerned, it was business as usual. The problems were far away and giving a bit of money to UNHCR would pass as responsible government policy in response.

Several things happened in 2015 to destabilize the situation. Putin decided that Russia had to be seen to be a world power, not simply a regional power as described by then President Obama,[27] and accordingly intervened decisively in the Syrian war with air power and mercenaries. Just as the relatively limited but nevertheless humiliating Black Hawk Down debacle in Somalia had paralyzed the United States, thus effectively disallowing the UN to intervene to prevent the mass genocide in Rwanda, so did the R2P intervention in Libya leading to anarchy dissuade the Obama Administration from intervening in Syria. In retrospect, these are examples of relatively small setbacks leading to major catastrophes. The result of the Putin intervention was that refugees in neighboring countries lost hope of a return to a country that would be led by a democratically elected government. Putting one's life on pause in a camp now made less sense.

Then, the Islamic State (IS) mounted its surprise offensive in Syria and Iraq taking a swathe of territory and subjugating the conquered populations to its obscurantist rule whereby slavery was permitted, and rape of infidels was a reward. Escape from IS was the logical response for minority groups. Even the pro-Assad Alawite people on Syria's Mediterranean coast took fright, and many escaped the country. Events fed the refugee flow.

Finally, the Recep Tayyip Erdoğan factor kicked in. By 2015, he had held the plebiscites necessary to change the constitution and install himself as President. The millions of refugees in Turkey were under his protection. And subject to his manipulation. Turkey has historically had a testy relationship with Europe and, despite the rhetoric, no realistic prospect of joining the European Union. Erdoğan was often criticized by European leaders because of his authoritarian instincts. He had begun his incumbency by declaring a policy of friendship with all. But, typical of an autocrat, Turkey's friendship with Syria soured not because of reasons of state, but because of a personal insult. During the friendship with all stage, the Erdoğans invited the Assads to share an Aegean holiday. The Turkish intelligence service later intercepted a personal email from Mrs. Asma Assad to her husband Bashar Hafez al-Assad, the Syrian President, "pleading never to be asked to do that again: this was a couple with no languages, he a thug who has read only one book, she a frump interested only in shopping."[28] Erdoğan's response was to join the chorus calling for Assad's removal. He was also subject to personal criticism from European politicians, and his response was to use his mastery over refugees in Turkey to annoy Europe. He opened the door.

Lampedusa may be 160 nautical miles from Tripoli, but the Greek island of Lesbos is less than 20 nautical miles from the Turkish coast. The steady flow of refugees to Europe now began to flood. The orderly process put in place through the Dublin agreement had been sorely tested by the Libyan exit, it now collapsed under the weight of the Turkish exodus. The internal territory encompassed by Schengenland was borderless, but the Dublin deal recognized the Westphalian reality whereby the state in which the asylum seeker first entered had the responsibility for registration and for restricting the seeker to within its national borders (minimal on the Schengenland frontier). Italy had barely managed the weight of this obligation, but the much smaller and more parlous economy of Greece simply could not cope. The Hobbesian response was to ignore the Dublin rules and simply wave the asylum seekers through to the next country.[29] A new domino theory took hold. Macedonia, Croatia, Hungary, and Austria would all see hordes of asylum seekers passing through their territory looking for a solution to their plight. The Alps did not stop Hannibal and nor was it a barrier to refugee entry into France from the other direction. Europe convinced itself that the sudden arrival of perhaps one million refugees was posing an existential risk.

Europe has five presidents: European Commission President Ursula Gertrud von der Leyen; President of the Euro Summit Charles Michel; the President of the Eurogroup Paschal Donohoe; President of the European Central Bank Christine Lagarde; and President of the European Parliament Roberta Metsola. But as everybody knew at the time, only one person exercised decisive power, German Chancellor Angela Merkel (who resigned in late 2021). She stepped in and offered to take asylum seekers making their way through Austria on their way to Germany. As Betts and Collier point out, it was a noble sentiment but one ripe for unintended consequences.[30] Assad had supplied the push factors which were compounded by Putin, IS, and Erdoğan, and now Merkel was adding significantly to the pull factors. By 2018, around 600,000 of the one million asylum seekers entering Germany were Syrian, with Iraqis and Afghans the next largest groups.[31] Even Syria got a slice of the action by selling passports to all comers for $400.[32]

The results of Merkel's noble gesture must have surprised even Merkel. She had attempted to solve an immediate problem of uncontrolled hordes trekking through Europe, but she had in effect unintentionally invited open migration to Germany. A definitive full stop needed to be found but Germany did not have the power to do so itself because, as a result of Schengen, Germany has no external borders. As can be seen from the source countries, the path to Germany ran through Turkey. Erdoğan needed to be convinced to cooperate. In a secretly negotiated deal, Merkel promised Turkey, already due €3 billion in a previous refugee deal, a further €6 billion to stop the flow and take back any that crossed from Turkey to Europe.[33] Further, Merkel promised Erdoğan the considerable prize of visa-free entry to Turkish passport holders for travel to Europe. The money was delivered, and the deal was respected on the Turkish side, thus ending the refugee crisis for the moment. But the visa-free deal is still under negotiation, with the EU adding the condition that first, Turkey had to recognize the Republic of Cyprus, causing Erdoğan to threaten to reopen the human sluice gate.[34]

What was the balance of Europe's reaction? In a word, Hobbesian. The Dublin deal was made obsolete; the EU burden sharing requirements were ignored; the treatment of asylum seekers deteriorated. Most concerningly, Hungary and Poland turned the issue into a religious question and others took a similar line while more politely describing it as civilizational. According to Betts and Collier, the perception among the people of Europe was of a loss of control over the basic issue of who can and cannot enter and remain in Europe, which in turn led to disparagement of the European decision-making processes, which in turn fueled the Brexit vote.[35] And one can add that the surprising Brexit vote and the migration issues behind it may well have fueled the surprising 2016 Trump vote.

Intolerant treatment of asylum seekers was certainly not limited to some European countries. Whereas Angela Merkel pursued a noble instinct, the tactic employed by succeeding Australian governments, can only be described as ignoble. Whereas the asylum seekers rushing to Europe numbered in the millions, those attempting the hazardous boat trip to Australia numbered not even in the tens of thousands. The public nevertheless wanted to see the government "in control." Australia adopted a game theory tactic to undermine the business model of the people smugglers with the aim of drying up the market for their services. This was achieved by making the lives of those who survived the boat journey so miserable that nobody could rationally wish to follow their example. The "Pacific solution" was to bribe Nauru and Papua New Guinea with additional aid money to allow Australia to hold the asylum seekers in isolated island camps for years on end while vowing that none would ever be allowed to set foot in Australia.[36] Having said that, however, it is only fair to note that Australia accepts for resettlement about 6,000 refugees annually through the (orderly) UNHCR processes.[37]

In 1980, the United States took in about one quarter of a million refugees, but the Trump administration's intake ceiling for 2020 was twenty thousand and unlikely to be filled.[38] What a precipitous drop! A recent documentary demonstrated what this means on the ground. The documentary film *Welcome to Chechnya* was released in 2020. It traces the attempts to rescue gay people from the violently homophobic regime in Chechnya, a self-governing Russian province. The film concludes with a graphic noting that in the two years of its making, 151 Chechen evacuees were resettled. Canada granted 44 refugee visas, the United States, none.[39]

## WHAT ROLE FOR THE LEVIATHAN?

We need to be honest in acknowledging that no Leviathan, however powerful, can solve the problem of one billion refugees. A Hobbesian response, however, will destabilize one nation after another and cause untold hardship. The role of the Leviathan is to give the calming impression of order and control. This is not easy even when dealing with dry economic issues, but it is immeasurably more difficult when dealing with as emotional an issue as migration.

I had an unhappy experience of this. Though I had not yet been appointed to the senior executive service, the highlight of my diplomatic career was being in charge of the East Europe desk at the end of the Cold War. I had not yet turned 40 and, given the vagaries of the staffing structure at the time, I was the key adviser to the Australian government on how to deal with all the issues being presented upon winning a war. I have already written on the myriad problems of recognition of states generated by the collapse of

Yugoslavia and the Soviet Union; we recognized 17 new states and withheld recognition from two.[40] And I have also previously recalled the frantic morning when I had to write two speeches on the fall of the Berlin Wall to be given that afternoon, one by the Foreign Minister in the Senate and one by the Prime Minister in the House . . . saying different things—the PM's speech dealt with the global implications while the Foreign Minister's speech provided an Asian regional perspective.[41] There was one episode that did not fit on the geopolitical chess board but was emotionally taxing.

The Soviet bloc was monolithic in some ways but idiosyncratic in others. Policy came down from the Kremlin, but on-the-ground management left room for the further perversity of individual actors. There is no better example than Nicolae Ceausescu's Romania which had to deal with communist orthodoxy while suffering from Ceausescu's megalomania. It was a closed country and hardly at the center of world affairs and our knowledge of it was limited. When communist legitimacy radiating from Moscow was expunged, Ceausescu was arrested, tried, and executed within a matter of days. Romania teetered close to anarchy, but its instincts were to gravitate towards the West Europeans for whom the doors of the previously closed country were opened. When the visitors arrived, led by diplomats and journalists, they found striking evidence of Ceausescu's megalomania, and they also found orphanages teaming with babies, white babies. It launched the adoption equivalent of a gold rush.[42] An airfare and a fistful of hard currency, could purchase a newly adopted baby within a week or two.

Australia is part of the global village and childless couples grappling with the many difficulties of domestic and foreign adoption, wanted to get in on the act. But Australia is a country of laws, including laws about legal adoption. And Australia had a simple but effective means of enforcement with regard to unauthorized foreign adoption by simply denying the child a visa. To authorize foreign adoption, Australia first required an agreement with the source country based on a close study of its adoption system. There was no such agreement with Romania and the government's reluctant response to the prospective parents was negative. At one stage I was with a government minister, meeting a delegation of these couples who insisted on being given "one good reason" why the government refused to relax its rules. The minister turned to me to respond. I said we don't have an Embassy in Bucharest and we know little about Romanian orphanages, but if they were like other Soviet bloc countries, it was likely that the children of political prisoners sent to the Romanian equivalent of the Gulag were being treated as orphans. What if an Australian couple adopted a child and not long thereafter liberated prisoners insisted on their child's return? The Australian government stuck to its guns.

It was a Labor government, and the policy may have been different with a conservative government, the philosophy of which might have been along these lines. We do not want to be a "nanny state" telling citizens what to do and pretending we know their own affairs better than they do. The government's job is to facilitate people's initiatives, not to stand in the way. If they can "lawfully" (meaning purchase adoption documents) adopt in Romania, the government should not stand in the way. I sometimes tell my students this story and ask them to debate which governmental approach is better. We only learned the tragic twist to this tale months later. Like other Soviet bloc countries, Romania had a medical practice of giving underweight babies infusions of blood. The blood infusion instruments were rarely sterilized, and the blood was unscreened, resulting in the widespread infection of nosocomial HIV and hepatitis B.[43] Many of the adopted Romanian babies were infected and would die in their adoptive parents' arms, or they would need lifelong medical attention. Adoption and travel to West Europe might be a preferred outcome from the children's perspective, but it was clearly not what the parents signed up for.

So, yes, migration, adoption, and refugee resettlement are emotionally taxing and therefore tricky issues for policy formulation. Whether politicians agree or not, these have become global issues. They flow from globalization for which the developed world has insisted that trade and investment move as freely as possible, while putting up walls to the movement of that other factor of production, labor. Market fundamentalists believe there should be no rules to distort the operation of comparative advantage . . . except when it comes to labor. Then the barriers are justified. Because the vision espoused in this book is based on the continued existence of nation states, it remains one of the attributes of the nation to determine entry to its territory. Even the UN Leviathan will not have the power to require nations to open their borders. But that still leaves a considerable role for the UN Leviathan in a world where dictators will continue to subjugate their people, where wars will continue to be fought, and where climate change will accelerate the forced movement of people.

The first step required is one that UNHCR will find difficult to swallow. We simply cannot continue to operate on the basis of individualized determination of refugee status as the trigger for protection. It was a system designed to rescue those who escaped from behind the iron curtain. It was envisaged as a temporary system, designed for European conditions, and unlikely to apply to large numbers. Betts and Collier explain the financial cost of operating such a system: the world spends \$75b a year on the 10% of asylum seekers reaching the developed world, while it spends \$5b a year on the 90% who remain in countries of haven in the global South.[44] Much of the \$75b is for resettlement costs, but an inordinate amount is spent on individual determination of status followed by the inevitable appeals during which time the applicant must live in suspended animation.

Is there another way? UNHCR needs to develop a risk management strategy applying to groups of people. There has been a tension from the outset between policies based on groups and those focused on individuals. The tension needs to be settled in favor of groups. We know there is a civil war in Syria, we understand the brutality of the Assad regime, we are aware of the cruel medieval justice meted out by IS, so let us simply designate escaping Syrians as refugees. Of course, this means giving the benefit of the doubt to all those people escaping Syria including some who may have been complicit in regime crimes. That is why it is called risk management rather than risk avoidance. In time, other Syrian refugees will point out Assad's accomplices. Germany is currently prosecuting three such cases.[45] But why should all the genuine refugees go through the lengthy, inefficient, and inexact individualized determination process so that a few bad apples can be weeded out at the outset. Surely it is better to designate groups that qualify for refugee status—the Rohingya of Myanmar, the Ahmadis in Pakistan and other Muslim-majority countries in Asia, and Darfuris in Sudan are examples—and extend protection to its members. Imposters may well free-ride for a while but most will eventually be unmasked. In many ways, this is already a de facto reality.

My next suggestion will also be unpalatable to UNHCR. Abandon the Huguenot definition! It is undeniable that political persecution is egregious in the extreme. But the status of refugee is, in fact, not triggered by this persecution. The need for a humanitarian response does not flow simply because of persecution. It flows from the fact that the individual has been forced from her home. That is an eminently sensible trigger because, unlike persecution, the fact of having been forced to leave one's home is readily demonstrable. As noted above, climate refugees are coming, in great numbers. The practical reality is that they need protection and assistance. Who should provide it? As in so many other radical sounding ideas in this book, the answer to this puzzle has already been answered . . . in embryonic form.

The 2004 tsunami devastated the coasts of a number of Asian countries and many people were lost and destitute as a result. The organization most adept at handling such cases was UNHCR, but there had been no allegation of persecution. The then Secretary-General asked UNHCR to intervene in Indonesia and Sri Lanka, and the organization did so while noting that this was unprecedented and exceptional.[46] Nevertheless, in the following years it also stepped in after natural disasters in Pakistan, Myanmar, the Philippines, Haiti, and Somalia, as well as the man-made disaster in Beirut in 2020.[47] This is the inevitable direction UNHCR must take. Climate refugees are refugees. Needless to say, no individualized determinations will be necessary. And a case before the Human Rights Committee in Geneva has given a soft law patina to these views. In its first ruling on a complaint by an individual seeking asylum from the effects of climate change, the UN Human Rights Committee has stated that countries may not deport individuals who face climate change-induced conditions that violate the right to life.[48] I am calling this soft law because the Committee only issues advisory opinions and because in the case before it, the Committee found that the country in question, New Zealand, had not violated the rights of the petitioner, a man and his family from Kiribati, though it had decided to deport him.

In adhering to the climate refugee concept, the UN will become the champion and Leviathan of forcibly displaced people. The "forcible" aspect remains critical. I do not believe there is a right of migration. But those forced from their homes for whatever reason are entitled to expect a humanitarian response from the international community. To avoid collective action miscues, free riders, and lack of coordination, a UN body needs to be in charge, building on its considerable experience to discharge its responsibilities. As in other cases discussed in this book, that UN body, let us continue to call it UNHCR, will require independent funding. Going cap in hand, crisis by crisis, donor by donor, is not a formula to handle one billion refugees, or even half or a quarter of that number. More on Tobin taxation in the final chapter.

Tobin taxes might in part resolve the funding problem, but they do not fully tackle the free rider issue. It is true that Tobin taxes may displace some national taxes thus establishing an indirect form of burden sharing. But the most difficult problem to solve will be resettlement. Victims of persecution dream of the day the civil war will be over, or the nasty regime will fall, at which point they can return home. Until that time, many are warehoused in camps run by UNHCR. We have already come across the sad figure of twenty years for the average duration of this refugee status. And we have come across the figure of 90% remaining in neighboring countries of haven. This situation might be tolerated by the international community under the Huguenot definition, but it simply cannot apply to climate refugees for whom there will be no place to return. For such refugees, resettlement will be the durable solution.

The UN Leviathan needs to convince the world that resettlement can be achieved as a win-win outcome. Counterintuitively, this can be demonstrated more readily in relation to the global North, than in the global South. The wealthy countries of resettlement in the global North are in demographic decline with below replacement birth rates, aging populations, and unsustainable welfare systems. They need an injection of energetic migrants to cure these ills. UNHCR therefore needs to elicit resettlement quotas from such countries. The United States, down to a miniscule 20,000 unfilled places, should get back to its previous quotas. The resettlement of hundreds of thousands of Indochinese refugees in the 70s and 80s enriched the country. A first step in that direction is to assign the 50,000 places, capriciously put aside for the green card lottery winners, to refugees. Indeed, a figure closer to two hundred thousand a year, as in 1980, would do the US no harm. Other countries of the developed world should also set high quotas. Assuming total resettlement in Europe, the Americas and Australasia is 500,000 per year, forty million refugees could be accommodated in the balance of this century.

But resettlement in the global North is not feasible for the great bulk of future refugees. Most will want to remain closer to "home." But this does not leave the global North off the hook. The burden sharing process needs to be strengthened to assist countries of haven in the global South. The responsibility of the global North goes beyond additional voluntary funding for UNHCR. These countries need to provide financial and trade preferences to allow the countries of haven to integrate the new populations into their economies, rather than to warehouse them in camps. Refugees need to be seen as producers and consumers, buyers and sellers, employers and employees. They need to be seen as the means to grow the local economy and make it more dynamic. Wealthy countries need to facilitate that outcome. This is the main burden of the Betts and Collier argument, and it is undoubtedly correct.

Climate change will lead to mass movements of people. The mass movements will be forced on these people because of the sudden climatic changes the Anthropocene has caused. Can the world simply wall these people out of neighboring countries? Can we deny our humanitarianism by hiding behind an inappropriate legal definition? We need to broaden our refugee systems to accommodate them. Only a UN Leviathan can manage this system.

## NOTES

1. United Nations, "Refugees," https://www.un.org/en/global-issues/refugees
2. Merriam-Webster, "The Origin of 'Refugee'," https://www.merriam-webster.com/words-at-play/origin-and-meaning-of-refugee
3. Peter Gatrell, "Refugees," *International Encyclopedia of the First World War*, https://encyclopedia.1914-1918-online.net/article/refugees
4. Ibid.
5. UNHCR USA, "Nansen - a man of action and vision," https://www.unhcr.org/en-us/events/nansen/4aae50086/nansen-man-action-vision.html
6. Elihu Lauterpacht and Daniel Bethlehem, "The scope and content of the principle of non-refoulement: Opinion," in *Refugee Protection in International Law UNHCR's Global Consultations on International Protection*, eds. Erika Feller, Volker Türk and Frances Nicholson, (Cambridge University Press, 2003) 87–177, 99.
7. Chauncy D. Harris and Gabriele Wülker, "The Refugee Problem of Germany," *Economic Geography*, Vol. 29, No. 1 (Jan. 1953), 10–25, 10.

8. Charles Wesley Sharpe, "The Origins of the United Nations Relief and Rehabilitation Administration, 1939–1943" (2012). *Publicly Accessible Penn Dissertations 696*, 292 https://repository.upenn.edu/edissertations/696

9. Ibid, 676.

10. Timothy Snyder, *Bloodlands: Europe between Hitler and Stalin*, (New York: Basic Books, 2010).

11. Sharpe, op. cit.

12. Article 2(a) Agreement for United Nations Relief and Rehabilitation Administration, November 9, 1943, http://www.ibiblio.org/pha/policy/1943/431109a.html

13. United Nations, https://undocs.org/en/A/RES/8(I)

14. Reproduced at https://www.unhcr.org/4d944e589.pdf

15. Mexico Declaration and Plan of Action to Strengthen the International Protection of Refugees in Latin America of 16 November 2004, and the 1984 Cartagena Declaration on Refugees.

16. Alexander Betts and Paul Collier, *Refuge: Rethinking Refugee Policy in a Changing World*, (Oxford University Press, 2017) 38.

17. Matthew J. Lister, "Who are Refugees?" *Law and Philosophy*, Volume 32, Issue 5, 2013, 645–671, 662.

18. Nidhi Nagabhatla, Panthea Pouramin, Rupal Brahmbhatt, Cameron Fioret, Talia Glickman, K. Bruce Newbold, Vladimir Smakhtin, *Water and Migration: A Global Overview*, UNU Institute for Water, Environment and Health, 2020.

19. Ibid., 6.

20. Ibid.

21. Abrahm Lustgarten, "Refugees from the Earth," *New York Times Magazine*, July 26, 2020, 13, 18.

22. Betts and Collier, op. cit, 134.

23. Bogumil Terminski, "Towards Recognition and Protection of Forced Environmental Migrants in the Public International Law: Refugee or IDPs Umbrella?" *Policy Studies Organization (PSO) Summit,* December 2011.

24. Betts and Collier, op. cit, 77.

25. Ibid, 56.

26. Ibid, 69.

27. Scott Wilson, "Obama dismisses Russia as 'regional power' acting out of weakness," *Washington Post*, March 25, 2014.

28. Norman Stone, "Turkey and Russia—friends for a while, now foes once again," *Financial Times*, 11 March 2016.

29. Betts and Collier, op cit, 65.

30. Ibid, 84.

31. Marion MacGregor, "Germany: Refugee numbers in context," *INFO Migrants*, https://www.infomigrants.net/en/post/17641/germany-refugee-numbers-in-context

32. Betts and Collier, op. cit, 109

33. Ibid, 92.

34. SchengenVisaInfo News, "Turkey Threatens to Suspend EU Migrant Deal Due to Lack of Visa-free Travel to EU," https://www.schengenvisainfo.com/news/turkey-threatens-to-suspend-eu-migrant-deal-due-to-lack-of-visa-free-travel-to-eu/

35. Betts and Collier, op cit, 135.

36. Janet Phillips, "The 'Pacific Solution' revisited: a statistical guide to the asylum seeker caseloads on Nauru and Manus Island," *Parliament of Australia*, 4 September 2012.

37. Elibritt Karlsen, "Refugee resettlement to Australia: what are the facts?," *Parliament of Australia*, 7 September 2016.

38. Migration Policy Institute, "U.S. Annual Refugee Resettlement Ceilings and Number of Refugees Admitted, 1980-Present," https://www.migrationpolicy.org/programs/data-hub/charts/us-annual-refugee-resettlement-ceilings-and-number-refugees-admitted-united

39. Jeanette Catsoulis, "A Moving Indictment of Brutal Persecution," *New York Times*, 30 June 2020.

40. Roland Rich, "Recognition of States: The Collapse of Yugoslavia and the Soviet Union," *European Journal of International Law*, 4 No. 1 (March 1993), 36–65.

41. Roland Rich, *Pacific Asia in Quest of Democracy*, (Boulder: Lynne Rienner Publishers, 2007), 9.

42. Kathleen Hunt, "The Romanian Baby Bazaar," *New York Times*, March 24, 1991.

43. Karen Dente and Jamie Hess, "Pediatric AIDS in Romania — A Country Faces Its Epidemic and Serves as a Model of Success," Medscape 2006, https://www.medscape.com/viewarticle/528693

44. Betts and Collier, op. cit, 129.

45. Christopher F. Schuetze and Ben Hubbard, "Syrian Doctor Accused of Torture Is Arrested in Germany," *New York Times*, June 22, 2020.

46. Betts and Collier, op. cit, 59.

47. UNHCR Press Release, "UNHCR rushes support for Beirut in the aftermath of massive blast," 7 August 2020.

48. OHCHR Press Release, "Historic UN Human Rights case opens door to climate change asylum claims," 21 January 2020.

# Chapter 11

# More Pandemics

When I began writing this book, I did not foresee that there would be a chapter on pandemics. If there was one aspect of global governance that lends itself to win-win outcomes it is health, and in particular, controlling infectious diseases. It was taken for granted that each nation would recognize the borderlessness of the bacterial and viral world. A corollary of that borderlessness is the essential interdependence of nations in fighting infectious diseases. The threat to win-win outcomes flows from ignorance. Clearly, if the germ theory of disease is not understood or if an Übermensch ideology holds that a population is naturally immune, then the self-interested motive for cooperation disappears. But science has defeated that ignorance . . . or so we thought. What the spread of COVID-19 has tragically taught us is that national policy can be built on politically constructed ignorance. So, though it was not part of my initial thinking, I am now convinced that we need a global health Leviathan.

## THE EBOLA RESPONSE

Everybody who follows even the sparest version of the news understands recurring instances of novel infectious diseases.[1] The AIDS epidemic began as a disease afflicting male homosexuals but soon spread beyond that cohort and beyond the wealthy North to the vulnerable South, and in particular to Africa. It took decades of effort by medical teams, social workers, and pharmaceutical researchers to find the package of social messaging, government policy and pharmaceutical products to achieve some sort of control over the disease.

Severe Acute Respiratory Syndrome (SARS) is a viral respiratory illness caused by a coronavirus first reported in Asia in February 2003. The illness spread to more than two dozen countries in North America, South America, Europe, and Asia before the SARS global outbreak of 2003 was contained through testing, tracing, and quarantining.

Middle East Respiratory Syndrome (MERS) is a viral respiratory illness that is new to humans. It was first reported in Saudi Arabia in 2012 and has since spread well beyond. It is a coronavirus and is spread from ill people to others through close contact. But the virus was not easily transmissible and the authorities in the affected countries came to grips with it through the well-known path of testing, tracing, and quarantining.

Zika is spread mostly by the bite of an infected Aedes species mosquito, but it can also be spread through sex or by a mother to her fetus, and infection during pregnancy can cause birth defects. In 2015 and 2016, large outbreaks of Zika virus occurred in the Americas. Zika can best be controlled by managing the range and density of the mosquito and protection against mosquito bites. The disease has not seen large outbreaks in more recent years.

Ebola virus disease is a deadly disease with occasional outbreaks that occur primarily on the African continent. Ebola most commonly affects people and nonhuman primates (such as monkeys, gorillas, and chimpanzees). Ebola virus was first described in 1976 near the Ebola River in the Democratic Republic of Congo and there have been about 20 outbreaks since that time. The years 2014–16 saw an acute epidemic of Ebola in West Africa. The first batch of these Ebola cases in West Africa was reported by the World Health Organization (WHO) on March 23, 2014, in the forested rural region of southeastern Guinea bordering Liberia and Sierra Leone but by late July, Ebola had reached the urban and densely populated capitals of all three countries. WHO reported 28,652 suspected, probable, and confirmed Ebola cases, including 11,325 deaths, far exceeding the combined total number of cases reported in approximately 20 previous outbreaks since the 1970s.

The international community responded, though there were criticisms as to the speed and competence of these efforts which will be elaborated below. It was only half a dozen years ago, but the world was a much different place at that time. In 2015, the United States might still be seen as a benign hegemon. The United States could still be seen as a guarantor of the international system it helped found in the post-WWII era. Accordingly, the United States was a key party to the international response mainly through the Centers for Disease Control (CDC). CDC worked with government agencies including national ministries of health, the WHO, and other international partners in an intensive effort to end the epidemic. For all the hesitations, delays, and missteps in dealing with the Ebola outbreak at that time, the international system seemed to work. The WHO took the basic coordination steps and the international community, led by the CDC, did the necessary legwork. The extent of the CDC's involvement can be seen in figure 11.1.[2]

The most recent Ebola outbreak took place in the Democratic Republic of Congo beginning in April 2018 and caused more than two thousand deaths.

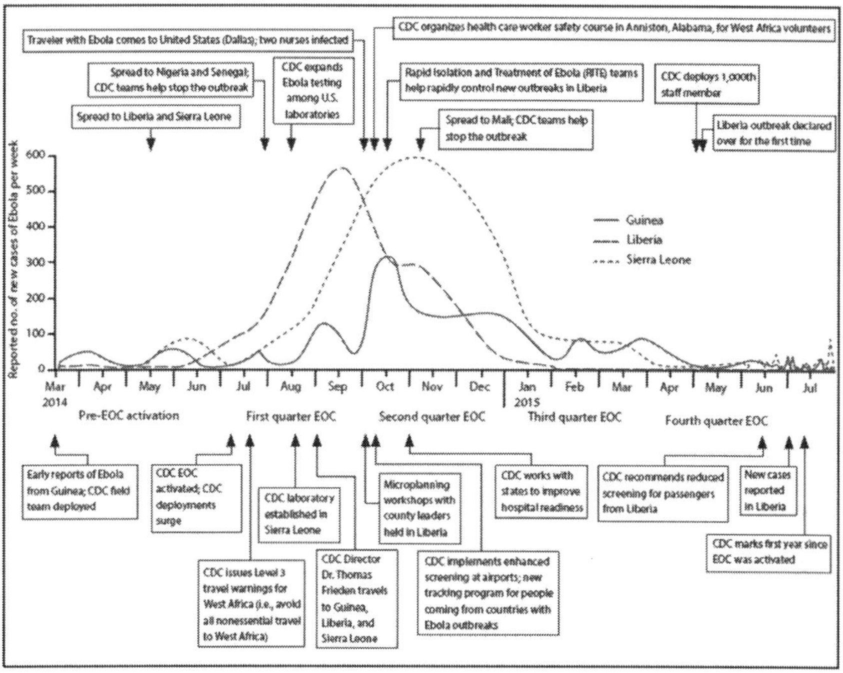


**Figure 11.1. Control Strategies, and Lessons Learned in the CDC Response to the 2014–2016 Ebola Epidemic.** ***Beth P. Bell, Damon IK, Jernigan DB, et al., "Overview, Control Strategies, and Lessons Learned in the CDC Response to the 2014–2016 Ebola Epidemic," MMWR, Supplements, July 8, 2016, 65(3):4–11. DOI: http://dx.doi.org/10.15585/mmwr.su6503a2.***

Learning from the lessons of the previous outbreak, the WHO reacted quickly and decisively. It was able to declare the outbreak over in June 2020.[3]

Ebola is a hemorrhagic disease. The symptoms of infected patients in the later stages of the disease are highly visible and terrifying. This generates concern and fear. But the reality is that, because Ebola is caught through direct contact with the bodily fluids of diseased patients, the infection rate can be controlled through personal hygienic practices inspired by careful social messaging. In Africa, one key to stopping the spread of the disease was limiting human contact with infected dead bodies, though this behavior was normal in local burial practices. While the disease has on occasion spread through several West African countries, there were only a handful of cases through infected travelers in the rest of the world and these were quickly contained. The key point is that this terrifying outbreak was eventually contained through sensible international cooperation. People in the US were shocked but not actually threatened by the disease, yet the US Government mounted a massive effort to combat it in association with the WHO and other partners.

As noted, approximately 4,000 CDC staff members directly participated in the response, and of these, 1,897 deployed to Guinea, Liberia, Sierra Leone, and other African countries affected by the epidemic.[4] President Obama expressed the nation's commitment to treating and tackling Ebola as both a national security priority, and an example of American global leadership.[5]

## THE WORLD HEALTH ORGANIZATION AND EBOLA

The key word in the previous paragraph is "eventually." A major outbreak around the world was averted but the Ebola epidemic of 2014–16 triggered warning lights, in particular in relation to the role and response by the World Health Organization. The first news of the reemergence of Ebola came to the WHO in March 2014 and it has been suggested that the organization's initial response was too slow and incompetent.[6] This sounds a little harsh given that within two months, the WHO had arranged for 112 epidemiologists to be on the ground.[7] The reasons for the criticisms lie less in the WHO's performance on the ground than in the inflated expectations of what a world health organization could or should do. In this sense, the world was looking for a global health Leviathan and instead it got a typical UN bureaucracy.

According to its constitutive charter, the WHO's core functions are providing leadership; shaping the research agenda and stimulating the exchange of knowledge; setting norms and standards; articulating ethical and evidence-based policy options; providing technical support; and monitoring health situation and trends.[8] These half a dozen tasks can be pared down to two basic responsibilities: normative goals, including leadership, research and standard-setting; and operational goals, including technical support and situation monitoring. The WHO does not claim to have yet another role, that of first responder, but many in the international community also expect that task to be fulfilled. The criticism of the WHO boils down to the fact that it was unable to be the normative leader, operational chief and first responder all at once.

But why should anyone be surprised? The WHO is a typical UN body in thrall to its Member States. It has no independent source of funding and is largely dependent for funding from governments, and much of this comes with strings tying up its use. The Director-General is selected by the governments at their World Health Assembly. The regional and country offices are hosted by these same governments. In other words, the WHO has 193 puppet masters often pulling strings in different directions. It turns out that the main skill required by the leadership of the WHO is not medical or organizational but diplomatic.

This attempt to balance the wishes of the various governments came through clearly in the response to the penultimate Ebola crisis. Why did the WHO leadership wait until August 2014 to declare a Public Health Emergency of International Concern? The answer was subsequently found in a trove of WHO emails demonstrating that the organization "held off on declaring an emergency in part because it could have angered the countries involved, interfered with their mining interests or restricted the Muslim pilgrimage to Mecca in October."[9] This was confirmed by the panel set up to assess the WHO's response to the crisis which found that the Organization was in effect caught in international political gridlock.[10] A medical expert put the matter starkly as follows: "For WHO, leadership failures, problems with regional and country offices in Africa, weak surveillance and response capacities, and incompetent staff made the Ebola outbreak a debacle."[11]

## NEW CHALLENGERS

The WHO inherited the dilemmas of its predecessor organization, the League of Nations Health Office (LNHO). Pandemics and plagues do not recognize national borders and maritime connected empires were particularly vulnerable. European colonial powers began discussions of mitigation issues in the nineteenth century ultimately leading to the establishment of the Office International d'Hygiène Publique in Paris in 1907 which advanced ideas on the establishment of an international sanitary system.[12] It was this work, together with some of those involved in it, that was folded into the LNHO which came into being in 1922.[13] From the outset, the LNHO was pulled in two directions. On the one side, it wished to continue the work of the Paris office on controlling infectious diseases. On the other side, it wished to assist poorer countries to develop their health systems.[14] This is the dilemma the WHO inherited.

In their excellent book on global health, Chelsea Clinton and Devi Sridhar, describe the two approaches as the vertical and the horizontal.[15] The vertical approach tackles specific diseases and in particular, infectious diseases. The horizontal approach aims at strengthening health systems and the normative principles underpinning them, such as health as a basic human right, the responsibility of the state in the provision of universal health care, and the availability of community based primary health care. The vertical approach is focused, measurable and even achievable. The horizontal approach is difficult, complex, long-term, and reliant on many factors associated with domestic politics and personalities. Success in the horizontal approach will necessarily lead to positive vertical results. But success in vertical ventures will not necessarily strengthen health systems. Ideally, both approaches would be pursued simultaneously, and diagonal links would be found. But the world of the WHO is not an ideal world. It is a world of limited resources, a world of fractious politics, and a world where pressing short-term needs will always overwhelm long-term objectives.

In the twenty-first century, two organizations have emerged to challenge the WHO's primacy in global health. They both adopt vertical approaches while paying lip service to horizontal needs. They have both taken a significant chunk of global health funding, much of which, prior to their emergence, would have been destined for the WHO. They have both pioneered new governance and funding mechanisms while the WHO remains locked into the twentieth century Westphalian model.

The Global Alliance for Vaccines and Immunization (Gavi) was established to answer the riddle of how to vaccinate the most children at the least cost. The answer was money. By establishing a well-endowed fund, vaccinators could negotiate with manufacturers and offer guaranteed sales in return for the lowest prices. Gavi was created in 2000 and was quickly off and running, acquiring in its first dozen or so years more than five billion dollars of vaccines.[16] Gavi did not see itself as an on-the-ground actor. The analogy it would select would be as the brains of the outfit. The attraction of this brain to donors is that it does not work on the basis of hunches or favors or routine, but instead, applies rational decision-making to solve the vaccination puzzle. It negotiates and purchases the vaccines which then go straight to its work horse, UNICEF, which does the vaccinating. The WHO continues to have a role in delivery, but its more consequential job is to assure quality control. Other actors, such as governments or civil society organizations, are coopted into the process as the need arises. Eligibility and priority are not decided through amiable chats over coffee or wine at the Palais des Nations in Geneva, but through numerical eligibility formulae. Success is judged by breadth of coverage, and rate of return on investment which has been measured at 18%, whereby for every dollar invested in the Gavi process, $1.18 of economic benefit is generated by the disease-free work force. Gavi has offices in Geneva but unlike most UN bodies, it does not have staff in any regional or national office. Why sleep under a bed net in sweltering equatorial Africa when one can happily crunch all the numbers in Geneva?

We have already come across the Global Fund to Fight AIDS, Tuberculosis and Malaria (Global Fund) in the Globalization chapter where it was described as a multi-stakeholder partnership. It was established in 2002 and, like Gavi, it also likes to think of itself as the brains of the outfit. Like Gavi it is based in Geneva and has no offices in the field. Also like Gavi, the Global Fund is a financial entity and in its first dozen or so years it raised $33 billion.[17] It also employs market forces to deliver its product. But unlike Gavi which does the negotiating at the purchasing start of the process, the Global Fund uses the power of competition at the distribution end of the process. It runs an application process for its grants which it has tweaked so as to obtain what it considers to be the best outcomes. The grant applicants are country coordinating mechanisms comprising governments and civil society bodies which are intended to deliver the products—antiretroviral drugs, testing regimes, antibiotics, counselling, and pyrethrum impregnated bed nets—to affected populations. The competition for funds together with the terms of reference established by the Global Fund are designed to produce the optimum results meritocratically. There is no doubt as to the Global Fund's significance: in 2010, the Fund accounted for 25% of all international disbursements to fight HIV/AIDS; 60% of international public funding for TB control; and 70% of all funds allocated to malaria management.[18]

I have to admit to some sympathy for the Global Fund approach. At the UN Democracy Fund, I developed a similar system of applications for funding, previously touched on in Chapter 3. We would receive around two thousand applications a year and finally select about 50 projects for funding (a slim one in 400 chance). Expert assessors went through the applications and short-listed about 250 and I would select the 50 projects to receive offers from this list which would then be submitted to the Board for approval. The good projects tended to jump out. Whereas many project applications were formulaic, employing fashionable buzz words and offering to perform similar sets of outreach and training activities, some applications were based on strong core ideas that were innovative and impactful. But a good application doth not a good project make. We would negotiate a project document or contract and provide funding in tranches based on performance indicators. The key to quality control was in-depth evaluation. I politely rejected offers from collegial UN bodies to undertake the evaluations and went to the commercial market. I would not believe a UN evaluation of itself, so why should others? The projects to be evaluated in depth were selected to provide for a representative range, thematically and geographically. The system demonstrated its rigor with the finding by the evaluators (a two-person team of international and local experts per project) that about 20% of the projects had failed to meet their designated goals. I used to make a number of points to the Board. First, I never pretended that we had selected the 50 "best" projects. There is no system that can guarantee that result. But I assured the Board that, given the competition, we had selected 50 excellent projects reflecting the range of applications. As to the 20% "failure" rate, unusual among UN bodies which normally report North Korean like figures of 99% success, I argued that it should be looked upon as an 80% success rate which was highly acceptable. The identification of failures meant that the Board could accept the veracity of the success rate. Finally, I made the point that, as an institution, UNDEF learned a great deal more from its failures than from its successes. As I once explained to a Russian friend, all good projects look the same, but every failed project has failed in its own particular way.

Why did the international community turn to the new global health approaches? The work being done was not based on a new silver bullet, a new medical discovery, or a new social mechanism. Yes, there were improvements in the effectiveness of drugs, but that is not the reason for the existence of Gavi and the Global Fund. The best way to summarize the reason is to say it was based on the idea of bringing private sector values to the delivery of public sector health goods. These values include competition, bargaining, evidence-based decisions, efficiency, higher volumes, and lower costs. These values were injected into a slow, inefficient, and entitled Westphalian system which venerated lowest common denominator decisions taken by general assemblies of governments, and then implemented by time-serving bureaucrats more interested in not making mistakes than in achieving effective delivery. The change was radical. The discourse switched from words to numbers. This is not a development I particularly value in the social sciences, but it lends itself to the health sciences. The documentation went from preambular paragraphs in resolutions to charts of breadth of coverage and rates of return. The expertise switched from medical doctors to logistics and management specialists. The results validated the new approach. Whereas vaccination rates had steadied and even declined in the 1990s, in the first decade and a half of the new century, under Gavi stewardship, an additional 200 million children, mainly from the poorest countries, were covered with a range of vaccines.[19]

I am not a believer in the great man version of history because it is circumstances that will cause a Napoleon to emerge, though it need not be Napoleon Bonaparte. And one need not be a Marxist to believe that history has its own dynamic, driven by geography, climate, economics, demography, and social movements. So, this is not a hagiography of Bill Gates as the great man who brought modernity to global public health, but he was the catalyst. It was Gates who made the initial grant to allow Gavi to be established, and the donor community followed. Of all the institutions supported by the Gates Foundation, funding to Gavi remains the highest at 25% of the budget, whereas the Gates Foundation meets some 3% of the massive Global Fund budget.[20] Gates brought the private sector values honed at Microsoft to the global public health field. No individual, whether speechifying at the UN, leading a UN agency, or even launching a government initiative, has had such an immediate and deep impact on the global health field. It helps to have an endowment of more than $45 billion.[21]

As head of the UN Office for Partnerships (UNOP), I was privileged to co-host the 2013 Forbes Philanthropy Summit in the Trusteeship Chamber of the UN at which both Bill Gates and Warren Buffett spoke.[22] When asked why he pledged to give the Gates Foundation $37b rather than start his own Foundation, Buffett said he had a day job, and that he couldn't do better than Gates, who, incidentally, worked for free. When asked his reaction, Gates said he had been very relaxed spending his own money but now that he was responsible for wisely spending Buffett's money, his job was more stressful. The giver got the better deal!

I do not want to pick on Bill Gates churlishly. He has done a great job. He chose a field that leant itself to his skill set. It is probably Melinda's influence that extended the foundation's work to softer and more nebulous fields like community and women's empowerment. But my message to Gates is that success breeds its own responsibilities. I believe the time has come for the Gates Foundation to depersonalize itself. Why? Because it needs to be the instrument and voice of American philanthropy in the global health space. Buffett's gift showed the way. American billionaires need to follow his example and forego the vanity of having foundations in their own names. To facilitate that process, the Gates Foundation needs to depersonalize itself. The Foundation began in 1997 as The William H. Gates Foundation but quickly changed its name to the current Bill and Melinda Gates formulation. It needs to change its name again. My suggestion, though admittedly a little corny, is to call itself the Through the Giving Gates Foundation. Its short name would remain the Gates Foundation thus maintaining that well-known brand. One meaning of the new name is that the money is being given through Bill and Melinda. But the two individuals will not be among us forever. Another meaning is to think of Gates as the door in a wall though which the various philanthropists will pass. One reason why American philanthropy needs to maintain a strong and rational voice in global public health is to balance the occasional vagaries in the voice and actions of the American government, such as the Trump Administration's decision to withdraw from the WHO. The Gates Foundation would never abandon the WHO. Though it has led the challenge to the WHO in the establishment of new institutions, the Gates Foundation understands the indispensable role played by the WHO and therefore remains its largest non-state financial supporter.[23]

## THE ROLE OF NON-STATE ACTORS

The establishment of Gavi and the Global Fund bought more than private sector disciplines to the global health scene, it brought a form of millennial modernity. A key aspect of that modernity concerns the role of non-governmental organizations (NGO). The better term is civil society organization (CSO) as it is preferable to describe an entity in the positive than in relation to one aspect of the negative. The non-governmental aspect of CSOs is only one of the things it is not. It is also not-for-profit. And, in the global South, the most important negative is that it is not part of the family, nor the clan, nor traditionalism. I was always attracted by the term used in the Philippines—cause oriented group—because this focused on what the group does rather than how it is comprised. But for the purposes of this discussion, we will stick to the CSO formulation though the most relevant negative in this case remains the non-governmental aspect.

Prior to the arrival of the Gates Foundation as a significant player, the only non-state actor to be accorded a seat at the Westphalian high table was the Red Cross, or more accurately for this discussion, the International Committee of the Red Cross (ICRC). The ICRC was born in the early era of the formation of civil society groups for political causes. The critical precedent was the establishment and activism of the British Anti-Slavery Society. Beginning in 1787, the Society would remain active until it achieved its goal of the British abolition of slavery in 1833.[24] The ICRC owes its birth to the witnessing by a Swiss businessman, Henri Dunant, of the plight of wounded soldiers in the aftermath of the 1859 battle of Solferino. By 1863, he had arranged a conference on the subject, marking the beginning of the Red Cross movement, which led, the following year, to the Swiss government convoking a meeting of states to draft the 1864 Geneva Convention on the protection of victims of war.[25] By pioneering the field of humanitarian law, the ICRC earned a place among states and would henceforth deal directly with governments in times of conflict.

But the ICRC, though a powerful precedent of non-state presence among governments, acted on the margins of the governance of global health, not at its center, which remained monopolized by governments. By the turn of the millennium, it became clear that other powerful non-state actors had emerged in the health field. The Gates Foundation was backed by its endowment and the vision of its founder. The pharmaceutical industry, brand and generic, was indispensable in the manufacture of vaccines, biologicals, and other remedies. In the field, civil society groups had become the major vehicle for delivering food and medicine since the early days of famine in the Horn of Africa. And among this cohort, Médecins Sans Frontières (MSF) emerged as the leading medical practitioner and the conscience of the international community. Non-state actors were thus funders of global health programs, producers of the medicines, and the deliverers of global health services, but they did not yet have a place in global health governance.

The response of the new institutions, Gavi and the Global Fund, was to provide that place as can be seen in the composition of their respective governing boards. The Gavi Board has 28 seats (pretty much at the outer limit of group effectiveness) of which four are permanent members—the WHO, UNICEF, the World Bank, and the Gates Foundation. Then there are nine independent individuals, five donor governments, five governments from developing countries, a representative of research institutes, a representative of the vaccine industry from industrialized countries, a representative of the vaccine industry from developing countries, one civil society organization and the Gavi CEO.[26] Accordingly, there are 18 institutional seats, nine individual seats and an *ex officio* non-voting seat for the CEO. Of the 18 institutional seats, ten go to governments, three to multilateral organizations, two to industry and one each to research and civil society groups, plus one for the Gates Foundation. Assuming that governments have the wherewithal to control the multilateral agencies, that still leaves only 13 "governmental" seats, not a majority. And even if the nine individuals were allied with the three civil society and research representatives, they would also not form a majority. According to Article 15 of the Gavi Statute, the board will try to make all decisions by consensus but if there is a vote, a two-thirds majority is required.[27] The dynamics of the structure means that no group can impose its view, but a group of ten can block a decision. Governments thus constitute a veto player as a group. The nine individuals would need to find an ally to similarly constitute themselves as a veto player. The Gavi board structure therefore rejects the dominant Westphalian paradigm but does allow that group to act as a veto player. The more likely cleavage in the board, however, is the North/South cleavage which also reflects a donor/recipient cleavage.

The Global Fund Board also comprises 28 members, eight of whom are, however, non-voting members. The Fund borrows from the Bretton Woods institutions the idea of constituencies. There are seven representatives from the six WHO regions (two for Africa) and eight from the donor governments either as individual countries or as part of a defined constituency. There are three CSOs, one from the North, one from the South, and one representing communities afflicted with one of the diseases. The private sector has a voting seat as does the Gates Foundation. Multilateral organizations such as the WHO and UNAIDS plus the World Bank are non-voting members, as are, the Chair and Vice-Chair of the Board. There is a non-voting place for a representative of partner organizations working on these issues and an *ex officio* non-voting spot for the Executive Director. As can be seen, 15 of the 20 voting seats are held by governments and so the Global Fund Board is more attuned to Westphalian notions of the centrality of governments. But as with Gavi, the key cleavage is North/South or in the Global Fund, a slight variation described as Donor/Implementor. The ten-member donor group comprises the Western governments, the Gates Foundation, and the representative of the private sector. The ten-member implementor group consists of the seven global South governments and the three CSOs (including the developed country CSO). According to paragraph 20.2 of the Fund's Operating Procedures:

> If all practical efforts by the Board and the Board Chair have not led to consensus, in order to pass, motions require a two-thirds majority of those present of both: a) the Donor Voting Group; and b) the Implementer Voting Group.[28]

Thus, neither the donors not the implementors can impose their views on the Fund and it would take four members of each group to vote together to block any decision. One notable inclusion on both boards is the private sector, with two vaccine manufacturers on the Gavi board and one private sector representative on the Fund's board. The representative on the Fund board at the time of writing is more of a CSO type, heading the Goodbye Malaria campaign after a career at Ernst & Young. Each board member has an alternate, and in the case of the private sector, he is from Merck, a "big pharma" corporation. As for Gavi, the developed country vaccine industry representative is from Pfizer, while the developing country vaccine industry is represented by Bharat Biotech of India. None of the current, at time of writing, nine individual members of the Gavi board has a background in the pharmaceutical industry, though the finance industry is well represented. Gavi faced controversy in 2011 when the vaccine manufacturer Crucell was invited to join the board. Gavi was Crucell's major client and questions of conflict of interest arose, with MSF arguing that some conflicts are too big to manage.[29] The solution was transparency with vaccine manufacturers thereafter publishing the quantities and prices of their sales to Gavi.

It is also worth recalling the central place of the Gates Foundation in the governance of these two bodies. It is the only entity with a guaranteed voting seat on each board. Of course, the United States and, probably, the United Kingdom, will also invariably have voting seats on the two boards, but they are on the Gavi board as non-permanent representatives of the donor countries constituency. The scale and impact of the Gates Foundation is unprecedented. Its annual budget is larger than that of the WHO, and a large slice of it goes to global public health. The Gates Foundation does not need to play the traditional political, personality and diplomatic games to have influence. It simply needs to spend and fund. The decisions taken by the Gates Foundation will have outsize impacts on global health. That impact can be seen in the move to the vertical axis. A study of Gates Foundation spending on child health showed that between 2010–14, 84% of funds went to vertical disease specific categories.[30] The international community has little option but to follow.

Unlike the Westphalian institutions that prefer to work directly with governments, the Global Fund has developed a mechanism that dilutes the influence of governments. Each eligible country establishes a Country Coordinating Mechanism (CCM) to develop grant applications to the Fund. The CCM comprises a mix of representatives of governments, donors, CSOs including faith-based groups and groups of people living with the diseases, academics, and the private sector. The CCM proposal will identify which part of the government or which CSO will be the deliverer of the project. About two-thirds of recipients have been government bodies but the Global Fund is encouraging dual track funding.[31] Civil society is thus a significant beneficiary of the Global Fund's massive funding. And, importantly, oversight of the work of the Fund is provided by a Kenyan CSO, Aidspan, which observes the Fund's board meetings and reports on developments on its website.[32]

Non-state actors have therefore brought a great deal to global public health. Private sector values inform decision making. The country direction of Global Fund grants is determined by a formula based on income level and disease burden, not through sweetheart deals with the local country director. The Fund has no staff in the field. And philanthropic funds, mainly through the Gates Foundation, also play a significant role. It is likely that public-private partnerships will play an increasing role in the field of global public health. The inclusion of civil society on boards and as deliverers has also had an impact. It has given voice to locals including those carrying the disease burden. And it has provided contestability to the previous philosophy that governments were responsible for health care. The government perspective must now engage with perspectives from industry and civil society.

But we should not lose sight of the continuing influence of governments in the two new health bodies. Public funds continue to be the main source for each of these bodies. Donor governments may not have a majority on the boards, but they continue to have the power of the purse. The United States threatened to withhold its voluntary contribution to the Fund until the office of Inspector-General was established to investigate claims and accusations, and Germany made a similar threat until alleged abuse of funds was investigated.[33] Using the power of the purse to ensure probity in the disbursement of public funds is appropriate. But vigilance is required to ensure the power of the purse is not used to gain a commercial or political advantage.

## ENTER COVID-19

The relatively successful international responses to TB, AIDS, SARS, MERS, Zika and even, in retrospect, Ebola, gave the impression that the global health system works fine. That it is based on science. That the WHO provided a useful forum for the transmission of information and coordination of policy responses. And that benign American leadership was an indispensable part of the formula. But all these assumptions would be found wanting when a more infectious and deadly virus appeared in 2019 and spread throughout the world in 2020.

Conspiracy theorists look for intentionality in the creation of the novel virus. Some Americans claim it came from a Chinese chemical weapons lab. Some Chinese accuse the US military of spreading it. All nonsense, of course. The existence of the virus is simply due to the operation of random Darwinian mutation followed by a viral version of survival of the fittest. And this virus is fit! It is relatively easily transmissible through airborne droplets and thus not dependent on direct fluid contact. Nor does it need to rely on the actions of a vector such as the mosquito. It is transmissible by asymptomatic people, so isolating the sick is no guarantee of containment. Because it is a novel virus, there was, initially, no cure or vaccine. And COVID-19 has a good public relations story. It does not generally attack children and it seemed to be deadly mainly to the old and infirm. My students called it the boomer remover. The only way to limit its spread is through mask wearing and physical distancing (not the misnomer social distancing). This has led to deep economic repercussions which may yet force humanity, when finally emerging from this pandemic, to rethink its unsustainable consumption of the Earth's resources. In my months of isolation, spent mainly finishing this book, I occasionally engage in whimsical thinking about the origin of the virus. In 1972, James Lovelock proposed his Gaia theory which sees the Earth as a holistic, self-regulating organism. Lovelock did not perceive of Gaia as a sentient being, but, because Disney has taught us to anthropomorphize just about anything, I imagine Gaia as a wizened old Mother Nature turning to an inconspicuous and unassuming little bat and saying, I've got a job for you . . .

The bat completed its mission, humanity did the rest. What we consequently learned is that in facing a deadly global pandemic, the nations of the world revert to Hobbesian behavior. Rational discussion, focused cooperation and joint action as envisaged to be the norm in the era of the UN Charter, was abandoned without much hesitation. In its place we saw a world of *bellum omnium contra omnes*, war of all against all.

The Director-General of the WHO, Dr Tedros Adhanom Ghebreyesus, declared "a public health emergency of international concern over the global outbreak of novel coronavirus" as early as 30 January 2020.[34] This would have been the time for the UN Security Council (UNSC) to step in and use its powers under Chapter VII to require certain behavior of the international community. The UNSC had already crossed this particular Rubicon in Resolution 2177 of 2014 in declaring the Ebola outbreak to be a threat to international security and thus trigger its Chapter VII powers of compulsion. The reasoning in the resolution was that the pandemic was "undermining the stability of the most affected countries concerned and, unless contained, may lead to further instances of civil unrest, social tensions and a deterioration of the political and security climate."[35] The Ebola outbreak being addressed by the Council killed 11,300 people.[36] The COVID-19 outbreak has killed more than five million people by January 2022 and shows few signs of abating.[37] One would have thought that it demanded the attention of the UNSC. The Secretary-General of the UN called for a global ceasefire to allow health authorities to tackle the disease and eventually the Council decided to meet. The result was meek. Not only did it not trigger Chapter VII, but it could not decide to draft even a non-binding resolution, settling for a Presidential statement which noted:

> The Members of the Security Council also expressed their support for all efforts of the Secretary-General concerning the potential impact of COVID-19 pandemic to conflict-affected countries and recalled the need for unity and solidarity with all those affected.[38]

The reason for this staggering inaction was Hobbesian. The United States and China were at each other's throats and so, could not agree on a text. And we cannot simply dismiss this as the amoral conduct of two autocrats at the helm of these countries because the European Union did not behave much better. The President of the European Commission had to apologize to Italy for the bloc's conduct in response to Italy's desperate pleas for assistance when the pandemic first hit, saying "yes, it is true that no one was really ready for this. It is also true that too many were not there on time when Italy needed a helping hand at the very beginning."[39]

The first nation to act badly was China. It did so for Leninist, not Hobbesian, reasons. Under Leninist dogma, nothing is more important than the party, not even people or nation. According to Dr Wang Linfa, an epidemiologist from the National University of Singapore and member of the scientific advisory board of the Wuhan Institute of Virology, Chinese doctors were aware of the novel coronavirus in December 2019 but information was suppressed so as not to disturb important communist party meetings then taking place in the city, thus allowing the infection to spread for weeks.[40] This strikes me as self-delusional because Chinese communist party meetings are as closely scripted as a Moscow show trial. In any case, the international wrong committed by China was not discharging its responsibility under Article 6 of the International Health Regulations to "notify WHO within 24 hours of all events which may constitute a public health emergency of international concern within its territory." The WHO acted quite expeditiously in declaring a public health emergency of international concern on January 30, 2020, but had China not suppressed the information, the outbreak may have been contained in Wuhan and, even if not, a proper notification would have allowed the WHO pandemic warning to come even sooner.

As country after country watched in horror as the virus entered its space and proliferated among its people, instead of leadership and global solidarity, we witnessed a Hobbesian struggle for personal protective equipment, drugs and vaccine research. It was blame of all against all. The institutions we rely on failed us. The UNSC did not meet for two months and then substantively absented itself. The WHO was neutralized in the blame game between the United States and China. With regard to critical medical supplies, the free trade rules of the World Trade Organization were thrown out the window and it became every country for itself. The G20 could only muster pious pronouncements and abdicated the leadership it had shown in 2008 during the sub-prime crisis. And, as noted, the European Union had its own Hobbesian moment.

The failure of the institutions demonstrated the extent to which the global system had relied on active and benign leadership from the United States. But President Trump ran on an America-first platform and meant it. He has no doubt never heard of Hobbes, but he acted out that author's worst nightmare. Instead of global leadership such as calling for vaccine research to be conducted under an open creative commons patent, Trump tried to buy the German company developing a vaccine, move its research wing to the United States and develop the vaccine "for the U.S. only."[41] The world then witnessed a virulent case of vaccine nationalism:

> Vaccine nationalism is not just morally and ethically reprehensible, it is contrary to every country's economic, strategic, and health interests. If rich, powerful countries choose that path, there will be no winners—ultimately, every country will be a loser.[42]

Trump then announced America's withdrawal from the WHO because of its favoritism towards China. Well, the WHO is deferential to all governments, that is at the heart of its problems. Then Trump turned his own country into a Hobbesian dystopia by engineering, through ignorance and willfulness, a system where every state competed against other states for PPE, supplies and drugs. His personal example to the nation was a refusal to wear a mask, and an insistence that he return to his indoor political rallies irrespective of the likelihood that these would simply spread the virus. Attendees had to assume the risks and promise not to sue. This is the politically constructed ignorance referred to at the beginning of this chapter.

## THE WORLD HEALTH LEVIATHAN

Trump has shown us the folly of maintaining a system of reliance on benign hegemonic stability supplied by the USA. That hegemonic status had been earned from being on the winning side in two world wars and then winning the Cold War. The United States had been the designer and guarantor of the UN Charter and Bretton Woods system. But when the USA began to squander its soft power, first in Vietnam and then in Iraq, the acceptance of its benign hegemonic status began to wither. Trump put an end to it. Our choice is now between Hobbes' *bellum omnium contra omnes*, or his Leviathan.

What do we want from a global health Leviathan? We need leadership in combating the next pandemic; we need acceptance of and compliance with that leadership from the global community; and we need cooperation and common purpose. We need a well-funded and confident global health Leviathan. And between now and the next pandemic, we need a Leviathan that will strengthen health systems around the world to make them more resilient when the emergency inevitably arrives. That means we need to complement our vertical action with far more horizontal action.

I had occasion to understand the reality of health systems in one of my postings. I am sitting at my desk at the Australian Embassy in Vientiane when the telephone rings. It is the well-known Adelaide Craniofacial Centre, and they are offering to fly a surgical team to Vientiane for a week in the not-too-distant future to repair cleft lips and palates. The correct bureaucratic response would have been to find some solid reasons why this generous initiative was not possible or timely. But, to the chagrin of my supervisors over the years, I rarely provided that sort of bureaucratic response. I said I would check it out and call them back. There actually were many good reasons why the initiative might not work. We would have to obtain the cooperation of the city hospital. And we would have to find the patients. The reality is that, in comparison to the rest of Laos, Vientiane is a wealthy city. Parents of babies born with cleft lips will find the money to cross the Mekong River and go to a Thai hospital and pay to have the condition rectified. So, the patients for the Adelaide initiative would need to come from the provinces.

There was no point passing the matter to the Lao authorities because, for reasons of either incompetence, inflexibility, or plain greed, it would die a slow death in their hands. So, I called a meeting of all the managers of Australian aid and commercial projects scattered around the country. Did they wish to help the people in their project areas? They would have to identify the patients and pay for their transport and upkeep in Vientiane. The Australian doctors would do the rest. There was considerable enthusiasm because it is not often that assistance can lead to such immediate and dramatic results. I called Adelaide and we set dates. Now it was time to deal with Lao officialdom. The Director of Mahosot Hospital was deeply unenthusiastic when I broached the question with him. "Ce n'est pas possible!" was the general tone of the response. I could see that rational discussion would get me nowhere, so, needless to say, I used my privilege as Ambassador to go above his head and raise the matter with the Minister for Health. A large slice of the Lao health budget drew on aid flows and the Minister had every reason to accede to a simple request from a significant donor. I suggested that he ring the Director of Mahosot in my presence which he promptly did and, after a rather gruff conversation in Lao, the required positive response was extracted.

The Adelaide team was due on the weekend, so on the previous Thursday I asked one of my local staff members to go to the hospital and make sure all was in readiness. She returned ashen-faced. Yes, the waiting, surgery and recovery rooms were available, but the hospital would not provide a single piece of equipment or any supplies . . . not a glove, a sheet or even a paper tissue. Ah, the Director's revenge. I rang Adelaide and asked them to fax me overnight a comprehensive list of all their supply needs. On Friday I dispatched the Embassy van to a medical supplier in Udon Thani, Thailand, after the company confirmed they could supply all the items on the list. I paid for it from Embassy discretionary aid funds. When the Adelaide team arrived, I told them everything has been smooth sailing. They needed to focus on surgery, not politics.

Well, the Adelaide team conducted surgery on more than 80 people in that week. I had a photographer, an Embassy spouse, take lots of before and after shots which would be the basis of that year's propaganda display for the big party held in the garden of the Residence on Australia Day. It all turned out very well.

Some months later, I had occasion to speak to a visiting Lao doctor then based in the private sector in Thailand. Why was Mahosot so uncooperative? He answered with a resigned sigh. Basically, our little initiative had humiliated the Lao doctors at the hospital. They can perform cleft lip surgery as competently as the Australian doctors, it is a relatively simple procedure. But by organizing this surgical visit, we had demonstrated all that was wrong with the Lao medical situation: the fact that those with money avoided Mahosot hospital and went to Thailand for their medical needs; that those in the distant provinces have little access to medical care and practically no access to surgical care; and that Laos' universal health care, as per communist ideology, actually meant negligible health care. As noted, there were lots of good reasons to decline the Adelaide request.

This little story has a coda. The aid project dealing with unexploded ordinance in Oudomxay brought to Vientiane a special case for the doctors to examine. She was a woman in her late teens who had suffered from a facially disfiguring childhood disease which became ever more accentuated with age. In an episode of *The Simpsons*, Lisa overhears a waiter calling her ugly! She visits the plastic surgeon who has a video program that extrapolates how she will look in adulthood—it is grotesque! Sadly, this is how the Oudomxay girl looked. She never left her room and had no prospects for marriage or a normal life. I was surprised at the alacrity with which the Adelaide team agreed to take the case and cover all the expenses. They flew the girl and her mother to Adelaide, where, over several months, they undertook five major reconstructive surgeries to transform her face to symmetrical features, straighten her teeth and ensure her lips covered them. When she got back to Vientiane, she came to the Embassy and gave me a big thankyou hug, no longer afraid to show her face.

I am not so crass as to conclude that Australian doctors are good people and Lao doctors are not. The Lao doctors' behavior flowed from simple human nature borne by resentment. The Australian doctors' behavior also flowed from simple human nature borne by the prospect of career advancement mixed with altruism. Cases like the Oudomxay girl do not come around often, and so it provided an opportunity for the Craniofacial unit to use its budget to demonstrate its capacities and publish the results. But I am free to comment on health systems. The Lao myth that its health system is free, creates all the wrong incentives. Patients have to bribe government doctors for services and if they have a choice, patients prefer to cross the Mekong River for better health and dental care. A more honest market-based system would at least keep the money, now flowing to Thailand, in the country to support the development of a more effective domestic health system. A global health Leviathan may have to step on a few political toes, but the horizontal requirement is to help turn this dysfunctional mess into a system that can plug into the rest of the world's vaccination, preventative, and curative processes.

Today's WHO is not the global health Leviathan we need. It has little independence and even less courage. It allows itself to be used as a political football between the United States and China. It took the WHO four months before deciding to support the general use of face masks.[43] Waiting for every study to come in and for all the evidence to line up neatly, like waiting for a consensus to form between all the states and stakeholders, is not leadership, it is cowardice. It is no use simply blaming the WHO for the current state of affairs. It is a hostage of states and their governments.

As in other situations, the elements of a solution to construct a benevolent global health Leviathan exist in embryonic form. That solution encompasses:

- independent funding
- tripartite World Health Assembly governance
- focused legal and enforcement powers
- competent staff

The Tobin tax idea has been discussed elsewhere and will be further elaborated in the concluding chapter. Suffice it to say at this point that global taxation would cover the costs of running the agency as well as its outreach activities. Governments would no longer hold the power of the purse over the agency.

The tripartite governance idea already exists among UN agencies at the International Labor Organization and in the major new global health institutions established this century. It needs to be formalized in the new WHO. Governments would continue to be one leg, business another, and civil society the third. It is the business side that raises the most difficult questions. I would list the philanthropic players like the Gates and Bloomberg Foundations as part of the business leg. That is where these foundations originated and where the values they imbue were formed. And, given their altruism, they would leaven the influence of the profit motive-based members. The next dilemma is whether to include "big pharma" in the governance structure. Recall Médecins Sans Frontières' comment that some conflicts of interest are too big to manage. But Thomas Pogge has said that "we will reach our common and imperative goal of universal access to essential medicines either in collaboration with the pharmaceutical industry or not at all."[44] This was also the view taken by Gavi. I think it is the better view. Apart from philanthropic bodies and big pharma, the business side should include representation from the finance and insurance industry, manufacturing, tourism, and hospitality. There should also be associations of health workers.

The civil society side is less problematic bearing in mind the need to avoid government organized NGOs and other strawman CSOs established by business lobbyists or political parties. Clearly Médecins Sans Frontières would be on the list. It will be important also to include CSOs from the global South, and following the Global Fund precedent, CSOs representing communities carrying the disease burden. A possible process for selecting and renewing the list has already been discussed in the General Assemblies chapter.

The next requirement is focused legal powers and, yet again, the system already exists in embryonic form. The World Health Organization Framework Convention on Tobacco Control is a treaty adopted by the 56th World Health Assembly in 2003. It remains the only World Health Organization treaty adopted under article 19 of the WHO constitution. Even more to the point are the International Health Regulations (IHR). Under Articles 21(a) and 22 of the Constitution of the WHO, the World Health Assembly may adopt regulations "designed to prevent the international spread of disease" which then apply to all WHO Member States. The most recent IHR of 2005 entered into force in 2007. These are some of the focused legal powers needed by a Leviathan. The tripartite World Health Assembly would be more active than the current version. We already came across Article 6 of the IHR requiring notification within 24 hours of any occurrence that may become a pandemic. The obligation rests on governments, but this is insufficient. It needs to also be an obligation of doctors and hospital administrators to report to the WHO in parallel with their governments and subsequently protected from those governments if the need arises.

Another question the tripartite World Health Assembly should determine is the future role of the WHO. As previously pointed out, it is currently convener, project deliverer, and even at times, first responder. To have so many roles is a recipe for failure in each of them. The WHO should be a Leviathan. It should set norms, require certain conduct of governments and practitioners, and enforce those norms. I am not sure the WHO should be a project deliverer. Would it not be better for that task to be undertaken by a mix of other bodies including governments, the private sector and civil society, at times working together in public-private partnerships? That is the Global Fund formula. But the WHO would use its independence to influence the direction and quality of those projects. It should work to balance the vertical with the horizontal.

Enforcement is invariably the most intractable question in international law, but in this case, there is a solid precedent—UNSCR 2177 of 2014 declaring the Ebola outbreak to be a threat to international peace and security. We also have Article 99 of the Charter granting the Secretary-General the power to bring a matter to the attention of the Security Council. So, in a case where a government is refusing to cooperate with the efforts of the international community and thus compounding the problem of the spread of infection, the Council could take Chapter VII measures. Of course, that is not a magic wand. Sanctions tend to be longer-term solutions whereas pandemics pose immediate concerns. But at least the Council has the power to seek the right mix of carrot and stick to gain the cooperation of a recalcitrant government. Other incentives and disincentives may also be crafted by a tripartite World Health Assembly given the participation of industry representatives.

The final requirement is competent staff. The Secretariat chapter has already explained the benefit of tripartite appointment of the head of the agency. The Director-General of the WHO would no longer be a hostage of governments. Nor would her (two women have held the post, Gro Harlem Brundtland and Margaret Chan) Secretariat be beholden to governments because the only criterion for their selection would be competence. A final word is required on staffing. It could be summed up in two Latin words: *cave medicus*, beware of doctors! There has been a tendency to stack the senior leadership of WHO with medical doctors. Yes, they know a great deal about health, but that is not the key skill required. Medical expertise is available from many professional, commercial, and academic sources. Management of a global health Leviathan requires a different set of skills—vision, diplomacy, oratory, leadership. A medical degree is not a job requirement to lead the WHO or to be a member of its staff.

I had not intended to write about the WHO. Even though there was serious criticism of its handling of the Ebola crisis, because the incentives for global cooperation were too weighty and apparent. There seemed to be no need to construct a Leviathan. But COVID-19 upturned that view. It showed the system to be broke and in need of fixing. The inevitable next pandemic may be even more deadly. The benign hegemon proved to be untrustworthy and without this underpinning, the system does not work. We cannot return to a national hegemon. The United States has abdicated, and China is the unacceptable pretender to the throne. We need a global health Leviathan.

In relation to COVID-19, the World Health Leviathan would work to ensure fair access to protective equipment and vaccines. The obvious solution is cooperation mediated by the UN on which a hesitant start has been made with the establishment of the COVAX coalition,[45] but more needs to be done:

> A framework agreement on vaccine sharing would also be more likely to succeed if it were undertaken through an established international forum and linked to preventing the export bans and seizures that have disrupted COVID-19-related medical supply chains.[46]

## NOTES

1. The following infectious disease information is from Centers for Disease Control and Prevention, https://www.cdc.gov/

2. Beth P. Bell, Damon IK, Jernigan DB, et al., "Overview, Control Strategies, and Lessons Learned in the CDC Response to the 2014–2016 Ebola Epidemic," *MMWR, Supplements,* July 8, 2016, 65(3):4–11. DOI: http://dx.doi.org/10.15585/mmwr.su6503a2

3. Abdi Latif Dahir, "Outbreak of Ebola is Over in Congo," *New York Times*, June 26, 2020.

4. Bell et al., op. cit.

5. The White House, "The (Obama) Administration's Response to Ebola," https://obamawhitehouse.archives.gov/ebola-response

6. Jason Gale and John Lauerman, "Ebola spread over months as WHO missed chance to respond," *Bloomberg Business*, 16 Oct. 2014. Editorial, "Reform after the Ebola debacle," *New York Times*, 10 Feb. 2015.

7. Adam Kamradt-Scott, "WHO's to blame? The World Health Organization and the 2014 Ebola outbreak in West Africa," *Third World Quarterly*, 37 (2016), 401–418.

8. Kelley Lee, *The World Health Organization*, (Oxford: Routledge, 2009), 20.

9. Maria Cheng and Raphael Satter, "Emails: UN health agency resisted declaring Ebola emergency," *Associated Press*, 20 March 2015, https://apnews.com/ea7199795faa48989449131404b7043e/emails-un-health-agency-resisted-declaring-ebola-emergency

10. Ilona Kickbusch, "Global health security: a cosmopolitan moment?" *G7G20*, http://www.g7g20.com/articles/ilona-kickbusch-global-health-security-a-cosmopolitan-moment

11. David P Fidler, "The Ebola outbreak and the future of global health security," *The Lancet* Public Policy forum, Vol 385 May 9, 2015, 1888–1889.

12. Mark Harrison, "Disease, Diplomacy and International Commerce: The Origins of International Sanitary Regulation in the Nineteenth Century," *Journal of Global History*, 1 (2006), 197–217.

13. WHO, "Archives of the League of Nations, Health Section Files," https://www.who.int/archives/fonds_collections/bytitle/fonds_3/en/

14. Ibid.

15. Chelsea Clinton and Devi Sridhar, *Governing Global Health: Who Runs the World and Why?* (Oxford University Press, 2017), 8–9.

16. Ibid., 41.

17. Ibid., 45.

18. Ibid., 46.

19. Ibid., 42.

20. Ibid., 117.

21. The Gates Foundation, https://www.gatesfoundation.org/Who-We-Are/General-Information/Foundation-Factsheet

22. See Forbes Magazine, "Forbes 400 Philanthropy Summit," https://www.forbes.com/conferences/2013/forbes400-2013.html.

23. Clinton and Sridhar, op. cit, 96.

24. Lynn Hunt, *Inventing Human Rights: A History*, (New York: Norton, 2007), 205.

25. David P. Forsythe, *The Humanitarians: The International Committee of the Red Cross*, (Cambridge University Press, 2005), Chapter 1.

26. See Gavi, "Gavi, the Vaccine Alliance Board," https://www.gavi.org/our-alliance/governance/gavi-board

27. See Gavi, "Gavi Alliance Statutes," https://www.gavi.org/sites/default/files/document/gavi-alliance-statutespdf.pdf

28. The Global Fund, "Operating Procedures of the Board and Committees," https://www.theglobalfund.org/media/4207/bm34_18-annex6operatingprocedures_report_en.pdf

29. Clinton and Sridhar, op. cit, 131

30. Ibid., 80.

31. Ibid., 54.

32. Ibid., 68.

33. Ibid.

34. WHO, "Director-General's statement on IHR Emergency Committee on Novel Coronavirus (2019-nCoV)," https://www.who.int/dg/speeches/detail/who-director-general-s-statement-on-ihr-emergency-committee-on-novel-coronavirus-(2019-ncov)

35. UNSCR 2177 of 18 September 2014, preambular paragraph 4

36. Centers for Disease Control, "2014–2016 Ebola Outbreak in West Africa," https://www.cdc.gov/vhf/ebola/history/2014-2016-outbreak/index.html

37. Our World in Data, "Total Confirmed COVID-19 Deaths," https://ourworldindata.org/grapher/total-deaths-covid-19

38. Jose Singer (Security Council President, Dominican Republic) on the Impact of COVID-19 on the issues that fall under the Security Council's mandate - Security Council Virtual Media Stakeout (9 April 2020), https://media.un.org/en/asset/k12/k12r1h26tf

39. BBC, "Coronavirus: EU offers 'heartfelt apology' to Italy," 16 April 2020, https://www.bbc.com/news/world-europe-52311263

40. Hannah Beech, "The Saturday Profile (of Dr Wang Linfa)," *New York Times*, 13 June 2020.

41. Aitor Hernández-Morales, "Germany confirms that Trump tried to buy firm working on coronavirus vaccine," *Politico*, March 15, 2020.

42. Thomas J. Bollyky and Chad P. Bown, "The Tragedy of Vaccine Nationalism: Only Cooperation Can End the Pandemic," *Foreign Affairs*, September/October 2020, 96–108.

43. Apoorva Mandavilli, "W.H.O. Backs Wearing Masks After Months of Reluctance," *New York Times*, June 6, 2020.

44. Thomas Pogge, *World Poverty and Human Rights*, (Cambridge: Polity Press, 2008), 255.

45. WHO, "COVAX: Working for global equitable access to COVID-19 vaccines," https://www.who.int/initiatives/act-accelerator/covax

46. Bollyky and Brown, op cit, 104.

# *Chapter 12*

# A Vision, Not a Roadmap

The concluding chapter will attempt to tie together the threads of a number of key issues described in this book. It begins by addressing why this book describes a vision, but does not explain how we get there. Is this a work of political science or science fiction? Thereafter, the chapter will deal with the two issues that recur throughout the book: Hobbesianism and the Leviathan. The former is at the heart of the problem, the latter is the key aspect of the solution. If one does not accept that international relations is increasingly Hobbesian, then there will be little confidence in the arguments in favor of a United Nations Leviathan. Finally, the chapter will rehearse the arguments why the Leviathan should be the UN. This will involve a discussion of cosmopolitanism, a philosophy in which this book hopes to find a place.

## NOT A ROADMAP

In the brilliant *Foundation* trilogy,[1] which Isaac Asimov rather devalued by churning out two sequels and two prequels, the mathematician Hari Seldon devises the discipline of psychohistory through which the future of populous polities can be determined, and even tweaked. That is science fiction. Describing possible improvements in governance, domestic or global, is a common aspect of political science. There is no attempt to employ psychohistory. Nor is there an attempt to plot a path to the future. As the military knows all too well, no plan survives first contact with the enemy. The book does not waste the reader's time by postulating tactics and back-up tactics to deal with inevitable set-backs. I do, however, make one exception.

The criticism in response will be to say that this is a cop-out. What is the point of describing a system that we know Putin will reject, and Xi will ignore, and the US Senate will not adopt? Granted, there will be no UN Leviathan in the immediate future. But history is full of intriguing examples of surprising decisions. Sticking with the UN, I ask my students why Stalin accepted the establishment of the UN. It certainly does not accord with Marxist philosophy and even less with Leninist ideas. Stalin focused almost exclusively on dominating the Soviet Union and its surrounds, not on any form of multilateralism. The Soviet experience of the League of Nations was not positive with Soviet propagandists calling it a "Holy Alliance of the bourgeoisie for the suppression of the Bolshevik revolution."[2] The USSR only reluctantly joined in 1934 while maintaining criticisms of the Covenant, and it was expelled in 1939 because of its war of aggression against Finland.[3] The establishment of the UN was not part of Stalin's post-war plans, it was the brainchild of Roosevelt. But Stalin did accept Roosevelt's plan and the reason was D-Day. Germany and the USSR had been *de facto* allies after the Molotov-Ribbentrop Pact and, in line with a secret Protocol to the Pact, they started the Second World War together in 1939 by invading and annexing Poland—Germany from the West, the Soviet Union from the East.[4] But two years later, Hitler decided to invade the Soviet Union in a *blitzkrieg* that turned into a war of attrition. For three years, the Soviet Union fought off German aggression on its own at tremendous cost, especially in blood. When the Allies opened a new front through the 1944 D-Day landing, Stalin knew Germany could not cope and he would win the war. His reward to Roosevelt was Soviet agreement to establish the UN, in which the Soviet Union, like the other Allies, would have a privileged position.[5] Even dictators can make surprising decisions.

Circumstances will dictate decisions. We do not know what those circumstance will be, but looking at the past, we can speculate that an event of global dimensions might be the catalyst for change. Will the COVID-19 pandemic be that catalyst? Will there be a particularly tragic weather event that will shock humanity into action? That is how Kim Stanley Robinson's hopeful science fiction book begins its plot and then in effect passes the action to body similar to a UN Leviathan.[6] Will Putin try to re-establish the territory of the Soviet Union? Will another Caligula-like American President be the last straw? Hopefully, it will not take a World War III to be the trigger.

The vision of a powerful, independent, and competent UN seems, at first glance, to be too dramatic a departure from today's reality. That reality can be summed up in one word—timidity. It is easy to blame individuals but much harder to recognize that the problem of timidity is systemic, and the solution needs to be structural. In attempting to craft a structure that will respond to the problems the world faces, I did not begin with a blank page. To my own surprise, I found that the UN had many of the desired structures in embryonic form:

- The tripartite governance structure already exists in the International Labor Organisation, and the global health structures established in the twenty-first century also have tripartite governance

- Independent Secretaries-General have been in office but were squashed by the P5
- Selecting Secretariat staff on the basis of competence is already in the Charter, it now needs to be given its full force
- The Secretary-General already has a military group that he can deploy at his discretion, it is the precedent for a far more robust structure
- The international community has already established an International Criminal Court and a doctrine of the responsibility to protect which stand ready to serve the needs of a UN Leviathan
- The concept of human development, as opposed to infrastructure development, has already been established, it now needs to be acted on
- The power to certify a domestic election has already been exercised and there is already a part of the Secretariat dealing with domestic elections, it now needs to be expanded and repurposed
- The World Health Organization already has the capacity to promulgate International Health Regulations
- The Office of the UN High Commissioner for Refugees claims to deal only with those subject to political persecution, but it has already jumped in after natural disasters in Indonesia, Sri Lanka, Pakistan, Myanmar, Haiti, the Philippines, Somalia and, most recently, the man-made disaster in Beirut
- The governance of globalization is weak, but there are dozens of bodies, in many of which the UN already plays a part, ready to enhance their roles and form a part of the UN Leviathan
- Taxing globalization to fund the UN may seem like a bridge too far, but France already has such a tax on domestic air travel.

The vision exists independently of the path. The path to that vision does not run through diplomats and dictators, but through "we the peoples." We the peoples want to have a formal voice at the UN through a General Assembly of Civil Society. We the peoples want human development. We the peoples want a global institution that can deal effectively with pandemics and climate change. We the peoples want globalization to be governed. We the peoples want democracy and human rights. If that is the case, then we the peoples will struggle for an acceptable vision of future world governance. My aim is to offer one such vision.

## HOBBESIANISM

Have I been exaggerating? Do we live in a Hobbesian world? Of course, Hobbes was referring to domestic society—London society of the seventeenth century. Hobbes' concern was about personal security, primarily of the physical kind. He wanted a Leviathan not for the sake of having one, but to deal with the problem of personal insecurity. Hobbes wanted a Leviathan because he saw it as the only way to deal with the most pressing problem of living in that era. Hobbes did not focus on international society. As have others before me, like Hedley Bull as mentioned in the introductory chapter, the Hobbesian construct is being elevated from the local to the global domain. Personal insecurity remains an issue in many places with weak law enforcement. But it is not the issue of concern in this book. Rather, I am borrowing Hobbes meta-question: is there a fundamental problem with which only a Leviathan can hope to successfully grapple?

I could simply rely for my evidence of the need for a Leviathan, on the general description of international society as anarchic. It has become a common concept in international relations, generally meaning the absence of international government, or international governance, or even international order:

- "anarchy is the defining characteristic of international politics"[7]
- "the field of international relations has, from its earliest years, been structured by a discourse about anarchy"[8]
- "Virtually all scholars agree that relations between states are anarchic and that this is one of the most unique, important, and enduring features of world politics"[9]

But this is not a decisive argument. Hedley Bull was not concerned directly with anarchy, but with order. He searched for systems of order within an anarchic context. Disorder may be a latent factor of the anarchic society, but it can be overcome in various ways. Jack Donnelly problematizes the term "anarchy" to cast doubt as to its meaning and utility.[10] Clearly, it is unconvincing simply to use the term anarchy to mean an absence of world government, as evidence that we need a world government. Global order may be achievable by other means such as a balance of power, or fear of mutually assured destruction, or through the decisions of a concert of powers. We need to look beyond the term anarchy to justify the description of international society as Hobbesian.

We need to return to the Hobbes meta-question: is there a fundamental problem with which only a Leviathan can hope to successfully grapple? Is there a problem causing comparable concern today to Hobbes' concern almost four centuries ago? Clearly, the problem is greater than personal insecurity caused by random violence. Our domestic Leviathans have largely dealt with that, though a by-product of Leviathan protection is that institution's own violence. The problems faced by today's world are multiple and complex, but if we were to attempt to distil them to a meta-problem, I would argue that it is the absence of international cooperation based on agreed premises and norms.

The preceding substantive chapters have provided various angles on that meta-problem. If there is a unifying theme of these chapters it is that as the world increasingly becomes a global village, its problems are increasingly taking on a global dimension. National economies are being gravitationally drawn to globalization by the forces of competition and comparative advantage. But globalization is being governed in an *ad hoc*, episodic, and ineffective manner. The need for governance has been demonstrated by these episodic attempts to provide it, but the delivery of governance is spotty and capricious. Finding gaps in governance through regulatory and taxation arbitrage has become a source of corporate success. The system thus loses legitimacy which then cascades into politics through a new xenophobic anti-globalization cleavage. The world must cooperate to govern globalization.

The COVID-19 pandemic has demonstrated the absence of international cooperation though the problem demands it. Governments did not meet their existing international obligations. Instead, they engaged in propagandistic blame games. Instead of cooperating on a vaccine under an open creative commons patent, the forces of national and corporate capitalism *sauvage* have been let loose. This will lead to controversy and consternation, the main result of which will be to strengthen the hand of the anti-vax charlatans. If there is any issue where global cooperation is indispensable, it is combatting pandemics.

The flow of refugees demonstrates the absence of international solidarity. Countries neighboring areas of crises bear the brunt of these flows, and wealthy countries elsewhere make meagre monetary contributions and accept a small trickle of refugees for resettlement. One million refugees spawned by the Syrian civil war seeking asylum in Europe was sufficient to overturn the European Union's relevant rules, and any sense of regional solidarity quickly evaporated. The main beneficiaries are demagogues and xenophobes. What will happen when increasing swathes of the planet become uninhabitable generating ever greater numbers of people forced from their homes? Lack of international cooperation will simply breed chaos.

Anthropogenic climate change is a fact. The world understands the problem and knows the elements of a solution. Those elements are becoming ever more complex and require increasing levels of cooperation. No Leviathan can solve this problem. Nor can governments, even if they were sincerely focused on doing so. The corporate world must take a stand, but even that is insufficient. Individuals must be a large part of the answer. We need to change our lifestyles—less aimless consumption, less meat consumption, less driving personal vehicles, less international air travel, more volunteering, more political participation, more human development. We need an audit of the planet's resources in terms of arable land, fertile soil, forests, oceans, water, and biodiversity. We need to stop thinking of these resources as inexhaustible. We need to revive the concept of the common heritage of humankind. I often wonder, for example, about our practice of burning oil. The flora and fauna that metamorphosed over the eons into the vast oil reserves represent an invaluable resource for the future. Should we be burning it for fuel? Being carbon-based, is it not transformable into food for the future? The most essential tool for dealing with anthropogenic climate change is planetary cooperation.

Democracy and human rights are often thought of as concepts existing within a national context. There may be some truth to that in terms of their formal delineation. But in the era of the Charter, human rights became a matter of international concern. Sovereignty did not bestow a license to kill, or to torture, or to arbitrarily deprive people of their liberty. Bit by bit, the machinery to deal with this problem was built, from the Universal Declaration of Human Rights to the International Criminal Court. Democracy has not enjoyed the same privilege. Arguments were made that democracy flowed naturally from human rights, but generally the processes of democracy were contained within their formal domestic contexts. In the post-Cold War world, things changed. Democracy came to be viewed as an instrument to deliver peace, human rights, and development. This linkage elevated it to the status of a matter of international concern. The machinery for this purpose is not as elaborate as that developed to protect human rights, but it nevertheless exists in the form of election observation practices and democracy promotion bodies such as the intergovernmental International Institute for Democracy and Electoral Assistance and the many political party foundations. We are beginning to realize that in a global village, a threat to democracy and human rights anywhere, is a threat everywhere. This adds weight to the need for cooperation between a wide array of actors.

One sector where this study makes modest claims concerns peace and security. Great powers at times behave badly, and the UN is unable, now or in the future, to police such conduct. The shock of the invasion of Ukraine is still with us. Putin imposed this unjustified war single-handedly. Maybe in the old USSR, the collective decision making of the Politburo would have been more circumspect. The visit of Putin to Beijing for the 2022 Winter Olympics and his promise to Xi not to start his war until the end of those Games in return for Chinese support,[11] will come to be seen as a modern equivalent of the Molotov-Ribbentrop pact. But modesty is not the same as immobility. This study proposes a more powerful Secretary-General of the UN with some enforcement capacity to deal with spoilers. It foresees the Security Council as moving towards the status of a concert of powers to ensure high-level deconfliction. But it does not foreshadow that state of affairs that has become known in popular culture as "world peace." That is because humanity will always find a reason for conflict, even when to follow this path is "folly."[12] And as the stressors, like globalization *sauvage*, inequality, pandemics, refugees, and climate change, multiply, the possible causes of conflict will also increase. But allow me to suggest an alternate thesis. What if humanity cooperated on these issues? What if humanity fell into the habit of cooperation? What if the standard operating procedure became to consult, to listen, and to coordinate? Would that not lessen the likelihood of war?

It is the absence of cooperation that is making the world Hobbesian. It may not yet be full blown Hobbesianism. It may be incipient Hobbesianism in some areas. But the direction is clear. The post-WWII order and the post-Cold War order are both being cast aside by the power that designed and guaranteed them. The United States no longer harbors the ambition to be the stabilizing hegemon. It has abandoned pretensions to be the indispensable power. For the first time in my life, a major political and military crisis, Libya in 2020, played out without a hint of American involvement. Strange bedfellow coalitions on either side fought it out militarily and diplomatically for control of the country. The United States saw no role for itself. It is abandoning the world to a Hobbesian future.

## THE NEW LEVIATHAN

In this section, key features of the new Leviathan will be examined. Are there alternatives available to solve the world's problems? How to ensure the independence of UN staff? Can Tobin taxation be made to work? And, where to start the process?

### Alternatives?

Can there be another stabilizing hegemon to take America's place and guarantee the international order? The Soviet Union once aspired to that role, but since its collapse, Russia has no global ideology, nor the economy to sustain a hegemonic role. Russia has military capacity, but uses it to prove its continued relevance, not to put its stamp on the world system. And Russia has no moral claim to leadership. Its domestic system is a corrupt oligarchy led by an amoral opportunist under cover of the meaningless tautology "sovereign democracy."

What about the old world? Britain was content to think of itself as Greece to America's Rome, thus passing the baton of world leadership. But the United (for the time being) Kingdom, no longer has any pretensions of mentorship of the hegemon. It is content to try to milk the "special relationship" for momentary national gain. The European Union, however, could fit the bill. It has reinvented itself on a continental scale and endowed itself with a pleasing universal ideology of openness and sophistication. The EU, however, remains a work in progress. It now has a foreign service but not a foreign policy. It has blended some military forces together but continues to rely on NATO. It has a seat on the Security Council, but it belongs to France. In the post-colonial era, it is difficult to see the former colonial masters attempting to reassert any form of global dominance. Europe's time has passed.

The only nation capable of filling the void being left by the United States is China. The conventional wisdom is that it is the rising power while the United States fades. China has an historic self-perception that would fit the role of hegemonic stabilizer—it is the center of the world, the Middle Kingdom, the last word in civilized behavior. It even has a system of relations with other polities that worked for many centuries—the tributary system. China was magnanimous to those who acknowledged its authority and enhanced its interests. In a choice between China as hegemon or Hobbesian anarchy, many countries, especially in the global South, might choose China.

But China would fail in the role of stabilizing hegemon. Its domestic model, where a corrupt elite extracts fealty from the population and delivers top-down governance, is not acceptable or applicable to the rest of the world. Its unrelenting materialism is unsustainable. Even more inappropriate for a hegemon, China simply does not understand the rest of the world. In a recent work, Edward Luttwak introduced the concept of "great state autism," a collective national lack of situational awareness that reduces a country's ability to perceive international realities with clarity.[13] When my students seek an example of Chinese autism, I refer them to the 1999 Chinese veto of the continuation of the peacekeeping force in North Macedonia, based on the fact that the country had recently recognized Taiwan.[14] Autism is a debilitating condition in dealings with others. It is not the same as ignorance of the rest of the world, a condition from which many Americans suffer. At least American ignorance could be balanced by its benign intentions and optimistic outlook. But Chinese autism has no balancing features beyond a universal love of its cuisine. It would not be a balancing hegemon so much as a hegemon bent on maximizing its interests at whatever cost.

The world needs a choice other than between a distracted and ineffective America and an autistic and authoritarian China to guarantee the international order. The option put forward in this book is the United Nations, not as hegemonic stabilizer, but as benign Leviathan. Not a Leviathan with a monopoly on the legitimate use of force, but with moral authority based on the support of the vast majority of the people of the world.

Another analogy to capture the concept of the benign Leviathan it is that of first responder. In some ways, this is already the UN role when dealing with emergencies, natural and human-made. But it is not analogous to the domestic first responders like police, firefighters, and medical auxiliaries. The domestic version has adequate resources, competent organization, and largely benefits from public confidence. The international community needs a similar first response capacity at the global level. First responders are not the government. Neither would the UN Leviathan be a world government though it would provide some of the requisite governmental services. To become an effective first responder, the UN would need to be fundamentally changed and enhanced.

## Independence

In discussing the UN Secretariat, reference was made to the requirement in the Charter that it be selected on the basis of "efficiency, competence, and integrity" but that, in reality, these requirements were subservient to the question of nationality. This can readily be fixed by returning to the intention of the Charter but giving no regard to geographic factors. Accordingly, the Secretariat would need to earn its legitimacy from the efficiency, competence, and integrity it displayed rather than from the passports it carried. Performance legitimacy runs far deeper than entitlement legitimacy. But there is one word that does not appear in Chapter XV of the Charter dealing with the Secretariat—independence. It is, however, implied in Article 100:

> In the performance of their duties the Secretary-General and the staff shall not seek or receive instructions from any government or from any other authority external to the Organization. They shall refrain from any action which might reflect on their position as international officials responsible only to the Organization. Each Member of the United Nations undertakes to respect the exclusively international character of the responsibilities of the Secretary-General and the staff and not to seek to influence them in the discharge of their responsibilities.

If there is one article of the charter that is violated every day, it is Article 100. Staff often surreptitiously seek instructions from their national missions to the UN; missions often seek to gain intelligence by reaching out to their own nationals; and it is standard operating procedure to try to influence Secretariat members, who are, in any case, in thrall to delegations. This is only to be expected when some members of the UN Secretariat are on leave from their foreign ministries and intend to return to their home base on completion of their UN stint. It is only to be expected when the national delegation, playing the equitable geographic distribution card, was instrumental in getting their national the job in the first place. And let us have some sympathy for the Secretariat member from an authoritarian state whose family members remaining home are, for all intents and purposes, hostages. These are the games governments play.

The only way to dilute the primacy of government delegations is to turn the UN into a tripartite organization. In the chapter on The General Assemblies, I explained the mechanics of establishing an assembly for civil society (UNGAC) and an assembly for business (UNGAB). As co-equals in the processes of norm development, enquiry, and oversight, the tripartite system would turn Article 100 into reality. It would ensure "the exclusively international character of the responsibilities of the Secretary-General and the staff" because government delegations would have their powers diluted, they would no longer be able to play their games and turn the UN into their puppet.

The three assemblies idea has further and deeper benefits. It would make the UN relevant to the civil society world and to the business elite. Civil society would readily embrace the idea. There have been attempts to provide civil society with a global forum, many of which, like the Civicus meetings, are quite successful. But these forums ultimately fall short of their universal goals for reasons of language or regional focus or simply personalities. The UN transcends these divisions. Civil society is currently in a nasty existential battle with authoritarian regimes. A UN General Assembly for Civil Society would be a powerful weapon in that battle. It would also bring the UN closer to "we the peoples." It would allow the UN to reach people more directly rather than only through governments.

The General Assembly for Business would be a critically important feature of the new UN. In the Climate Change chapter, I referred to the involvement of the corporate world as the Davos gambit as they would work to mitigate global warming because this is the right business goal from a longer-term perspective. A similar story can be told with regard to globalization, pandemics, refugees, human rights, and even democracy. In each of these areas, the longer-term business goal is to work for global cooperation. That is the case for the world's two biggest industries, insurance and pensions, and for the vast majority of other industries which prefer an environment of greater certainty and rule of law that only cooperation can ensure.

Knowing a little bit of how big businesses work, I suspect that the UNGAB would be less involved in the normative side of the UN's work. There may be certain issues, particularly in regard to globalization and development, that would be within its normative wheelhouse. But the normative side would generally raise far greater passions in the other two general assemblies. Nevertheless, I believe the business assembly will become the most powerful of the three because, through its members and the corporations and industries it represents, the world will see a new type of enforcement develop. This will be a form of enforcement that does not require Chapter VII or boots on the ground. It will often not even take formal shape in terms of treaties or resolutions. But it will be devastatingly effective because it will be a key determinant in the flow of trade and investment. Through their business networks, the business assembly will encourage countries, their citizens, and their businesses, to cooperate in the global project or face the consequences of becoming economic pariahs. An example of the distinction between being a formal part of the world community as opposed to being an engaged part can be seen in the difference between North Korea and Taiwan. The former has sovereignty, international status and a seat at the UN but plays no role in the world economy. The latter has none of these formal attributes but is a significant player in the world economy. Of course, North Korea's isolation is partly self-imposed and partly due to sanctions, but the example nevertheless remains telling from a business community perspective which is less concerned with the official trappings and more concerned with behavior.

North Korea is an outlier. And within the business community there will also be outliers that will see short-term profit in situations of chaos. But they must be prepared to be outliers within the business community itself. A company selling guns to spoilers, will not be accepted in the formal gun market. Yes, some individuals and corporations will be prepared to become the equivalent of economic *personae non gratae* because their business model prefers chaos, just as some people decide to become professional criminals. But the vast majority will seek to succeed in the formal global economy just as the vast majority of people are law-abiding.

The tripartite structure of the UN will not only make it more independent of governments, but it will also bring the UN closer to the people and the business community. It will give the UN a legitimacy beyond its current role of being a forum where governments engage with each other. And it will give the UN far greater effectiveness. UNGAC will give it reach beyond governments to the people and UNGAB will give it a reach into the business community, each of which bring the UN new powers of persuasion and enforcement. The two new assemblies will also revive domestic UN associations which are currently moribund, except in a few capitals in northern Europe. Once they have their own UN assembly, one can expect UN civil society associations and UN business associations to proliferate in just about every country in the world.

## Tobin Taxation

Independence, however, will not be achieved without independent financing of the UN, and that means Tobin taxation. There will be no issue which governments will fight harder to disallow. Taxation is a sovereign right, they will argue, and it should remain the preserve of sovereigns. Global organizations, they will insist, must continue to come cap in hand to governments for their funds. Yet the reality is that there can be no true global cooperation without an independent Leviathan to oversee it. And there can be no independence without freedom from government interference. The UN Leviathan must be able to raise taxes.

Before we come to the principles on which that tax should be raised, we need to think about the purposes of the UN budget. The general assemblies must fund themselves. If they want studies done or reports prepared, they will have to pay for them. This will establish some contestability in relation to such reports which may graduate from the bland lowest common denominator product currently produced by the UN Secretariat. The peacekeeping and peace enforcement budget will need to continue to be raised according to the current formula for which the five permanent members of the Security Council shoulder a particular responsibility. The UN Secretariat, apart from those servicing the needs of the assemblies and the Security Council which will be part of the costs of these bodies, must be independently funded. This must include the S-G's military force. It will also include the staff at the various UN headquarters as well as UN staff based in Member States. The practice of the Global Fund only to have staff in Geneva will not work for the UN as that body needs to maintain links with local civil society, business, and governments. And the UN needs to keep its ear to the ground.

Let us try to put some figures to that. The total staff of the global UN Secretariats as of 31 December 2018 was 37,505.[15] For purposes of comparison, the State Department has around 75,000 employees, double the size of the UN.[16] The budget for the UN in 2020 was $3 billion.[17] The budget for the State Department for 2020 was $40 billion.[18] It is not expensive to fund the UN Secretariat by a form of global taxation. But this does not contain all the funding requirements for the UN Leviathan.

As previously noted, the UN should get out of the development project game. It does not have comparative advantage in this field and should leave it to smaller more agile bodies. But the UN Leviathan should become a deliverer of various world requirements like the governance of globalization, first responder in emergencies caused by natural and human-made disasters, dissemination of normative information, as well as the Secretary-General's security force. It will not be the sole funder of these initiatives. The traditional donors remain, and they need to share the burden, but the UN needs to be able to step in independently. The exact amount of the annual UN Leviathan budget is for future determination, but to be able to conceptualize the taxation burden, we need a figure. Let us, for the purpose of this exercise, put forward the figure at $100 billion annually, hardly a Leviathan-like figure in an age when the trillion has become the unit of description in the major economies, but a realistic amount to make the UN Leviathan function effectively.

Global taxation cannot follow the same concepts as domestic taxation. In the national context, policy decisions need to be taken about how progressive or regressive taxation should be; whether taxation should focus on income or also include wealth and inheritance; whether indirect taxes should cover all goods and all services or only some or none. Global taxation should not reach down to the issue of income or wealth. It should cover that part of the world economy that benefits from globalization. In effect, the UN should be funded by a tax on globalization as well as a small tax on international arm sales to fund the S-G's armed force. Focusing on taxing globalization, apart from the classic Tobin tax on international financial transactions, three obvious sources of tax revenue are air travel, container shipping and air freight.

The total number of passengers carried on scheduled services was 4.3 billion in 2018. A five-dollar surcharge per passenger would bring revenue of around $20 billion.[19] There are almost 400,000 air cargo flights a year.[20] A five-hundred-dollar levy on each flight would bring in $20 billion. About three billion containers are transported by sea each year.[21] A ten-dollar surcharge per container would bring in $30 billion. A study by UNDP on the Tobin tax and its collection, estimated in 2010 that the tax could bring revenue of $40 billion.[22] These back-of-the-envelope calculations bring the revenue from taxing globalization to $110 billion. And the collection of the taxes would be directly from industry, not through governments. The airline industry, the container ship industry and the air cargo industry only have a handful of major players. These industries are necessarily transparent. A taxation system is clearly feasible. The UNDP study goes in considerable detail to demonstrate the means whereby the Tobin tax could be collected by relatively simple electronic means. This is not science fiction; it is readily available revenue for the global system.

While the tax could be collected without the intermediation of governments, it would need the consent of "we the peoples." Ultimately, the one hundred billion dollars would be paid by people because the concerned industries would pass on these taxes to consumers. The people indirectly paying the taxes are, however, the direct beneficiaries of globalization. The taxes are not capricious, they are targeted at those who can easily pay them, and they would be spread around mainly to the four or five billion urban consumers in the world, each of whom might indirectly pay an average of $25 a year. It would require the equivalent of a global social contract to obtain the necessary consent. The deal would not be dissimilar to that which Hobbes proposed: support the Leviathan to deal with our most pressing global problems that only a Leviathan can tackle. The main difference would be the benign nature of the UN Leviathan. Sounds like a good deal.

Benign, perhaps, but how can the world ensure that this Leviathan is not corrupt? Once again, the problem has been encountered and resolved. And although the sums involved in this case are "only" in the hundreds of million per year, the system employed seems more like having the status of a pilot project than simply an embryonic idea. We have already discussed the Global Fund to Fight AIDS, Tuberculosis and Malaria in the Pandemics chapter. In its first dozen or so years, the Global Fund raised $33 billion.[23] The view taken was that the world needed the centralization and focus of a new entity to minimize the spread and impact of these three diseases. The Global Fund thought of itself as the brain, and it directed and funded all the on-the-ground functions. Come to think of it, it is something of a Leviathan in its global health field. The question arose about oversight of the Global Fund and the answer was the establishment of the office of Inspector-General.[24] The website of the office explains its mission and processes:

> Through audits, investigations and consultancy work, the Office of the Inspector General promotes good practice, reduces risk and reports on abuse. The scope of work for the Office of the Inspector General includes all systems, processes, operations, functions and activities of the Global Fund and of the programs it supports. The Inspector General has the authority to:
>
> - Access all books and records maintained by the Global Fund
> - Access all books and records relating to grants funded by the Global Fund, whether maintained by grant recipients or Local Fund Agents
> - Access the sites where these records are kept and where the programs are implemented, as permitted under applicable arrangements
> - Seek any information required from any personnel involved in the Global Fund's projects and require such personnel to cooperate with any reasonable request made by the Office of the Inspector General
> - Obtain independent professional advice and secure the involvement in its activities of outside persons with relevant experience and expertise, if and when determined necessary
> - The Office of the Inspector General is independent of the Global Fund Secretariat and reports directly to the Board through its Audit and Finance Committee.[25]

The UN already has a number of oversight and investigation offices, but they lack credibility. They are either subservient to governments or apologists for their Secretariat colleagues. A powerful Inspector-General is the answer to the problem of oversight of a UN Leviathan. Incidentally, I would recommend the practice developed in Australia for similar institutions, that the person heading this office have a generous salary; be appointed for a relatively long fixed term; not be subject to re-appointment; and have the expectation of retiring from public life at the conclusion of her term. In such circumstances, the office-holder has nobody to please but herself.

## The Veto

Where to start the process of establishing the Leviathan? I believe we need to start by dealing with the problem of the Security Council veto. In chapter 5, I laid out the mechanism to limit the scope of the veto. It is deceptively simple. There is no veto on procedural issues, so simply enlarge the scope and meaning of procedural issues in relation to the work of the Security Council. Henceforth, only action under Chapter VII will be considered *not* to be procedural. All other decisions and resolutions will require the existing special majority of nine of the fifteen votes regardless of which members cast them, a not inconsiderable hurdle. I can already hear the howls of indignation coming from P5 capitals, so let us try to unpack this idea.

It has been more than 75 years since the Battle of Britain, the siege of Leningrad, and the capture of Iwo Jima. We remain grateful to the WWII allies for saving us from the catastrophe of fascism. We demonstrated that gratitude by granting each of the allies a veto over the major substantive work of the United Nations. Now, two and half generations later, it is time to reassess the deal. Have the permanent members of the Security Council exercised that veto responsibly? Sometimes, but not nearly often enough. The reality is that the veto has mainly been used to further national priorities. The P5 delegations usually dress this up in internationalist sounding rhetoric which nobody believes. China's autism has already been discussed. The United States insists everybody comply with Security Council resolutions, but then invaded Iraq in defiance of the Council. Russia has even stopped pretending to be a peace-loving state, invading, destabilizing, and harassing its neighbors at will. Is the UN a better institution because of the veto? I doubt anybody outside the P5 would argue the affirmative case. The reality is that the P5 have betrayed the trust placed in them by the international community.

The proposal being put forward is a compromise. The P5 would retain the veto for action under Chapter VII. Many will see this as a cop-out because it does not advance the use of the doctrine of the responsibility to protect. But I consider it a practical compromise. The P5 would retain the veto for enforcement decisions. It is practical because enforcement would be just about impossible without the support of the P5. The United States and China are great powers. Russia is a great spoiler. France and the UK retain influence and importance. Chapter VII will simply not work without P5 concurrence. But the P5 would lose the veto on issues such as normative pronouncements, criticism of certain national behavior, and, crucially for the purposes of this book, the appointment of the Secretary-General. There can be no UN Leviathan with the P5 exercising the veto as currently occurs.

I have eschewed attempting to plot a roadmap to the emergence of the UN Leviathan. But, because others have tried without success to limit the veto, and because it is a threshold issue, it is necessary to demonstrate that this path is not impenetrable. It would have to occur in the current UN 2.0 context because the veto power will block the possibility of establishing a UN Leviathan. The first step is a resolution in the General Assembly articulating the understanding that henceforth the veto power will only apply to resolutions under Chapter VII and that all other resolutions will be considered to be procedural within the meaning of Article 27 (2). Not only will the P5 squeal like stuck pigs, but they will mount a major campaign to block this resolution. This is where "we the peoples" must assert ourselves by insisting that this matter is not business as usual and that the normal bribes and threats will not be effective. Any nation that has served as an elected member of the Security Council will be predisposed to vote in favor, given their humiliating experiences at the haughtiness of the permanent members. But that will be insufficient. The key will be to resist the threats and blandishments of the P5. Germany must face down its friend and neighbor France, the rest of Europe will follow. Australia, Japan, and South Korea must learn to say no to the United States. The Monroe doctrine must be side-stepped by Latin America. Francophone Africa will need to demonstrate its independence from the former colonial power. Russia's neighbors must redouble their courage. And Africa will need to resist Chinese commercial threats to call in debts and abandon infrastructure projects. There is a prisoners' dilemma quality here, if everybody resists, the threats and blandishments become ineffective.

Success in the General Assembly must mean more than a majority of votes. My sense is that the resolution should garner as many as 125 votes in favor to make the case and force the next steps. Why not 188 votes? Because we need to be realistic and accept that some countries will consider it impossible to resist their superpower boss. That is why civil society is so important. Foreign policy is not an arcane subject only understood by diplomats and beyond the reach or ordinary people. It is an existential subject affecting everybody and on which we should all be involved.

Armed with a massive vote in favor in the General Assembly, the action moves to the Security Council. Wait for a non-P5 President of the Council—that occurs at least for seven months of the year. Introduce a resolution in identical wording as that passed by the General Assembly. Ideally, there should be ten votes in favor, but nine will suffice. The P5 will claim that they have vetoed the resolution. The President of the Council will disagree saying it was a procedural vote that gained the required majority. The question would then be considered by United Nations Legal Counsel, currently, Miguel de

Serpa Soares of Portugal. He would no doubt consult his countryman, the Secretary-General. Here is one of those moments in history where an individual can make the difference. Let us hope that these two men would be able to stand up to the inevitable GRU attempts at *kompromat*, the CIA disinformation campaign, and Chinese hacks and bribes. If the Legal Counsel finds that the resolution is validly adopted, then the UN machinery will act accordingly, giving it a number and publishing it. It would be on the books. The P5 could contemplate seeking a ruling from the International Court of Justice to overturn the decision. But, here, the Westphalian nature of the court works against them as they currently have only four guaranteed votes out of fifiteen.

The P5 will be left with the Samson tactic of threatening to pull the entire house down. The precedent of boycotting the UN is not promising. The P5 need to be present to defend their interests. Eventually, after all the sulking and simpering, they will accept the compromise. One key roadblock to the creation of the UN Leviathan will have been dismantled.

As indicated at the outset, for a UN Leviathan to take shape, there needs to be a global social contract. We cannot expect governments to lead the discussion or even moderate the arguments because they will see themselves as the losers in a zero-sum game. There was a time when progressive political parties around the world might have included this objective in their national election manifestos. That may still be possible, but political parties no longer have a vice like grip on the political agenda. One of the most intriguing recent developments in political science has been the eclipse of parties and the rise of movements. One reason is the explosion of social media thus broadening the audience. It would be heartening to believe that a social contract can be achieved on a global scale by a positive vision of a new global society, but it is far more likely that the catalyst will be fear for survival in the face of anthropogenic threats. Once the enormity of the problem is appreciated, people will search for solutions. The battle over the veto power may well be the early consolidating force in the search for a global social contract.

## COSMOPOLITANISM

I recall a conversation with an airport official on leaving Dakar, Senegal. The French is simple. He was intrigued by my documents: "vous avez un passport Australien, la carte verte Americaine, et vous parlez comme un Français. Comment ça se fait?" I replied, "parce que je suis un citoyen du monde." Upon hearing this, a faraway look crossed his eyes, he was savoring the notion of being a citizen of the world, trying it on for size. It is the progressive notion. It is the inclusive notion. And, perhaps counter intuitively, it is the practical notion.

Given all the criticism heaped upon governments in this book, readers may conclude that your author is some kind of anarchist who wants governments to wither away. That is not the case. I believe in governments—national, regional, and local. I worked for a national government for a quarter of a century. Governments are an essential ingredient to a properly functioning society. I simply do not have the imagination to conceive of a world without them. But just as I do not believe in the divine right of kings, I cannot accept the boundlessness of sovereignty. As we have seen, it cannot be a license to kill. And it cannot be allowed to become a license to kill the planet. The world must invent a new system of subsidiarity in which the appropriate issues are governed by the appropriate entities. A benign UN Leviathan belongs at the apex of that system. And just as we can belong to a city and to a country, so can we belong to the world. We can all be citizens of the world.

This is how I view the concept of cosmopolitanism. It is not a concept of a world government. Once again, my imagination cannot stretch to that concept. I know that some believe humanity has the capacity to formulate and support not simply world government, but a democratic world government.[26] I simply cannot encompass that thought. It is difficult enough to make democracy work nationally and it has taken heroic efforts to try to make it work regionally in Europe among like-minded people. To establish it as a world system is, I believe, beyond our capacities. But cosmopolitanism can also mean the sense that we are all citizens of the world.[27] That we belong to the world and that the world is our nest, or as Buckminster Fuller put it half a century ago, our spaceship.[28] In my view, cosmopolitanism, though in contradistinction with communitarianism, need not be in contradiction with it. One can belong to a family, a clan, a tribe, a religion, a city, a country, and still belong to the world. None of those ascriptions need to be in denial of the others. The problem is not the overlapping memberships, as these can readily be managed. The problem is the claims to exclusivity made by one or other of the membership groups. The problem arises when the family teaches that one's loyalty is to the family and to no other group. Or if the clan insists that one's loyalty is exclusively to the clan . . . and so forth. It is these claims of exclusivity, including by religions and nations, that must be rejected.

But there is a dilemma. Spaceship Earth needs to be piloted but it is beyond our capacities to have a world government at the controls. My answer is the United Nations as Leviathan. This does not deny the responsibilities of the other levels of governance. We need city government, federal nations need provincial government, and countries need national government. They already share their respective powers, often divided by way of a constitution interpreted by an apex court. The European Union goes one step further and has a continent-wide government. It simply fits in with the other levels, though obviously there are growing pains in the process. In pure logic, the next step should be world government, but as I have said, I cannot envisage it. The UN Leviathan fits in its place. It is not government, but it achieves many of the same outcomes by setting norms, acting as a first responder, being a forum of national governments as well as for global civil society and business, and requiring cooperation to deal with global problems. It even has some coercive powers though Chapter VII, through treaty-making, and through less formal processes powered by trade and investment. The overarching principle establishing a division of labor between the various levels of governance is subsidiarity—matters ought to be handled by the smallest, lowest or least centralized competent authority. That authority needs to be competent to deal with the issue. On the issue of the climate emergency, city, national and regional governments can contribute to a solution but none of these levels is competent to deal with the breadth of the problem. For that, one must go to the global level.

## A PRACTICAL SOLUTION

Some readers, whether they agree with the substance or not, will dismiss the structures set out in this book as impossible to implement. The Permanent Five will never allow their powers to weaken; the General Assembly will never share its powers with civil society and business; Tobin taxation will never be accepted . . . and so forth. One simple response is never say "never." The world keeps changing and opinions change with it. We are at a hinge in history. None of the previous certainties can be guaranteed to retain their salience. The post-WWII order has had a good run. It survived the Cold War, it went through a Kantian moment in the post-Cold War period, but, through the actions and rhetoric of the Bush and Trump Administrations, the United States has abdicated its leadership role leaving the system rudderless. We are left with American resentment, Chinese assertiveness, Russian opportunism, and European equivocation. This is a formula for anarchy and chaos.

The United Nations as Leviathan is a practical solution. It does not require the P5 to lose their beloved vetoes over enforcement decisions, but on other issues, global opinion may prevail. It does not require the General Assembly to disband, but it will need to learn to work with the other two assemblies. And the UN itself need not be reinvented, but simply renewed. Much of the dead wood need to be shown the door. Delegate interference in the workings of the Secretariat will not be tolerated. And an independent and, therefore, powerful Secretary-General will head the organization and speak directly to and for "we the peoples." Collecting $100 billion in tax sounds exorbitant at first blush. But the great bulk of it should be seen as a global social safety net. By taxing globalization, the UN could perform a great service to national governments by taking the sting out of the rhetoric that is making globalization the new political cleavage. Yes, globalization does not directly benefit everybody, but the UN is taxing it to provide global social safety nets. The sovereigntists will bellow against the tough new human rights and democracy machinery, but it will only negatively impact those with something to hide. It will be popular with "we the peoples." Does not every individual wish to have his or her human rights protected? And when the incumbent tries to steal the election, would not everybody wish to have an impartial referee call him out? And, if I may belabor the point one last time, many of these innovations already exist in embryonic form.

I can hear my friend Daniele Archibugi complain that my vision is anti-democratic. I have not supported the idea of a general assembly of parliaments. But my reasoning is practical because we already have the Inter-Parliamentary Union, however flawed it may be, and it would be better to forge closer UN ties with that body than to establish yet another assembly. The criticism would then have it that the UN Leviathan does not have the legitimacy of being elected in a formal process. Agreed. I recall a comment made to me once by Francis Fukuyama that there is a limit to how far democracy can successfully be scaled up. Europe is having difficulty with extending electoral democracy to a continent, I do not believe it is practical to extend electoral democracy to the whole world. But democracy is more than elections. The UN Leviathan would achieve far broader representativeness than does the UN 2.0 version. It would have representation by civil society and business as well as executive branches of government. The method of selecting the civil society and business representatives would not be Westphalian so as to avoid Gongos and cronies. Instead, it would be self-selecting, thus assuring its genuineness, and enhancing its representativeness even without an electoral process. The presence of the three assemblies will also enhance the deliberative quality of the debates and the contestability of decisions in the UN. One can currently attend formal meetings at the UN for a full week without hearing anything interesting being said. The UN Leviathan would be accountable in a way that is lacking under the domination of governments which prefer sweetheart deals and fake whipping boy outrage. The presence of civil society and business within the organization will be an enormous step in providing accountability. The UN already has a culture of transparency in that it cannot keep a secret, so that culture should continue. Finally, the Inspector-General will be a force in favor of financial accountability and efficiency. I believe that representativeness, deliberation, transparency, accountability, and contestability add up to a high-quality democratic structure. As to legitimacy, that will need to be earned by performance.

Where does this leave sovereignty? The vision of the UN Leviathan presented in this book does not extinguish to concept of national sovereignty.

Sovereignty will not wither away. It will continue to be an important part of global governance. But its scope will be circumscribed by the doctrine of subsidiarity. The gravitational pull of subsidiarity is to the bottom, to the local, closer to the people. Within this system there remains an indispensable role of national governments. They continue to assure national security and they continue to provide national social safety nets. In relation to day-to-day governance, national executives will have the most prominent place. This is not simply realistic; it is the practical solution. There will, however, be a layer of governance above national executives to deal with those issues that require a global response. Preceding chapters have spelled this out in the fields of climate change, epidemics, refugees, and globalization. The global domain must be extended to direct involvement in dealing with human rights violations as well as certification of national election results. It might sound neat, but in practice it will be messy. The dividing boundaries of the subsidiarity hierarchy are not always clear cut. There will be contestation. Politics will resolve some questions, others may remain in limbo, and perhaps some will be resolved by decisions of the International Court of Justice (ICJ).

The ICJ may also require evolution. It is currently far too Westphalian with the P5 claiming to have permanent slots among the fifteen seats.[29] The trilateral character of the assemblies may not be the best means of appointment, though it could act as a confirmation process. It might be wise to borrow an idea from India where the Supreme Court has an important role in the appointment process.[30] But that discussion may be for another book.

The UN Leviathan is the practical solution because it is not revolutionary or other worldly, but it is a step beyond our current system. A major step. The existing system can still be discerned. The major powers remain major powers and retain responsibility for national defense. The world economic system continues to function on the basis of global comparative advantage. Sovereignty will continue to have salience, but aspects will be shared with a global level of governance. Global governance will not be provided by a newly minted world government or a world parliament with coercive powers. It will be provided by an institution the world has known for a century. Just as UN 2.0 was a significant leap beyond UN 1.0, so will UN 3.0 be a quantum leap forward.

## NOTES

1. Isaac Asimov, *Foundation; Foundation and Empire; Second Foundation*, (New York: Gnome Press, 1951, 1952, 1953 respectively).
2. David L. Bosco, *Five to Rule them All: The Security Council and the Making of the Modern World*, (Oxford University Press 2009), 18.

3. Boris Yeltsin Presidential Library, "USSR Joins the League of Nations," https://www.prlib.ru/en/history/619549
4. Timothy Snyder, *Bloodlands: Europe Between Hitler and Stalin*, (New York: Basic Books, 2010), 116
5. Bosco, op. cit, 19.
6. Kim Stanley Robinson, *The Ministry of the Future* (London: Orbit Books, 2020.)
7. Stephen D. Krasner, "Realism, Imperialism, and Democracy: A Response to Gilbert." *Political Theory* 20 (1) 1992, 38–52, 48.
8. Brian Schmidt, *The Political Discourse of Anarchy: A Disciplinary History of International Relations*, (New York: SUNY Press, 1998), 41.
9. David A. Lake, *Hierarchy in International Relations*, (Cornell University Press, 2009), 2.
10. Jack Donnelly, "The discourse of anarchy in IR," *International Theory* (2015), 7:3, 393–425.
11. Edward Wong and Julian E. Barnes, "Report Suggests Chinese Knew of Plan to Invade," *New York Times*, March 3, 2020.
12. Barbara Tuchman, *The March of Folly: From Troy to Vietnam*, (New York: Random House, 1987).
13. Edward Luttwak, *The Rise of China vs. the Logic of Strategy*, (Harvard University Press, 2012)
14. Nicole Winfield, "China Vetoes," *Associated Press*, February 25, 1999.
15. United Nations General Assembly, "Composition of the Secretariat: staff demographics: Report of the Secretary-General," A/74/82, 22 April 2019.
16. US Department of State, "Workforce Statistics (2017)," https://2009-2017.state.gov/documents/organization/254217.pdf
17. UN News, "General Assembly approves $3 billion UN budget for 2020," https://news.un.org/en/story/2019/12/1054431
18. US Department of State, "FY 2020 Department of State Agency Financial Report," November 16, 2020, https://www.state.gov/reports/fy-2020-department-of-state-agency-financial-report/ This figure includes USAID.
19. International Civil Aviation Organization, "The World of Air Transport in 2018," https://www.icao.int/annual-report-2018/Pages/the-world-of-air-transport-in-2018.aspx
20. International Air Transport Association, "The Value of Air Cargo," https://www.iata.org/contentassets/62bae061c05b429ea508cb0c49907c4c/air-cargo-brochure.pdf
21. Statista, "Number of ships in the world merchant fleet as of January 1, 2019, by type," https://www.statista.com/statistics/264024/number-of-merchant-ships-worldwide-by-type/.
22. Rodney Schmidt and Aniket Bhushan, "Human Development Research Paper 2011/09 The Currency Transactions Tax: Feasibility, revenue estimates, and potential use of revenues," http://hdr.undp.org/en/content/currency-transactions-tax
23. Chelsea Clinton and Devi Sridhar, *Governing Global Health: Who Runs the World and Why?* (Oxford University Press, 2017), 45.
24. Ibid., 68.

25. The Global Fund Office of Inspector-General, "Overview," https://www.theglobalfund.org/en/oig

26. Daniele Archibugi, "Cosmopolitan Democracy: A Restatement," 2011, SSRN: https://ssrn.com/abstract=1460678

27. Sometimes referred to as ethical cosmopolitanism. Toni Erskine, "Normative International Theory," Tim Dunne, Milja Kurki, Steve Smith (eds.), *International Relations Theories*, (Oxford University Press, Third Edition 2013), 36–58. 42.

28. R Buckminster Fuller, *Operating Manual for Spaceship Earth*, (Baden, Switzerland: Lars Müller Publishers, 1969.)

29. In 2017 however, the UK, facing defeat at the hands of an Indian candidate for the final seat on the court, withdrew its nomination. https://ijrcenter.org/2017/11/21/after-contested-election-uk-withdraws-icj-candidate/

30. Memorandum showing the procedure for appointment of the chief justice of India and judges of the Supreme Court of India, https://doj.gov.in/sites/default/files/memosc.pdf

# Bibliography


Alston, Philip, "Report of the Special Rapporteur on extrajudicial, summary or arbitrary executions," A/HRC/14/24/Add.6 of 28 May 2010

Anderson, Kenneth, "United Nations Collective Security and the United States Security Guarantee in an Age of Rising Multipolarity: The Security Council as the Talking Shop of the Nations," *Chicago Journal of International Law*, Vol. 10, No. 1, 2009, 55–90, 71–72.

Andreassen, Bård A. and Gordon Crawford, *Human Rights, Power and Civic Action: Comparative analyses of struggles for rights in developing countries*, Oxford: Routledge, 2013.

Annan, Kofi with Nader Mousavizadeh, *Interventions—A Life in War and Peace*. New York: Penguin Press, 2012.

Annan, Kofi, *In Larger Freedom: Towards Development, Security and Human Rights for All*, UN Doc. A/59/2005, 21 March 2005.

Archibugi, Daniele, "Cosmopolitan Democracy: A Restatement," 2011, SSRN: https://ssrn.com/abstract=1460678

Asimov, Isaac, *Foundation; Foundation and Empire; Second Foundation*, New York: Gnome Press, 1951, 1952, 1953 respectively.

Avi-Yonah, Reuven S. and David M. Uhlmann, "Combating Global Climate Change: Why a Carbon Tax is a Better Response to Global Warming than Cap and Trade" *Stanford Environmental Law Journal*, Vol. 28, No. 3, 2009, 3–50.

Becker, Gary, *Human Capital: A Theoretical and Empirical Analysis, with Special Reference to Education*, Cambridge, MA: Harvard University Press, 1964.

Beech, Hannah, "The Saturday Profile (of Dr Wang Linfa)," New York Times, 13 June 2020.

Bell BP, Damon IK, Jernigan DB, et al. *Overview, Control Strategies, and Lessons Learned in the CDC Response to the 2014–2016 Ebola Epidemic*. MMWR Suppl 2016; 65(Suppl-3):4–11. DOI: http://dx.doi.org/10.15585/mmwr.su6503a2,

Betts, Alexander and Paul Collier, *Refuge: Rethinking Refugee Policy in a Changing World*, Oxford University Press, 2017.

Bhagwati, Jagdish, *The Economics of Underdeveloped Countries*, London: Weidenfeld & Nicholson, 1966.

Bhagwati, Jagdish, "The New Thinking on Development," *Journal of Democracy* 6.4, 1995, 50–64.

Bishop, Matthew and Michael Green, *Philanthrocapitalism: How Giving can Save the World*, New York: Bloomsbury Press, 2008.

Bollyky, Thomas J. and Chad P. Bown, "The Tragedy of Vaccine Nationalism: Only Cooperation Can End the Pandemic," *Foreign Affairs*, September/October 2020.

Bosco, David L., *Five to Rule them All: the Security Council and the Making of the Modern World*, Oxford University Press, 2009.

Boutros-Ghali, Boutros, *An Agenda for Democratization*, New York: UN Department of Public Information, 2006.

Boutros-Ghali, Boutros, *Unvanquished—a U.S.-U.N. Saga*. New York: Random House, 1999.

Bradley, Curtis A., "U.S. Announces Intent Not to Ratify International Criminal Court Treaty," *The American Society of International Law Journal*, Vol. 7, Iss. 6, May 11, 2002.

Buckley, Chris, "China Takes Aim at Western Ideas," *New York Times*, August 19, 2013.

Bull, Hedley, *The Anarchical Society: A Study of Order in World Politics*. London: Macmillan Press, 1977.

Burns, William J., "The United States Needs a New Foreign Policy," *The Atlantic*, July 14, 2020.

Calamur, Krishnadev, "Trudeau Reaches His Breaking Point with Trump," *The Atlantic*, June 2, 2018.

Carey, Chris, "The Puzzles of Thermopylae," *History Today*, 10 October 2019.

Cartwright, Mark, "The Seven Voyages of Zheng He," *Ancient History Encyclopedia*, 07 February 2019, https://www.ancient.eu/article/1334/the-seven-voyages-of-zheng-he/

Catsoulis, Jeanette, "A Moving Indictment of Brutal Persecution," *New York Times*, 30 June 2020.

Chaisse, Julien and Mitsuo Matsushita, "China's 'Belt and Road' Initiative: Mapping the World Trade Normative and Strategic Implications," *Journal of World Trade* 52, no. 1 (2018), 163–186.

Chappell, David A. "The Noumea Accord: Decolonization without Independence in New Caledonia?" *Pacific Affairs*. Vol. 72, No. 3 (Autumn, 1999). 373–391.

Cheng, Maria and Raphael Satter, "Emails: UN health agency resisted declaring Ebola emergency," *Associated Press*, 20 March 2015, https://apnews.com/ea7199795faa48989449131404b7043e/emails-un-health-agency-resisted-declaring-ebola-emergency

Chesterman, Simon (ed.) *Secretary or General? The UN Secretary-General in World Politics*, Cambridge University Press, 2010.

Chollet, Derek, and Samantha Power. 2012 *The Unquiet American*, New York: Public Affairs. 257.

Clinton, Chelsea and Devi Sridhar, *Governing Global Health: Who Runs the World and Why?* Oxford University Press, 2017.

Crane, Elizabeth, "China's New Philanthropy: A New Form of Revolution?," lecture, Douglass Campus, Rutgers University, 10 March 2020.

Croissant, Aurel, book review of Roland Rich, "Democracy in Crisis. Why, Where, How to Respond," *Democratization*, 2019, 26:7, 1325–1327.

Dahir, Abdi Latif, "Outbreak of Ebola is Over in Congo," *New York Times*, June 26, 2020.

Dahlburg, John-Thor, "Mobutu lost his power - but not his wealth," *Deseret News*, May 17, 1997. https://www.deseret.com/1997/5/17/19312407/mobutu-lost-his-power-but-not-his-wealth

Danielle Kehl, "Dot What?," *Slate*, 7 May 2015, https://slate.com/technology/2015/05/icann-transition-the-interesting-history-of-the-internet-domain-name-system.html

Delahunty, R.J. "Towards a Concert of Asia? A Proposed International Security Régime," 11 U. *Penn. Asian Law Rev.* 1 (2017).

Dente, Karen and Jamie Hess, "Pediatric AIDS in Romania — A Country Faces Its Epidemic and Serves as a Model of Success," *Medscape*, 2006, https://www.medscape.com/viewarticle/528693

Diamond, Jared, *Guns, Germs and Steel: The Fates of Human Societies*, New York: Norton, 1999.

Donnelly, Jack, "The discourse of anarchy in IR," *International Theory* (2015), 7:3, 393–425.

Easterly, William, "The Ghost of Financing Gap: How the Harrod-Domar Growth Model Still Haunts Development Economics." *World Bank Policy Research Working Paper No. 1807*, July 1997.

Easterly, William, *The Tyranny of Experts; Economists, Dictators and the Forgotten Rights of the Poor*, New York: Basic Books, 2013.

Edmondson, Amy C. and Jean-Francois Harvey, *Haiti Hope: Innovating the Mango Value Chain*, Harvard Business School, 2016.

Eggers, William D. and Paul Macmillan. *The Solution Revolution: How Business, Government, and Social Enterprises Are Teaming Up to Solve Society's Toughest Problems*. Boston: Harvard Business Review Press, 2013.

von Einsiedel, Sebastian, David Malone, Bruno Stagno Ugarte (eds.) *The UN Security Council in the 21st Century*, Boulder: Lynne Rienner Publishers, 2016.

Enyedi, Z., "The Social and Attitudinal Basis of Political Parties: Cleavage Politics Revisited," *European Review*, 16(3), 2008, 287–304.

Erlanger, Steven, "Macron Says NATO Is Experiencing 'Brain Death' Because of Trump," *New York Times*, 7 November 2019

Erskine, Toni, "Normative International Theory," Tim Dunne, Milja Kurki, Steve Smith (eds.), *International Relations Theories*, Oxford University Press, Third Edition 2013), 36–58.

Faure, Michael G., and Jurgen Lefevere, "Compliance with Global Environmental Policy," in *The Global Environment Institutions: Law and Policy*, eds. R.S. Axelrod, J.D.L Down, N.J. Vig, California: CQ Press, 2004, 172–191.

Fidler, David P, "The Ebola outbreak and the future of global health security," *The Lancet* Public Policy forum, Vol 385 May 9, 2015, 1888–1889.

Forsythe, David P., *The Humanitarians: The International Committee of the Red Cross*, Cambridge University Press, 2005.

Franck, Thomas M., "The Emerging Right to Democratic Governance," *The American Journal of International Law*, Vol. 86, No. 1. January 1992, 46–91.

Frankovits, Andre, "Rules to Live by: The Human Rights Approach to Development" *PRAXIS The Fletcher Journal of Development Studies*, Volume XVII, 2002, 9–17.

Friedman, Lisa, "What Is the Green New Deal? A Climate Proposal, Explained," *New York Times*, Feb. 21, 2019.

Friedman, Thomas, *The World is Flat: A Brief History of the Twenty-First Century*, New York: Farrar, Straus and Giroux, 2005.

Fuller, R Buckminster, *Operating Manual for Spaceship Earth*, Baden, Switzerland: Lars Müller Publishers, 1969.

Gale, Jason and John Lauerman, "Ebola spread over months as WHO missed chance to respond" *Bloomberg Business*, 16 Oct. 2014.

Gatrell, Peter, "Refugees," *International Encyclopedia of the First World War*, https://encyclopedia.1914-1918-online.net/article/refugees

Giddens, Anthony, *The Consequences of Modernity*, Cambridge: Polity, 1990.

Grono, Nick, "The Deterrent Effect of the ICC on the Commission of International Crimes by Government Leaders," *International Crisis Group*, October 5, 2012.

Guilluy, Christophe, *Twilight of the Elites: Prosperity, the Periphery, and the Future of France*, Yale University Press, 2019.

Hale, Thomas and David Held (eds.), *Handbook of Transnational Governance: Institutions and Innovations*, Cambridge: Polity Press, 2011.

Hall, Shannon, "Exxon Knew about Climate Change almost 40 years ago: A new investigation shows the oil company understood the science before it became a public issue and spent millions to promote misinformation," *Scientific American*, October 26, 2015.

Harris, Chauncy D. and Gabriele Wülker, "The Refugee Problem of Germany," *Economic Geography*, Vol. 29, No. 1, 1953, 10–25.

Harrison, Mark, "Disease, Diplomacy and International Commerce: The Origins of International Sanitary Regulation in the Nineteenth Century," *Journal of Global History* 1 (2006), 197–217.

Held, David, A. McGrew, D. Goldblatt and J. Perraton, *Global Transformations: Politics, Economics and Culture*, Cambridge: Polity, 1999.

Hernández-Morales, Aitor, "Germany confirms that Trump tried to buy firm working on coronavirus vaccine," *Politico*, March 15, 2020.

Hochschild, Adam, *King Leopold's Ghost: A Story of Greed, Terror, and Heroism in Colonial Africa*, New York: Mariner Books, 1999.

Hoggan, James with Richard Littlemore, *Climate Cover-Up: the Crusade to Deny Global Warming*, Vancouver: Greystone Books, 2009.

Hopkins, A. G. (ed.), *Globalization in World History*, London: Pimlico, 2002.

Hopper, Paul, *Understanding Development*, New York: Polity Press, 2012.

Human Rights Council of Australia, "The Rights Way to Development: A Human Rights Approach to Development Assistance," HRCA, Sydney, 1995.

Hunt, Kathleen, "The Romanian Baby Bazaar," *New York Times*, March 24, 1991.

Hunt, Lynn, *Inventing Human Rights: A History*, New York: Norton, 2007.

Huntington, Samuel P. *The Third Wave—Democratization in the Late Twentieth Century*, Norman and London: Oklahoma University Press, 1991.

Jammeh, Basainey E., "The Post-War Economic Miracle in West Germany," Berlin: Hochschule für Technik, 2009.

Johnson, Chalmers, *MITI and the Japanese Miracle: The Growth of Industrial Policy 1925–1975*, Stanford University Press, 1982.

Kamradt-Scott, Adam, "WHO's to blame? The World Health Organization and the 2014 Ebola outbreak in West Africa," *Third World Q*. 37 (2016) 401–418.

Karlsen, Elibritt, "Refugee resettlement to Australia: what are the facts?," *Parliament of Australia*, 7 September 2016.

Kavanagh, Michael and Dan McCarey, "All the President's Wealth: The Kabila Family Business," *The Pulitzer Center*, July 20, 2017. https://pulitzercenter.org/reporting/all-presidents-wealth-kabila-family-business

Kickbusch, Ilona, "Global health security: a cosmopolitan moment?" *G7G20*, http://www.g7g20.com/articles/ilona-kickbusch-global-health-security-a-cosmopolitan-moment

Kirby, Michael, "Ombudsman—The Future." Speech delivered on 7 September 1985. *Canberra Bulletin of Public Administration*, vol XII no 4.

Krasner, Stephen D., "Realism, Imperialism, and Democracy: A Response to Gilbert." *Political Theory* 20 (1) 1992, 38–52.

Kumar, C. Raj, "Corruption and Transparency in Governance and Development: Reinventing Sovereignty for Promoting Good Governance," in *Reinventing Sovereignty: The End of Westphalia?* in Trudy Jacobsen, Charles Sampford and Ramesh Thakur (eds.), Farnham, UK: Ashgate, 2008, 251–265.

Lake, David A., *Hierarchy in International Relations*, Cornell University Press, 2009.

Lauterpacht, Elihu and Daniel Bethlehem, "The scope and content of the principle of non-refoulement: Opinion," in *Refugee Protection in International Law UNHCR's Global Consultations on International Protection*, in Erika Feller, Volker Türk and Frances Nicholson (eds.), Cambridge University Press, 2003, 87–177.

Lawson, Andrew, David Booth, Meleki Msuya, Samuel Wangwe, and Tim Williamson, "Does General Budget Support Work? Evidence from Tanzania," in *Budget Support as More Effective Aid? Recent Experiences and Emerging Lessons*, in Stefan Koeberle, Zoran Stavreski, and Jan Walliser (eds.), Washington: World Bank publication, 2006, 121–138.

Layne, Christopher, "This Time It's Real: The End of Unipolarity and the 'Pax Americana'," *International Studies Quarterly*, Vol. 56, No. 1 (March 2012), 203–213.

Lee, Kelley, *The World Health Organization*, Oxford, Routledge, 2009.

Lipset, Seymour Martin and Stein Rokkan, "Cleavage Structures, Party Systems, and Voter Alignments: an Introduction" in S.M. Lipset and S. Rokkan (eds) *Party systems and voter alignments: cross-national perspectives*. New York: Free Press, 1967, 1–64.

Lister, Matthew J., "Who are Refugees?" *Law and Philosophy*, Volume 32, Issue 5, 2013, 645–671.

Lustgarten, Abrahm, "Refugees from the Earth," *New York Times Magazine*, July 26, 2020.

Luttwak, Edward, *The Rise of China vs. the Logic of Strategy*, Harvard University Press, 2012.

Lynch, Colum, "The U.N.: Russia's den of spies." *Foreign Policy*, June 29, 2010.

Lynch, Colum, "U.N. Human Rights Chief to Leave, Citing 'Appalling' Climate for Advocacy." *Foreign Policy*, December 20, 2017.

MacGregor, Marion, "Germany: Refugee numbers in context," *INFO Migrants*, https://www.infomigrants.net/en/post/17641/germany-refugee-numbers-in-context

Mandavilli, Apoorva, "W.H.O. Backs Wearing Masks After Months Of Reluctance," *New York Times*, June 6, 2020.

Maren, Michael, *The Road to Hell: The Ravaging Effects of Foreign Aid and International Charity*, New York: The Free Press, 1997.

Marinoff, Lou. 2019. "Thomas Hobbes: A grim portrait of human nature." *The Times Literary Supplement*, 11 January.

Marks, Stephen and Rajeev Malhotra, "The future of the right to development," Harvard University monograph, https://cdn1.sph.harvard.edu/wp-content/uploads/sites/134/2018/06/Marks-Malhotra-The-Future-of-the-Right-to-Development-2017.pdf

Mbaye, Kéba, "Le Droit du Developpement comme un Droit de l'Homme," *Revue de Droit de l'Homme* 5, 503–534, 1972.

McKibben, Bill, "130 Degrees," *New York Review of Books*, August 20, 2020.

McLuhan, Marshall and Bruce R. Powers, *Global Village: Transformations in World, Life and Media in the 21st Century*, Oxford University Press, 1992.

Mehling, Michael, "Emmanuel Macron's carbon tax sparked *gilets jaunes* protests, but popular climate policy is possible," *The Conversation*, December 10, 2018.

Milanovic, Branko, *Global Inequality: A New Approach for the Age of Globalization*, Cambridge: Belknap Press, 2016

Myrdal, Gunnar, "Development and Under-development: A Note on the Mechanism of National and International Economic Inequality," Cairo: National Bank of Egypt, 1956.

Nagabhatla, Nidhi, Panthea Pouramin, Rupal Brahmbhatt, Cameron Fioret, Talia Glickman, K. Bruce Newbold, Vladimir Smakhtin, "Water and Migration: A Global Overview," *UNU-INWEH Report Series*, Issue 10, 2020.

Naím, Moisés, *The End of Power*, New York: Basic Books, 2013.

Newman, Edward and Roland Rich (eds.) *The UN Role in Promoting Democracy—Between Ideals and Reality*, United Nations University Press, Tokyo, 2004.

Nunnenkamp, Peter, Gustavo Canavire-Bacarreza and Luis Triveño, "Targeting aid to the needy and deserving: nothing but promises?," *Kiel Institute for the World Economy Working Papers* No. 1229, 2004.

Oberhaus, Daniel, "China Is Still Building an Insane Number of New Coal Plants," *Wired*, November 27, 2019.

Ostrom, Elinor, "A Polycentric Approach for Coping with Climate Change," World Bank Policy Research Working Paper 5095, 2009.

Palmer, Geoffrey, "An International Regime for Environmental Protection," 42 *Journal of Urban and Contemporary Law* 5, 1992, 5–19.

Paul, Delia, "Elders Present Four Proposals for UN Reform" IISD, SDG Knowledge Hub, 11 Feb. 2015, http://sdg.iisd.org/news/elders-present-four-proposals-for-un-reform/

Phillips, Janet, "The 'Pacific Solution' revisited: a statistical guide to the asylum seeker caseloads on Nauru and Manus Island," *Parliament of Australia*, 4 September 2012.

Piketty, Thomas, *Capital in the Twenty-First Century (Le Capital au XXIe siècle),* Harvard University Press, 2013.

Pogge, Thomas, *World Poverty and Human Rights*, Polity Press, Cambridge, 2008.

Raymond, Adam K. 2017. "Report: Tillerson Called Trump a 'Moron' for Comparing War to Renovating a Restaurant." *New York Magazine*, October 4.

Rich, Roland, "Bringing Democracy into International Law," *Journal of Democracy* 12, No. 3, July 2001.

Rich, Roland, "Crafting Security Council Mandates," in *The UN Role in Promoting Democracy—Between Ideals and Reality* eds. Edward Newman and Roland Rich, Tokyo: United Nations University Press, 2004.

Rich, Roland, "Recognition of States: the Collapse of Yugoslavia and the Soviet Union," *European Journal of International Law* 4 No. 1, March 1993, 36–65.

Rich, Roland, "Situating the UN Democracy Fund" *Global Governance* 16 (2010), 423–434.

Rich, Roland, "The Right to Development as an Emerging Human Right," *Virginia Journal of International Law* 23, No. 2 (Winter 1983): 287–328.

Rich, Roland, "The Right to Development: A Right of Peoples?" in James Crawford (ed.), *The Rights of Peoples*, Oxford University Press, 1988, 39–54.

Rich, Roland, book review of William Easterly, *The Tyranny of Experts: Economists, Dictators, and the Forgotten Rights of the Poor,* New York: Basic Books, 2013, *Population and Development Review*, 40(3): 559–572 (September 2014).

Rich, Roland, *Pacific Asia in Quest of Democracy*, Boulder: Lynne Rienner Publishers, 2007.

Rich, Roland, *Democracy in Crisis: Why, Where, How to Respond.* Boulder: Lynne Rienner Publishers. 2017.

Robinson, Kim Stanley, *The Ministry of the Future*, London: Orbit Books, 2020.

Rosenberg, Eli, and Carol Morello, "U.S. withdraws from UNESCO, the U.N.'s cultural organization, citing anti-Israel bias," *Washington Post*, October 12, 2017

Routley, Nick, "Meet China's 113 Cities with More Than One Million People," *Visual Capitalist*, February 6, 2020.

Rowlings, Bill, "Dead to rights: how an Aussie hero framed the world's conscience," Civil Liberties Australia, 24 April 2012.

Rudd, Kevin, "UN 2030: Rebuilding Order in a Fragmenting World," Chair's Report, Independent Commission on Multilateralism, 2016, https://asiasociety.org/sites/default/files/I/IPI-ICM-UN-2030-Chairs-Report2FINAL.pdf

Ruggie, John, *Constructing the World Polity: essays on international institutionalisation.* London: Routledge, 2020.

Sahle, Eunice N. "On Kéba M'Baye and the Right to Development at 30," in *Human Rights in Africa Contemporary Debates and Struggles*, ed. Eunice N. Sahle, New York: Palgrave Macmillan, 2019.

Sands, Philippe, *East West Street*, New York: Vintage Books, 2017.

Sands, Philippe, "Britain's Colonial Legacy on Trial at The Hague," *The New York Review of Books*, June 23, 2020.

Scheidel, Walter, *The great leveler: violence and the history of inequality from the Stone Age to the twenty-first century*, Princeton and Oxford: Princeton University Press, 2017.

Schmidt, Brian, *The Political Discourse of Anarchy: A Disciplinary History of International Relations*, New York: SUNY Press, 1998.

Schmidt, Rodney and Aniket Bhushan, "Human Development Research Paper 2011/09 – The Currency Transactions Tax: Feasibility, revenue estimates, and potential use of revenues," http://hdr.undp.org/en/content/currency-transactions-tax

Schuetze, Christopher F. and Ben Hubbard, "Syrian Doctor Accused of Torture Is Arrested in Germany," *New York Times*, June 22, 2020.

Scott, James C., "'Stilled to silence at 500 metres'—making sense of historical change in Southeast Asia," *IIAS Newsletter*, No. 48, Autumn 2008.

Sen, Amartya, "Democracy as a Universal Value." *Journal of Democracy* 10.3 (1999), 3–17.

Sen, Amartya, *Development as Freedom*, New York: Anchor Books, 1999.

Sen, Amartya. 2010. *Human Development Report 2010, 20th Anniversary Edition.*

Sengupta, Arjun, "On the Theory and Practice of the Right to Development" *Human Rights Quarterly* (2002) 24.4.

Seyedsayamdost, Elham, "MDG-based National Planning: An Assessment," 2015, https://oxfamblogs.org/fp2p/wp-content/uploads/2015/07/MDG-Assessment_ES.pdf

Sharpe, Charles Wesley, "The Origins of the United Nations Relief and Rehabilitation Administration, 1939–1943" (2012). *Publicly Accessible Penn Dissertations 696*, 292 https://repository.upenn.edu/edissertations/696

Shevchenko, Arkady. *Breaking with Moscow*. New York: Knopf, 1985.

Snyder, Timothy, *Bloodlands: Europe between Hitler and Stalin*, New York: Basic Books, 2010.

Soledad, Fely I. 2001. "The Philippine Council for NGO Certification." *The International Journal of Not-for-Profit Law*. Vol. 3, Issue 2, Dec.

Stone, Norman, "Turkey and Russia—friends for a while, now foes once again," *Financial Times*, 11 March 2016.

Tarrow, Sidney, *The New Transnational Activism*, Cambridge University Press, 2006.

Tarullo, Daniel K., "Logic, Myth, and the International Economic Order," *Harvard International Law Journal* 26(2) 1985.

Terminski, Bogumil, "Towards Recognition and Protection of Forced Environmental Migrants in the Public International Law: Refugee or IDPs Umbrella?" *Policy Studies Organization Summit,* December 2011.

Tett, Gillian. "Ethical investing has reached a tipping point: Environmental, social and governance considerations are finally moving into the mainstream," *Financial Times*, 18 June 2019.

Tobin, James, "A Proposal for International Monetary Reform." *Eastern Economic Journal*, vol. 4, Jul/Oct. 1978, 153–159.

Traub, James, *The Best Intentions: Kofi Annan and the UN in the Era of American Power*, New York: Farrar, Straus and Giroux, 2006.

Tuchman, Barbara, *The March of Folly: From Troy to Vietnam*, New York: Random House, 1987.

Tung, Nguyen Vu, "Vietnam's Membership of ASEAN: A Constructivist Interpretation." *Contemporary Southeast Asia: A Journal of International and Strategic Affairs*, Volume 29, Number 3, December 2007, 483–505.

Uvin, Peter, "On High Moral Ground: The Incorporation of Human Rights by the Development Enterprise" *PRAXIS The Fletcher Journal of Development Studies* Volume XVII, 2002, 1–11

Vasak, Karel, "A30-Year struggle The sustained efforts to give force of law to the Universal Declaration of Human Rights," *UNESCO Courier*, XXX 11, 28–32.

Vromen, Simone. "The Council Committee on NGOs: An analysis of the reports of the Council Committee on NGOs between 2005 and 2015." *Utrecht Law Review*, Volume 13, Issue 1, 2017, 82–98. http://doi.org/10.18352/ulr.373

Wachtel, Ted, "Governance and the use of authority: encompassing diverse definitions of 'Restorative'," *European Forum for Restorative Justice*, September 2016 Newsletter, Volume 17(3), 7–9.

Waller, P., "Aid and Conditionality," *D+C Development and Cooperation* 1, January–February 1994.

Waltz, Kenneth N., "Toward nuclear peace," in Kenneth N. Waltz, (Ed.). *Realism and international politics*, New York: Routledge, 2008, 260–275.

Watson, Peter, *The Great Divide: Nature and Human Nature in the Old World and the New*, New York: Harper, 2013.

Weart, Spencer, *The Discovery of Global Warming*, Harvard University Press, 2008.

Weber, Max. 1918. "Politics as a Vocation." From H.H. Gerth and C. Wright Mills (Translated and edited), *From Max Weber: Essays in Sociology*, 77128, New York: Oxford University Press, 1946.

Weiss, Thomas G., *What's Wrong with the United Nations and How to Fix It*. Cambridge: Polity Press, 2016.

Wiess, Thomas G., Tatiana Carayannis and Richard Jolly. 2009. "The 'Third' United Nations." *Global Governance* 15. 123–142

de Wilde, Pieter, Ruud Koopmans and Michael Zürn, "Conflicts or Cleavage? Contesting Globalization in Western Europe and Beyond" in a Paper presented at the ECPR General Conference, Glasgow, 4–7 September 2014, https://ecpr.eu/Filestore/PaperProposal/ce7978ec-3492-4c4f-ba81-459b6ad76667.pdf

William A. Schabas, *An Introduction to the International Criminal Court*, Cambridge University Press, 2001.

Williams, Susan, *Who Killed Hammarskjold?* Oxford University Press, 2014.

Wilson, Scott, "Obama dismisses Russia as 'regional power' acting out of weakness," *Washington Post*, March 25, 2014.

Wong, Edward, "China Admits Building Flaws in Quake," *New York Times*, Sept. 4, 2008.

# Index

# About the Author

**Professor Roland Rich** is the Director of the United Nations and Global Policy Studies Master of Arts Program of the Political Science Department at Rutgers University, New Brunswick, New Jersey. He is also a Visiting Fellow at the Australian National University.

Prior to joining Rutgers in 2015, Dr. Rich was, from 2007, the Head of the United Nations Democracy Fund and concurrently Executive Director of the United Nations Office for Partnerships from 2010 to 2014.

He was the Foundation Director of the Centre for Democratic Institutions at the Australian National University from 1998 to 2005.

Dr. Rich was an officer of the Australian Department of Foreign Affairs and Trade for 25 years including postings in Paris, Rangoon, Manila and as

Ambassador in Vientiane. At headquarters, he held various positions, including Legal Advisor and Assistant Secretary for International Organisations.

Dr. Rich holds Arts and Law (Hons.) degrees from the University of Sydney, and Master of International Law and Doctor of Philosophy (Political Science) degrees from the Australian National University.

His two most recent books are *Democracy in Crisis: Why, Where, How to Respond* (Lynne Rienner Publishers, 2017) and *Parties and Parliaments in Southeast Asia: Non-Partisan Chambers in Indonesia, the Philippines and Thailand* (Routledge, 2013).